EXTREME ARCHITECTURE
RUTH SLAVID

Published in 2009
By Laurence King Publishing Ltd
361–373 City Road
London EC1V 1LR
Tel +44 (0)20 7841 6900
Fax +44 (0)20 7841 6910
E-mail enquiries@laurenceking.com
www.laurenceking.com

Text © Ruth Slavid 2009
This book was produced by
Laurence King Publishing Ltd

All rights reserved. No part of
this publication may be reproduced
or transmitted in any form or by
any means, electronic or mechanical,
including photocopy, recording or
any information retrieval system,
without permission in writing from
the publisher.

A catalogue record for this book is
available from the British Library.

ISBN-13: 978-1-85669-609-8

Designed by Co Studio Design

Printed in China

EXTREME ARCHITECTURE
RUTH SLAVID

Laurence King Publishing

CONTENTS

6 INTRODUCTION

08 HOT

Chapter 1
Hot introduction

Cape Schanck House
Victoria, Australia
Paul Morgan Architects

House RR
Itamambuca, São Paulo, Brazil
Andrade Morettin Arquitetos

Casa Segura
Sonoran Desert, Arizona, USA
Robert Ransick

Magma Arts and Congress Centre
Costa Adeje, Tenerife, Canary Islands, Spain
Artengo Menis Pastrana

Nk'Mip Desert Cultural Centre
Osoyoos, British Columbia, Canada
Hotson Bakker Boniface Haden Architects + Urbanistes

Engbarth Residence
Scottsdale, Arizona, USA
Jeffrey H. Page RA

Sacred Sands Strawbale B&B
Joshua Tree, California, USA
Janet Armstrong Johnston

Walmajarri Community Centre
Djugerari, Western Australia
iredale pedersen hook

School Buildings
Gando and Dano, Burkina Faso
Diébédo Francis Kéré

Central Market
Koudougou, Burkina Faso
Laurent Séchaud

56 COLD

Chapter 2
Cold introduction

Delta Shelter
Mazama, Washington, USA
Olson Sundberg Kundig Allen Architects

Echigo-Matsunoyama Museum of Natural Science
Matsunoyama, Niigata, Japan
Takaharu + Yui Tezuka

Remota Hotel
Puerto Natales, Patagonia, Chile
Germán del Sol

Svalbard Science Centre
Longyearbyen, Norway
Jarmund/Vigsnæs AS Architects MNAL

Svalbard Global Seed Vault
Spitsbergen, Norway
Peter W. Søndermann/Barlindhaug Consult AS

Ice hotels and bars
Jukkasjärvi, Sweden; Sainte-Catherine-de-la-Jacques-Cartier, Canada; London, UK; Stockholm, Sweden
Various architects

Snow Show
Sestriere, Italy
Curator: Lance Fung, various artists and architects

Halley VI Antarctic Research Station
Antarctica
Hugh Broughton Architects

Amundsen-Scott South Pole Station
South Pole, Antarctica
Ferraro Choi and Associates

104 HIGH

Chapter 3
High introduction

Aurland Lookout
Sogn og Fjordane, Norway
Todd Saunders and Tommie Wilhelmsen

Prekestolhytta
Stavanger, Norway
Arkitektfirma Helen & Hard

Mountain Lodge
Hemsedal, Norway
div.A arkitekter AS

SnowCrystals
Architecture and Vision

Nordpark Cable Railway
Innsbruck, Austria
Zaha Hadid Architects

Carmenna Chairlift Stations
Arosa, Switzerland
Bearth & Deplazes Architekten

Galzigbahn
St Anton am Arlberg, Austria
driendl*architects

Ski Jump and Judges' Tower
Vogtland Arena, Klingenthal, Germany
m2r-architecture

SkiBox and Chalet C7
Portillo, Chile
dRN Arquitetos

Tschuggen Bergoase Spa
Arosa, Switzerland
Mario Botta Architetto

Olympic Ski Jump
Garmisch-Partenkirchen, Germany
terrain: loenhart&mayr BDA architects and landscape architects

Manned Cloud
Jean-Marie Massaud, Studio Massaud

154 WET

Chapter 4
Wet introducion

La Maison Flottante
Paris, France
Ronan & Erwan Bouroullec – designers

Floating Sauna
Stockholm, Sweden
Scheiwiller Svensson Arkitektkontor/Ari Leinonen

Yacumama Lodge
Yarapa River, Peru
Travis Price

Floating Housing
Maasbommel, The Netherlands
Factor Architecten bv

Floating Cruise Terminal
Dubai, United Arab Emirates
Waterstudio.NL

Digital Water Pavilion
Zaragoza, Spain
carlorattiassociati

Poseidon Underwater Hotel
Fiji
Poseidon Undersea Resorts

SeaOrbiter
Jacques Rougerie Architecte

180 SPACE

Chapter 5
Space introducion

Concordia Station
Antarctica
SERVEX

Spaceport America
New Mexico, USA
Foster + Partners

Galactic Suite
Caribbean/Space
Equip.Xavier Claramunt

MoonBaseTwo
Architecture and Vision

Lunar Hotel
Hans-Jurgen Rombaut–Lunar Architecture/Wonka

MarsCruiserOne
Architecture and Vision

200 ENDMATTER

Project credits

Index

Picture credits

Author's acknowledgements

INTRODUCTION

Left Foster + Partners has designed an iconic building for the remote Siberian city of Khanty-Mansiysk.

Norman Foster is a British architect who has become a global brand and is admired, unusually, for both his business savvy and his design skills. He seems to be set on world domination; on having projects in all the key places. Once, perhaps, it would have been enough to be present in New York, London and Beijing, but Foster's practice has a far wider spread than that with a seaside resort in Mauritius off the coast of Africa, a towering mixed-use scheme that will soon rise above the Siberian city of Khanty-Mansiysk, and a housing scheme in the Swiss resort of St Moritz. People all over the globe are likely to encounter his buildings. But, even more dramatically, if you choose to pay for a trip into space you will pass through a Foster creation.

Foster is the lead architect for Virgin Galactic's Spaceport America under construction in the desert of New Mexico (page 186). A long way from any sizeable town, in a challenging environment, it is an example of 'extreme architecture' which I define for the purposes of this book as architecture in extreme environments. It is also, of course, the jumping-off point for the most extreme environment of all – the one beyond our world, the limitless and totally demanding environment of space.

The fascination of architecture in extreme environments is that it is so demanding technically, yet offers so much potential. There are few projects in this book that have had to make obeisance to historic neighbours, or even to any neighbours at all. The greatest constraints usually come from the need not to spoil the natural environment, and that demands far more judgement, and is far more open, than the need to match the brickwork of an adjoining building, or keep to a planner's height restriction.

Instead, the architects of many of these projects have to deal with more fundamental questions. How do you make a building liveable in a brutal climate? How do you transport materials and manage the building process? And, in many cases, how do you provide energy and power and dispose of waste when it is not simply a matter of plugging in to the electricity grid, to mains water and to an infrastructure of waste disposal?

Non-connected buildings can be described as 'infra-free', a term that is subtly different from the 'off-grid' beloved of some evangelical environmentalists. Being off-grid is usually a conscious choice; with infra-free buildings there is normally no infrastructure to which one could connect. Studies on 'infra-free systems' were launched at the University of Tokyo in April 2006, and the subject formed the basis of an international conference held in Istanbul in December 2006 and chaired by Tokyo University's Dr Serkan Anilir. Speakers included poetic Japanese architect Kengo Kuma, who is concerned with designing in harmony with nature, and architects working on projects in the Antarctic and in space.

What is driving those projects and the others in extreme environments shown on these pages? Part of it is technological – we can launch into space, we can make hot places liveable, and we can support scientists working in the Antarctic. Architecture often follows engineering as a second wave. Whereas the importance of architecture has been acknowledged for centuries in urban centres, some of these extreme environments seemed at first so demanding that they were treated purely as engineering problems. As long as people didn't die on their journeys into space, or while cut off and living in the extreme cold, what did it matter what these places looked like? Mountain dwellings and tropical schools could surely be left to ageless vernacular techniques?

Belatedly, there is a realization that architecture has a crucial role to play. As planned space journeys become longer, decent living conditions will not just be an indulgence but may be the key to staying sane. The Antarctic may be freezing cold, but it is a hothouse environment for the scientists there, who will be happier and more productive if they inhabit some liveable spaces that acknowledge their social needs. The ever more competitive tourist industry demands novelty and luxury in the most beautiful and, ironically, unspoilt places, and the world's top architects are best placed to meet these demands.

Many of these projects are not just exciting in their own right, but are in environments that offer lessons for the future. Understanding the horrific consequences that will ensue if their missions go wrong part-way through, space agencies are trying to learn as much as they can through simulation – by isolating potential astronauts under water, in the desert, near the poles and at altitude.

Extreme architecture on earth will have lessons for the even more extreme architectural conditions in space. And it may transform the CV of the high-achieving architect. Norman Foster made his reputation with the Willis Faber Offices in Ipswich, the Hongkong and Shanghai Bank in Hong Kong and the Millau Viaduct in France, and only designed the spaceport late in his career. British architect Hugh Broughton is making his reputation with Antarctic stations for British and Spanish scientists. The next generation may become famous not for anything on earth but for buildings on Mars and the moon, or even in orbit.

CHAPTER 1
HOT

Right and below right
The Moulmein Rise Residential Tower in Singapore, by WOHA Architects, won an Aga Khan Award for its reinterpretation of the traditional monsoon window (shown in detail at top).

In the early 1980s, I visited the construction site of the Sultan Qaboos University in Oman. There were two levels of accommodation for the staff working on the project. The Brits (both the architect and the contractor were British) lived in houses that would subsequently be homes for the faculty. The labourers, who were referred to as TCNs (third-country nationals) and came predominantly from India and other Asian countries, were housed in barrack-style dormitories.

There was great pride in the fact that, unlike other TCN accommodation in the Middle East, these dormitories had air conditioning. I was conscious that this was not entirely altruistic. With summer temperatures in the nearby capital Muscat regularly hitting 48°C (118°F), ensuring that workers who were outside all day could at least get a decent night's sleep worked wonders for productivity.

In the 1980s this seemed an obvious solution. For permanent accommodation in hot countries (as, indeed, at the university itself) enlightened architects used shade and encouraged cross breezes as far as possible to increase the levels of comfort. But the use of air conditioning to ameliorate the heat just made sense. For the first time, areas of the world that had been either uncomfortable or uninhabitable could be brought up to the standards of comfort that were the norm in temperate climes. The whole of the Gulf boom was built on air conditioning.

Fast-forward to today and it all looks very different. Rising energy costs and concern about carbon emissions make air conditioning undesirable (although the Chinese, with their growing affluence, are still retrofitting it like mad to substandard accommodation in hot cities). In temperate climates, we can couple clever design with a tolerance of a few uncomfortable days, and decide that we can manage. In hot countries this is not enough.

The projects shown in this chapter in Burkina Faso (pages 46 and 52) are for a country so poor that any increase in comfort provided by the architecture will be welcomed. But the buildings, admirable though they are, would probably not be considered as offering adequate thermal comfort in more affluent countries.

The Koudougou Market in Burkina Faso won an Aga Khan Award in 2007. Another Aga Khan Award that year went to WOHA Architects for the Moulmein Rise Residential Tower in Singapore. This 28-storey building is remarkable largely for its reinterpretation of the traditional monsoon window, an opening that allows breezes in while keeping out the rain.

Opposite Researchers now believe that in desert environments, dense settlements such as the proposed Masdar in Abu Dhabi, planned by Foster + Partners, produce an 'urban cool island' effect.

Far left Wind turbines on Atkins' World Trade Centre in Bahrain generate between 10 and 15 per cent of the total energy requirement.
Left SOM has designed Bridging the Rift, on the Israel–Jordan border, to produce its own energy.

On a far more ambitious scale is Foster + Partners' masterplan for the city of Masdar in Abu Dhabi, which aims to be the world's first zero-carbon, zero-waste city. A dense, walled, car-free city, it will be built in two phases, the first phase being a large photovoltaic power plant that will be used to power not only the finished city but also the construction process. Foster's city has heavily shaded streets, with people rarely experiencing direct sunlight. One could argue that this compact approach is not a good idea. After all, in temperate cities dense living leads to an 'urban heat island' effect. Could this also happen in the desert?

The answer is not obvious, as there are conflicting factors to do with movement of air and build-up of heat. David Pearlmutter, a researcher at the Desert Architecture and Urban Planning Unit at Ben-Gurion University of the Negev, Israel, studied these in depth. In 2000, writing in *The Aridlands Newsletter* published by the University of Arizona, he concluded: 'What emerges from this case study, then, is evidence that a compact urban fabric in the desert can in fact contribute to a relative "cool island", in sharp contrast to what is so often emphasized in non-arid cities. Like the urban heat island in general, the micro-scale heating effect shown here is primarily a nocturnal phenomenon, and has far less relevance than it would in more tropical regions. (It is interesting to note that in winter, when the heat island effect is desirable, the compact street canyon was seen to reduce heat loss from the body during nearly all hours – primarily due to protection from cold winds.)'

Pearlmutter is writing about deserts, and Masdar is in a desert, as are some but not all of the projects shown here.

There is an enormous difference between designing for desert and humid tropical environments. Although both can experience very high temperatures in daytime, and shading from the heat of the sun is essential in both, they demand almost opposing approaches.

Deserts have high daytime temperatures, with very low humidity, and cold nights. Thermally massive buildings can therefore be used to modulate the temperature, heating up slowly in the day and cooling in the evening. In some areas there will be cold desert winters, in which case this cycling of temperatures can work seasonally as well as diurnally.

But in the tropics, or in countries that have a hot rainy season, the opposite is the case. If heat builds up during the day, there is no time at which it can dissipate, since the nights are also hot. Instead, lightness and ventilation are key – shelter rather than enclosure – unless the architect goes to the extreme of the air-conditioned sealed box. Houses such as House RR (page 16) epitomize an approach to living with humid weather rather than fighting against it.

Of course, generation of energy is another route towards sustainability, although it can still rarely justify its reckless dissipation. On smaller buildings, any approach beyond using the sun to heat water is likely to be tokenistic, but at the scale of Masdar it is certainly worthwhile. The huge World Trade Centre in Bahrain, designed by global consultancy Atkins, has three 29 metre (95 foot) diameter wind turbines sitting between the two towers of accommodation, generating between 10 and 15 per cent of the building's total energy requirement. A proposed international learning centre, called Bridging the Rift, designed by American practice SOM, will sit in the desert on the Israel–Jordan border. It will use underground aquifers to help in a cooling strategy, and solar power to generate heat and electricity. This will allow it to operate independently of both neighbouring countries.

Deserts offer wonderful opportunities to generate power. As well as the potential for large solar arrays, there are proposals such as that by the German engineering practice, Schlaich Bergermann, for a 'solar updraft tower'. Effectively a large glazed roof that slopes up gently to a central giant chimney, this would operate by converting the wind energy of hot air rushing up the tower into electricity. A prototype was constructed in Manzanares in Spain, but so far, despite much discussion, especially in Australia, a full-scale version has not yet been built.

But for the architect of a normal-sized individual building, such solutions are likely to be beyond reach. Instead, working intelligently to ameliorate the extremes of heat will be the most rewarding solution, whether on a school in Burkina Faso (page 46), an eccentric-looking house in Australia (page 12) or a congress centre in the Canary Islands (page 24).

VICTORIA, AUSTRALIA
PAUL MORGAN ARCHITECTS

CAPE SCHANCK HOUSE

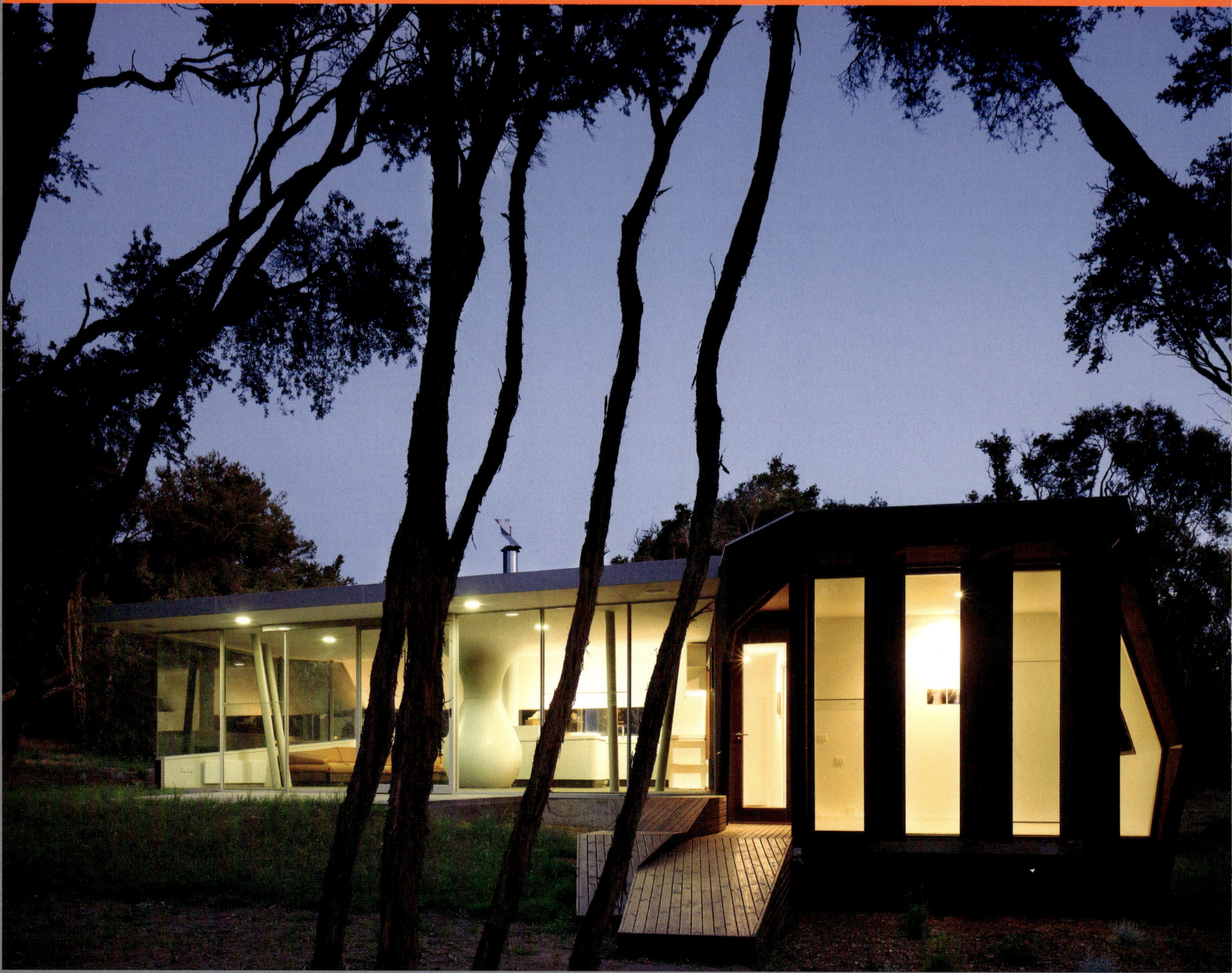

Height above sea level
79m/260ft

 Average annual rainfall
751.7mm/30in

Average high and low temperatures
40.2°C/104°F – 10°C/50°F

A bulbous water tank, like a huge drop of milk that has fallen from the ceiling and just hit the floor, dominates the large white living room of this house which overlooks the rugged coast on the edge of Melbourne, Australia. At night, you can see it through the glazing, at the end of a naturally occurring tunnel of tea trees.

Combining an ingenious solution, structural support and symbolic gesture, this tank is the most immediately obvious element in a design that responds to the site-specific conditions. Designed by the architect for his own family and that of his sister, it is a one-off design that carries a certain burden of theorizing but is also an intelligent solution to the problems not only of its situation but also of the environment in Australia today.

The first decade of the twenty-first century has brought Australia hideous tales of drought and bush fires, with record high temperatures and low rainfall. Global warming is expected to make the situation even worse. So the ability to capture water, the most precious of resources, makes eminent sense. And in this case the water is not only stored, but also helps to cool the house – not to mention replacing an open fire (too hot) or television (too uncool) as the centrepiece of the main room.

The house has two very different parts. The main living area is open and largely glazed, with all internal finishes in white. Set at a right angle to it, like the bar of the letter 'T' with a rather squat base, is the sleeping accommodation, with bedrooms and bathrooms contained in a block clad in dark ply.

This bar of sleeping accommodation is not, however, rectilinear. The entire house is designed in relation to the prevailing wind which has distorted the surrounding vegetation, largely tea trees. In a similar way it has distorted the form of the house. These distortions are a response to the changes in pressure, as the wind's path is interrupted by the house which has been designed to be as aerodynamic as possible. The building has won several architectural prizes in Australia, and one jury wrote of it: 'The resultant shaping provides a drag coefficient bettered only by a CX Citroen.' On the south elevation there are wind scoops, which Morgan describes as 'a kind of peeling of the skin'. They trap cooling winds in summer, while providing shade from the afternoon sun.

Opposite The house is surrounded by tea trees distorted by the prevailing wind.
Above The rugged coast near Melbourne is the site for the house.
Right The water tank dominates the living room.

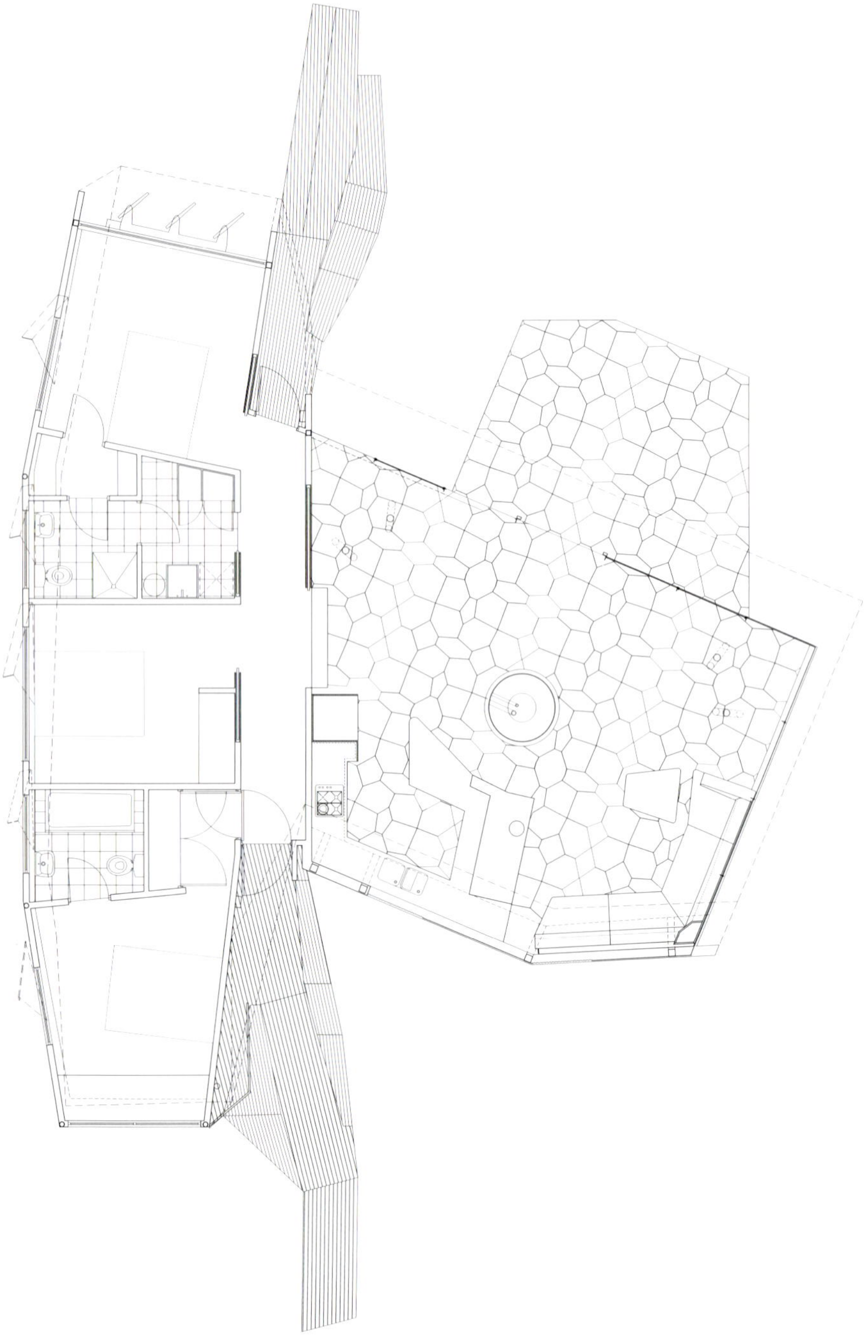

But however well considered other elements of the building are, attention will always focus on the water tank. Made of steel, and containing 1,700 litres (374 gallons) of water, it acts as a passive cooling system for the house, providing ambient cooling that is assisted by the carefully designed cross-ventilation. Excess water drains to an external tank and is used for irrigation, flushing lavatories, washing wetsuits or even drinking.

Morgan's neighbour was a builder who volunteered to undertake the construction, which included the extremely challenging freehand plastering around the top of the steel bulb. He has done this to perfection, prompting Morgan to describe him as 'extremely skilled'. The pavers on the floor are in a pattern that is meant to be reminiscent of cooling lava.

This is a surprising house, not just because of the massive tank but because it encapsulates so much innovation. There are dark elements and light elements, and every façade is distinctively different. Yet there is a harmony to it, and a sense of inspiration, which means that this very site-specific building will probably inspire other architects on other sites to combine ingenuity and romance in a similar approach.

Top left Seating within the main living area.
Above left The surprising angles of the house are an aerodynamic response to the wind.
Above Plan, showing sleeping areas on the left and the living space in the tiled area on the right.

Right Junction between the dark-clad sleeping accommodation and the white living space.

ITAMAMBUCA, SÃO PAULO, BRAZIL
ANDRADE MORETTIN ARQUITETOS

HOUSE RR

 Height above sea level
0m/0ft

 Average annual rainfall
1500mm/59in

 Average high and low temperatures
32°C/89°F – 20°C/68°F

Opposite The relatively blank ends of the house are clad in corrugated steel.
Right Andrade Morettin Arquitetos has designed the house to cope with the hot and humid surroundings.

Shelter rather than enclosure is the driving force for buildings in hot and humid climates. There is a need to dodge direct sunlight, to keep out the rain and to exclude the annoying and biting insects that revel in the conditions humans find so trying. But total enclosure is not the answer, as any breeze is to be welcomed, both for cooling and to reduce condensation which can lead to mould and rotting.

This is very much the thinking behind House RR, which Andrade Morettin Arquitetos designed just a few metres from the coast in the northern part of the state of São Paulo. It is a culmination of a number of houses by the practice, both in and around the capital. While those in the urban setting have a certain tough solidity, the architect has gone for a much lighter touch with the houses in the countryside, in some cases deliberately evoking a very basic shelter.

House RR is more sophisticated than that, but works on the same principles – a simple light structure that provides comfort without cutting off the residents from the external landscape. It is very much a box within a box; a long linear two-storey structure, with a shallow veranda to one side, and a wide veranda, equivalent in depth to the house itself, on the other. The staircase to the upper floor sits on this veranda, allowing all the internal space to be used. The verandas are enclosed with mosquito screens, consisting of glass fibre with a PVC coating, contained within steel frames.

Structurally, the house is of timber with galvanized steel joints. Floors are also of timber and there is a widespread use of OSB (oriented strand board) for the 'exterior' of the internal house, continuing the woody appearance. These walls can open up, to make the most of the cross-ventilation, while the external screens will remain closed at times when mosquitoes are present. In contrast to the long open sides to the house, the ends are relatively blank, with just small horizontal strip windows interrupting the profiled steel-sheet cladding, which is also carried over the roof. The whole structure is raised by 75 centimetres (30 inches), on concrete pillars that were cast in situ, to lift it above the surrounding dampness.

As much as possible of the structure was prefabricated, as the architect wanted to reduce assembly time and errors, minimizing waste and reducing environmental impact on the surrounding site as far as possible. Prefabrication also allowed the builders to create a waterproof shelter quickly, under which construction could take place.

Right Insect mesh encloses the outer space, allowing windows to the inner box to remain open whenever required.

One interesting aspect of building in this environment is that the materials were deliberately chosen to be as lightweight as possible. Whereas in a hot, dry environment thermal mass is desirable, because the building can heat up during the day and then cool at night (and to a lesser extent, heat up in summer and cool in winter), this is not the case in the humid tropics. Nights there are almost as hot as days, and so any accumulation of daytime heat will just serve to make the nights more uncomfortable; conversely, there will not be enough heat loss during the night to create a reservoir of 'coolth' for the daytime.

Having tackled these issues and worked quite extensively with steel, it is not surprising that Andrade Morettin was one of the three winners of the 2007 Living Steel competition, to design sustainable housing using steel. The site for its entry is in Recife, Brazil (the other two sites are in London and China). On Brazil's northwest coast, Recife has a humid tropical climate, where average night-time temperatures never fall below about 23ºC (73ºF). The challenge was to design affordable lightweight housing (soil conditions were poor) with a minimal need for mechanical cooling. Andrade Morettin's solution arranged three-storey blocks with their long sides facing the prevailing wind. It uses vented outdoor screens, open apartment interiors, and medium-height room dividers to optimize cross-ventilation. Oversailing roofs and the use of shutters minimize solar gain.

There is a great tradition in architecture, from the first Modernists in the early twentieth century, of designing one-off houses that are not only achievements in themselves but can also act as laboratories for ideas that can then be used on a larger scale. This is exactly what Andrade Morettin has done. The delightful private house by the sea could well help to make housing more comfortable in a difficult climate for many of the less affluent in Recife.

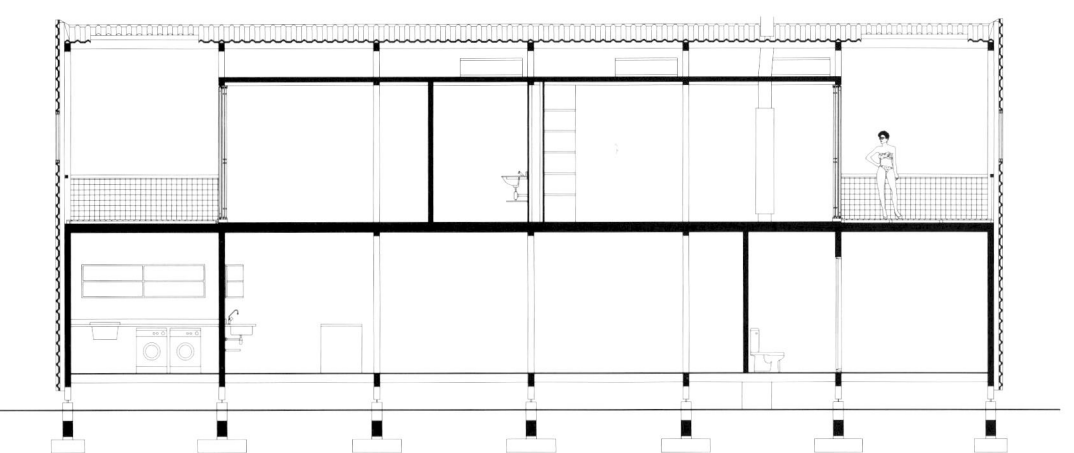

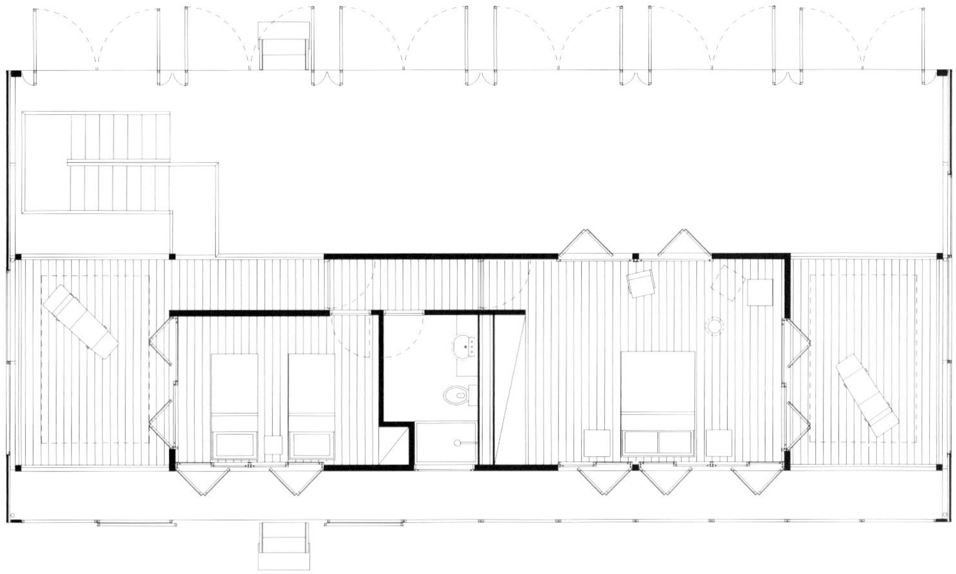

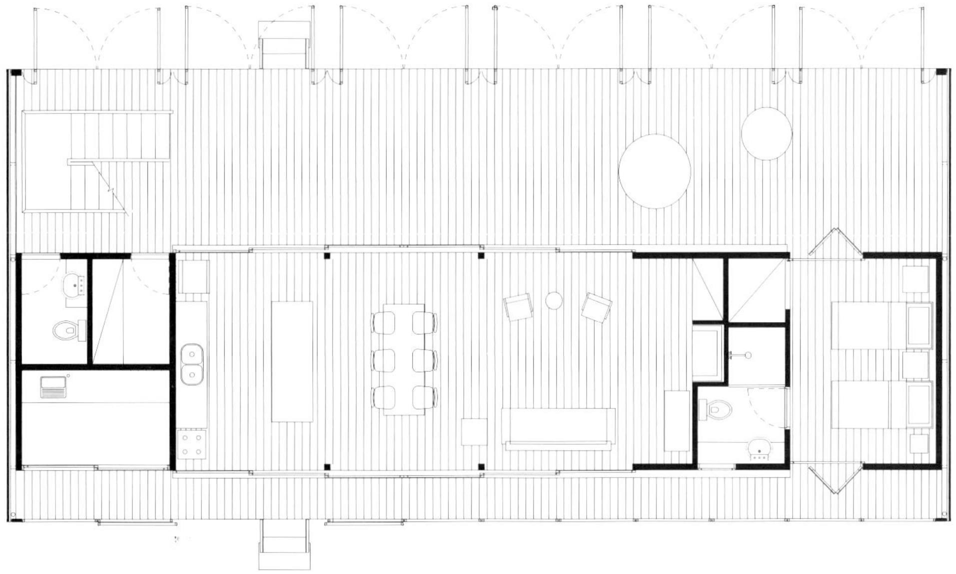

Left, from top Long section, first-floor plan and ground-floor plan.
Overleaf In contrast to the very open ground floor, the upper floor is more enclosed to provide some privacy for the bedrooms.

SONORAN DESERT, ARIZONA, USA
ROBERT RANSICK

CASA SEGURA

Height above sea level
2,171m/7,123ft

Average annual rainfall
465mm/18in

Average high and low temperatures
32.7°C/90°F–5.6°C/42°F

Opposite Only the solar panel on top of the rugged enclosure reveals that this is anything more sophisticated than a simple store.
Far left and left Robert Ransick designed Casa Segura's interior to provide as many facilities as possible within a limited space.
Below Section.

Southern Arizona's Sonoran Desert is one of the favoured crossing points for illegal immigrants trying to enter the United States from Mexico. It is also physically one of the harshest. With high temperatures, unrelenting sun and no access to water or food, this route into the country has become known as the 'Camino del Diablo' – the devil's highway.

In May 2004, the New York Times reported that 43 people had died near the Mexican border since the previous October. As entry in urban areas has become more difficult with fences, improved technology and enhanced patrols, the attraction of crossing the Sonoran Desert has increased. Crossing the border itself is fairly easy – just a matter of getting over a barbed-wire fence – but it is followed by a walk of two or three days, covering up to 80 kilometres (50 miles). The problem is that most people need a 4.5 litres (1 gallon) of water for every 8 kilometres (5 miles) they walk, and most start with only about 9 litres (2 gallons), weighing about 8 kilograms (17 pounds).

It was the danger to the immigrants, coupled with the distrust landholders feel for them that led artist Robert Ransick to come up with his concept of the Casa Segura (safe house). Initially an art project, displayed at the Eyebeam Gallery in New York, it was also intended to be installed for real, as a building that could offer refuge, both physical and emotional, to people who had been struggling across the desert.

Working with a landowner, Ransick developed the simple structure, powered by solar energy, in which water and food would be provided, along with clean clothes and basic medical supplies. In addition, a touch-screen interface would allow the migrants to create stories and images using ready-made graphic icons that could then be uploaded to a website. These icons, developed with artists Alberto Morackis and Guadalupe Serrano, were based on Mexican myths and belief systems, and on the history of votive offerings.

Wood-framed, insulated and clad with plywood panels, the Casa Segura is like an icon of a dwelling, with only the solar panels above the roof suggesting a more hi-tech existence.

Exhibited in New York in autumn 2007, documentation of the project also subsequently went to the Te Tuhi Centre in New Zealand as part of an exhibition called 'Land Wars'.

All this, however, was a mere preliminary to the installation for real in the Sonoran Desert. While there is considerable hostility to illegal migrants, Ransick's collaborating landowner took a different view. He explained: 'Not long ago, our house was broken into while we were away. The only things taken were some jeans and shirts, a few pairs of walking shoes, and food. We were expecting to feel outraged and violated when we returned to the house, but when we realized that it could only have been desperate migrants, we felt sad – for not being able to do more for them – their taking only necessities spoke eloquently of their need and their desperation. The border patrol suggested protecting our house with motion detectors, alarms, leaving a car outside at all times, keeping a radio going inside, even purchasing a shotgun. "If you don't hit them, you'll blow a hole so wide, they'll have no trouble finding their way out."

'We asked if it would be okay (within the law) to leave a box of supplies outside our house for them. No one objected, so we bought warm clothing, shoes, canned goods, bottled water, a can opener, and left a note in Spanish. It has been emptied a number of times. Some neighbours have taken to doing the same.'

Keen to find more such compassionate landowners, Ransick has published the plans of the Casa Segura and technical information on solar panels and touch-screen connections at http://casasegura.us. If take-up is sufficient, these modest houses could have an enormous impact, reducing the unforgivable loss of life.

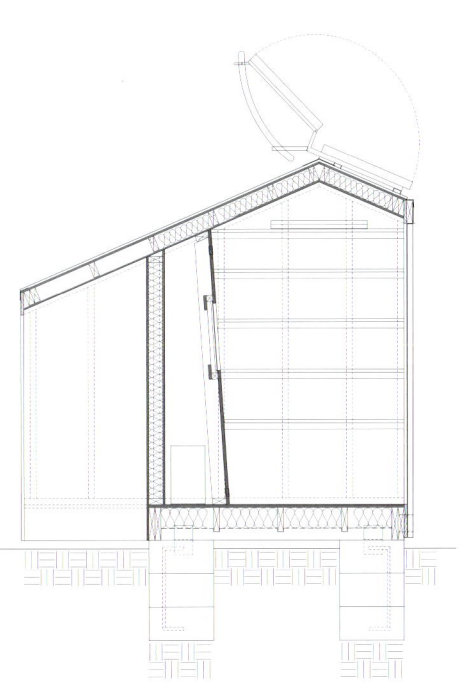

COSTA ADEJE, TENERIFE, CANARY ISLANDS, SPAIN
ARTENGO MENIS PASTRANA

MAGMA ARTS AND CONGRESS CENTRE

 Height above sea level
100m/328ft

 Average annual rainfall
412mm/16 1/4 in

 Average high and low temperatures
27°C/80°F – 18°C/64°F

Opposite Local volcanic ash used in the concrete helps the building to blend into its surroundings.
Right Site plan.
Below The curvaceous roof covers a series of complex but logically planned spaces.

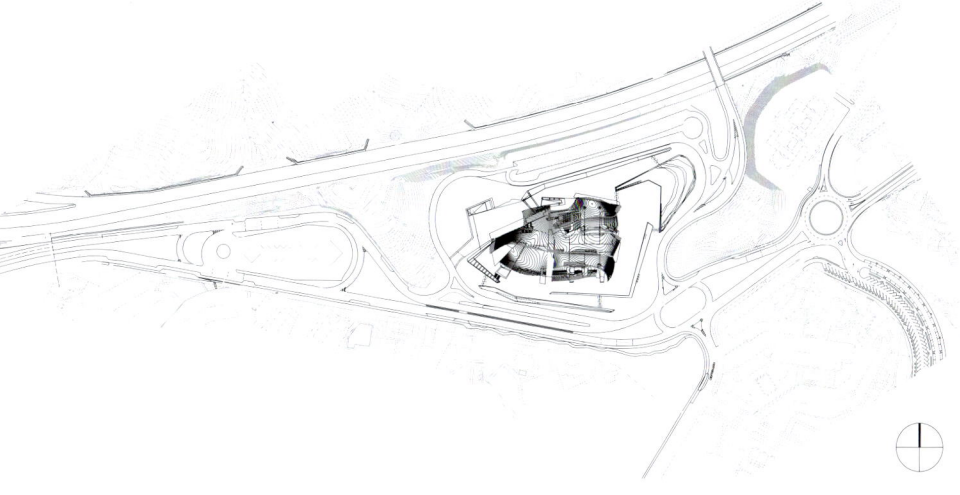

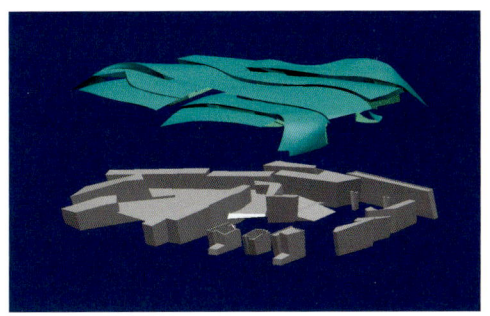

Tenerife is often seen as synonymous with cheap tourism, especially by the English who make up the largest proportion of the 3.5 million visitors it receives every year. Administratively part of Spain, it is the largest of the seven Canary Islands that sit off the northwest coast of Africa, offering winter sunshine in a slick and unthreatening way.

Geographically there are two parts to Tenerife: a humid, lush northern section, and the much drier, near-desert south. It is in the latter that the Magma centre sits, looking rather like a collection of rocks that have been thrown up by a volcano.

Planted around with cacti and other succulents, the building seems at home in its uncompromising environment, a solid but complex collection of heavy elements topped by a lighter undulating roof that has been described, a little unkindly, as 'like overflowing custard'.

The spatial planning is in fact highly rational, with the principal volumes at the centre and other elements either thrown to the edges, where they can enjoy natural light or, for functional areas such as WCs and cloakrooms where this is less important, protruding into the central space.

Initially the building was intended purely as a convention centre, but during the planning stage the brief evolved to allow it also to be used for theatre and music. The main elements are therefore two multifunctional halls that can satisfy a wide range of uses, with reconfigurable seating and movable partitions.

The larger of these two halls can hold up to 2,500 people for concerts or plays. When it is being used by an orchestra, the fly tower is blocked off. The huge steel trusses concealed by the ceiling allow a free span of nearly 80 metres (262 feet), and the lack of symmetry that is desirable for the best acoustic performance also sits well with the sculptural form of the building.

In the performance spaces and elsewhere, the roof is cleft, allowing shafts of light to enter. Where this is not technically feasible, concealed artificial lighting is used to give the impression of the entry of daylight.

The architect has revelled in the appearance of the concrete, combining diagonal board-marking with bush-hammering to provide a range of textures that can reflect the light externally and internally, or show their detail in the shadows cast by the overhanging roof.

One simple way in which the architect has rooted the building in its surroundings is by the use of a local stone for aggregate. Called 'chasna', this is a sandy coloured, compressed volcanic ash.

So, from a distance, the building blends into the terrain while presenting an intriguing combination of forms and textures. Close to, it is an impressive structure, reminiscent of the sturdy tombs of primitive societies. And once the visitor is inside, they are absorbed and overwhelmed by the massive elements and the soaring spaces these enclose.

Although in environmental terms the building provides a respite from the harsh environment around it, visually it echoes the strength of those surroundings. Tough and magnificent, there is nothing pretty or yielding about it. And despite the fact that it makes one feel that it may have been thrust from the ground in the last volcanic eruption, it has an air of solidity and permanence that contrasts impressively with much of the less considered development around it, whose ephemeral nature is its only virtue.

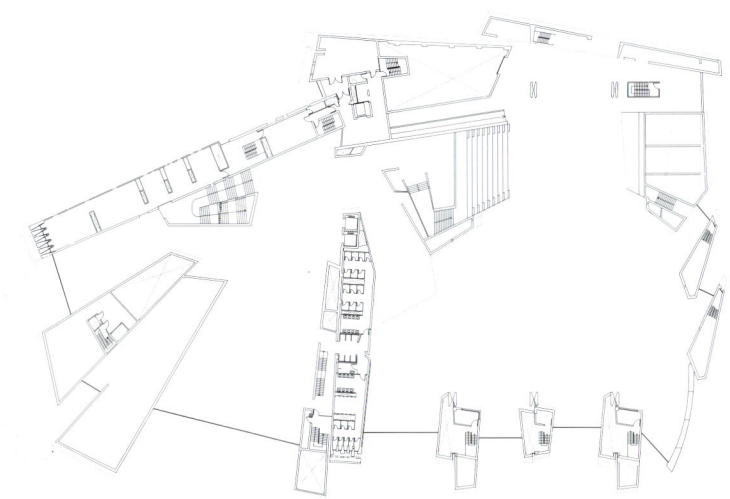

Top First-floor conference room. Light, both natural and artificial, is used cleverly to enhance the sculptural forms.
Above Ground-floor plan with the performance space at top right.
Left The magnificent spaces of the interior have a tough sensuality, with the use of polished concrete on the floors and bush-hammered and board-marked finishes on the walls.

OSOYOOS, BRITISH COLUMBIA, CANADA
HOTSON BAKKER BONIFACE HADEN ARCHITECTS + URBANISTES

NK'MIP DESERT CULTURAL CENTRE

▲ **Height above sea level**
277.7m/911ft

 Average annual rainfall
250mm/9¾in

Average high and low temperatures
45ºC/113ºC – 1.3ºC/34ºF

Stripes of sedimentary colour make up the long rammed-earth wall that is the defining element of the Nk'Mip Desert Cultural Centre in Osoyoos, British Columbia. Seeming to have been formed from the surrounding environment, this wall is, in fact, the product of clever technology and some artificial colourants, a seeming contradiction that is appropriate for the paradoxes that surround the centre.

It sits on the edge of the Nk'Mip Desert, probably the only desert in the world that is sandwiched between a lake and a thriving vineyard. Nk'Mip is in turn part of the Okanagan region of British Columbia, seen as Canada's only desert area. Indeed, the nearby town of Osoyoos is twinned with Palm Springs.

However this is not a vast untamed area, but a habitat that is under attack. As it is about the hottest place in Canada, with the longest growing season, the temptation has been to irrigate it and replace the indigenous semi-arid vegetation. Also, given the severity of much of the country's climate, the area is a draw for tourists, particularly since the dryness makes the high summer temperatures tolerable.

A further complication comes from the fact that the area forms part of the Osoyoos Indian Reserve. It was a change in the law, allowing joint ownership of land, which led to the development of the Nk'Mip resort, an attempt both to generate revenue and to preserve some of the historic environment. And dominating the resort is the cultural centre, the most highly applauded building there, which acts as an interpretation centre and, hence, a starting point for exploration and understanding of the desert.

The stated aim of Hotson Bakker Boniface Haden Architects + Urbanistes was to represent the Osoyoos people 'as part of a living culture', and so it deliberately eschewed any imitation of traditional architecture, instead choosing a collection of buildings both protected and advertised by the rammed-earth wall, which makes the complex seem part of the land but in a contemporary manner.

At 80 metres (262 feet) long and 5.5 metres (18 feet) high, this is one of the largest rammed-earth structures ever built. And, just to increase the challenge, the architects decided to incorporate a continuous slot window along part of its length, which meant that the upper part of the wall had to be suspended from the concrete roof slab.

Opposite A continuous slot window in the rammed-earth wall increases the technical complexity of the structure.
Above The retaining wall both protects the buildings within the complex and advertises their presence.
Right Ground-floor plan. 1. entry; 2. WCs; 3. administration; 4. lecture/performance theatre; 5. stage; 6. exhibition gallery; 7. outdoor amphitheatre; 8. terrace; 9. desert stream

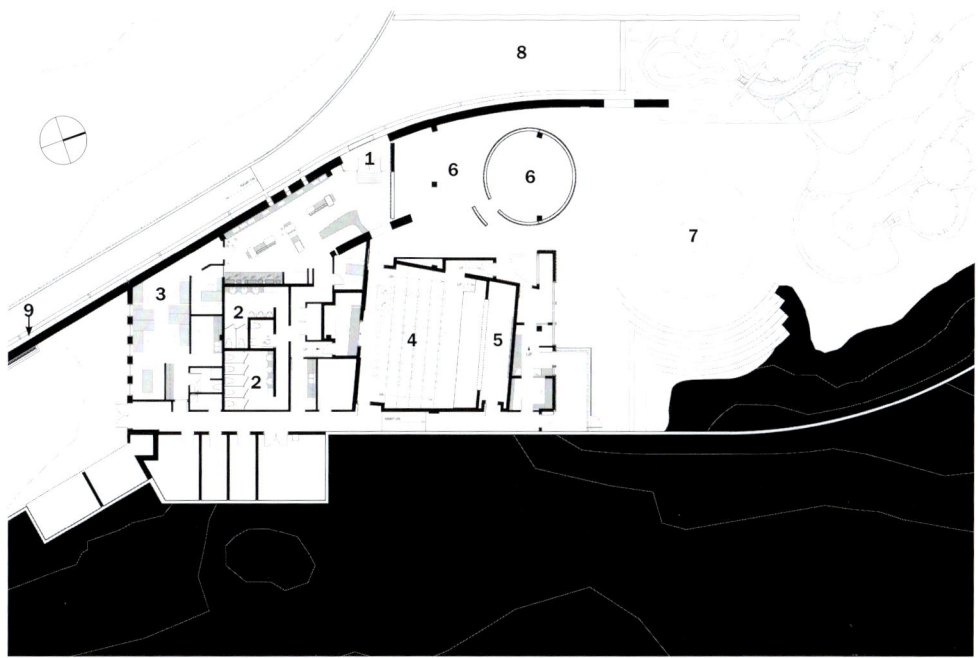

Strictly speaking, the material used is stabilized rammed earth, a more durable form of the primitive construction material. Adding a small amount of cement to the mix makes it less vulnerable to rain damage – yes, it does rain sometimes, even in the desert. The material is shaped in formwork, like concrete, and like concrete the wall also contains reinforcement as well as a layer of polyisocyanurate insulation. But the reinforced earth itself also has considerable insulating properties, and the thermal performance of the complex is further enhanced by partially burying elements of the structure.

Although the wall uses local soil, the colours were made more dramatic by the inclusion of some chemical dyes – natural colours would have been more muted.

But these colours blend well with the surprisingly successful use of Cor-ten weathering steel on some building elements, a material more often used to romanticize urban grittiness than in a natural setting. Internally, pine and polished concrete continue the aesthetic of tough luxury. The pine, also used for some external applications, is local bluestain pine, which looks as if it has received a blue wash. The architects are keen to use this as a demonstration project, to show that the material can be as useful as the yellow pine that is normally preferred.

The concrete roof to the centre is planted with scrubby desert plants, reinstating the desert that was destroyed by the building works.

With exhibition spaces, a lecture theatre and an outdoor amphitheatre, the building has the full range of facilities that one would expect in such a centre. But the most impressive element, acting both as a draw and as a reinterpretation of the surroundings, is the building itself. The architects were eager that the construction should both teach usable skills to local people and act as a demonstration of sustainable techniques. It has achieved both these aims, but the building would be admirable even if one knew nothing about them.

Above Local bluestain pine has been used on the interiors.
Left The outdoor amphitheatre.

Above From inside the complex, visitors are aware of the surrounding scenery.
Right Although artificial colours were used in the creation of the rammed-earth wall, it still blends with the surrounding soils and vegetation.

SCOTTSDALE, ARIZONA, USA
JEFFREY H. PAGE RA

ENGBARTH RESIDENCE

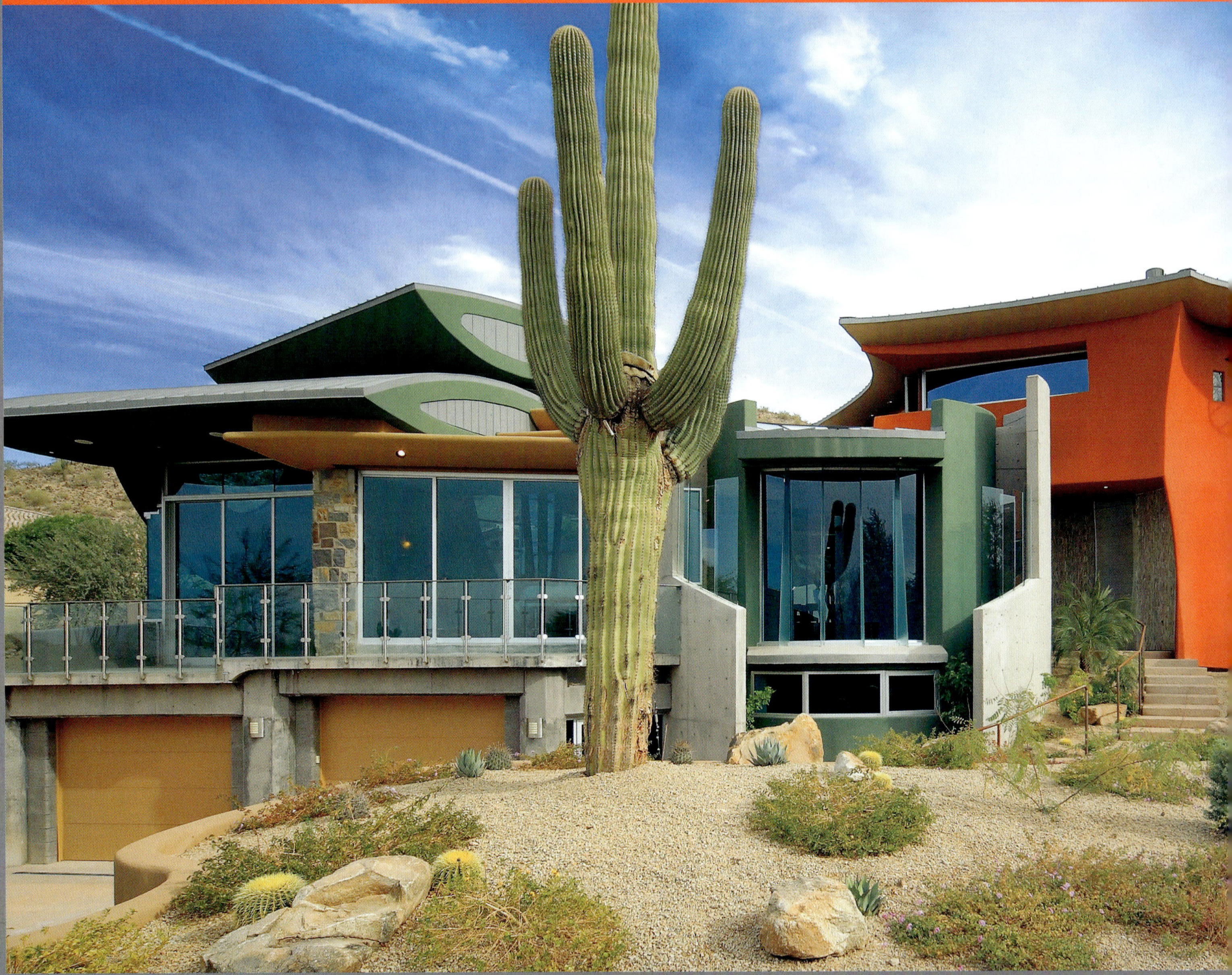

Height above sea level
513m/1,683ft

Average annual rainfall
254mm/10in

 Average high and low temperatures
46.11°C/115°F – -1.11°C/30°F

Below Set on the edge of Scottsdale, the house straddles a dry desert wash and is rendered in sage green, burnt orange and aubergine (the last not visible in this image).
Right Ground-floor plan.
1. entry; 2. dining room; 3. billiard room; 4. deck; 5. great room; 6. patio; 7. breakfast room; 8. kitchen; 9. bedroom; 10. meditation room

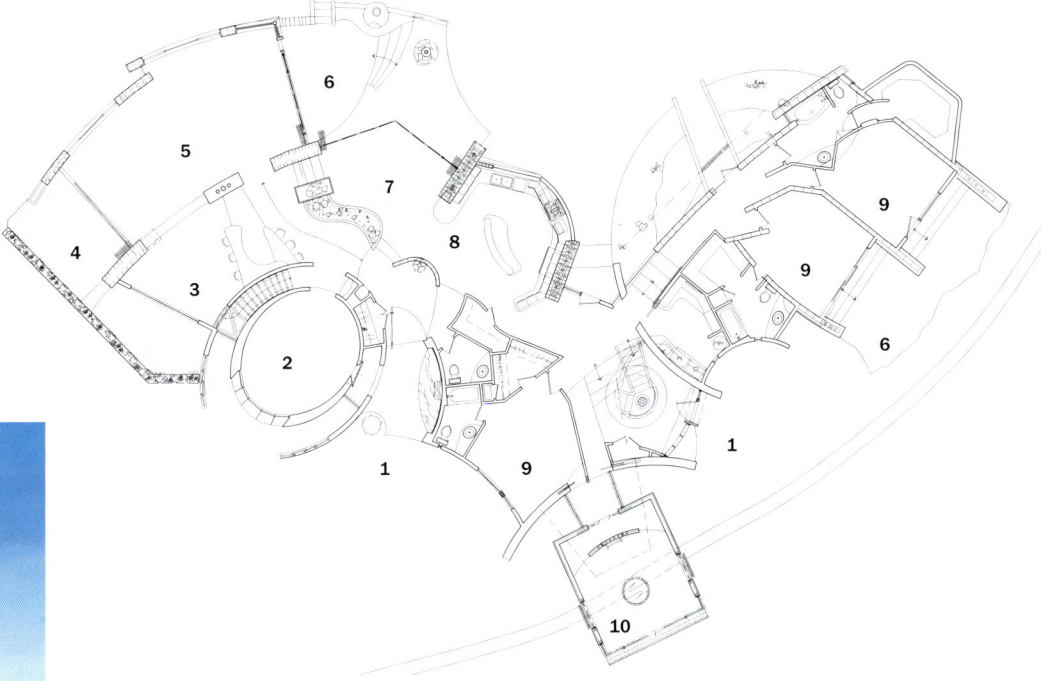

There is an angle from which you can approach the Engbarth Residence, on the edge of Scottsdale, Arizona, where it almost seems to blend in with the desert surroundings. If your first view is of the guest house/office, you will see a curving, dry-dirt red form looking at ease with the rounded shapes of the cacti and the arid environment. But this is the only approach that gives that impression. Otherwise this house, in the city dubbed the 'Beverly Hills of the Desert', aims to keep its residents in touch with desert and mountain views but in a way that contrasts with nature rather than accommodating it.

Built for a family with three children, who also wanted a home office, the house is a deliberate mixture of clashing forms and bright colours, with the sun welcomed in certain spaces and kept out elsewhere. All this is under an overhanging roof planted with soil and desert plants to provide some temperature moderation.

Jeffrey H. Page, whose office is nearby in Cave Creek, another but smaller satellite of Phoenix, has experience of designing for the particular demands of the desert. These are not only extreme heat and, sometimes, cold (the highest ever recorded temperature in Scottsdale was 48°C (119°F), the lowest –7°C (19°F)), but also dryness interspersed with a sudden influx of water.

Indeed, this contrast formed a vital part of Scottsdale's history. The original Old Town, now the most southern part, was built around Indian Bend Wash, a dry riverbed that carried extreme flows of heavy rains. Because Scottsdale was a relatively poor town in the first half of the twentieth century, there was no money to build bridges, so roads ran straight across the riverbed. This meant that when the river was in flood people's homes were simply cut off. When, in the 1960s, these '99 year' floods started happening more frequently, the municipality rejected proposals to put Indian Bend Wash into a concrete canal. Instead, it invested in creating a natural flood plain of parks and golf courses. It was this development, coinciding with the development of cheap air conditioning to moderate the summer temperatures, that kick-started the development of Scottsdale.

The Engbarth Residence also runs across a dry creek bed, although on a smaller scale. But here, too, this is used to facilitate leisure, although in a more esoteric manner. A cantilevered circular glass floor forms the basis of a meditation room, from which one can look down to the creek bed known a desert wash (and occasional rushing water) below.

Left Lightweight steel framing creates clashing geometric forms.
Below White plaster finishes, coupled with local stone and a careful control of natural light, give the interior a feeling of refuge from the desert heat.

Entrance to the main house is in the centre, through a water court and an interior garden to the 'great room' which has a ceiling of white rendered planes and high-level glazing of extraordinary complexity – reminiscent on a smaller scale of the intricacy of EMBT's Scottish Parliament in Edinburgh. Like that project, this one seems to cram a great number of ideas into a relatively small space – and a lot of materials. Page has used lightweight steel framing, exposed concrete, rough-hewn stone, timber ceilings, blockwork and render. Internally the render is largely white but on the outside it is in sage green, burnt orange and aubergine, in addition to the ox-blood of the separate but linked guest house/office.

Page talks of an 'orchestrated collision of geometric forms' and these are used to create 'leftover' spaces including an oval, largely glazed dining room, and a separate children's wing reached up a ramp and through an irregular archway that looks as if it has been hammered out by some villain, or just never finished. The master bedroom occupies the entire upper level, up a staircase supported by reinforcing bars in an inverted cone form designed to be reminiscent of the ocotillo shrub, a local drought-resistant plant with whip-like stems.

Other local vegetation, tamed a little for the desert garden, includes saguaro – the tree-sized, branched cacti native to the region, yellow-flowering palo verde trees, spiny velvet mesquite trees, barrel cactus and other forms of cacti. The situation is magnificent, at the foot of the McDowell Mountains.

Energy conservation was a priority – the house is wrapped in insulating synthetic stucco and has exterior wall cavity insulation. Exterior glazing is double-insulated solar coated low-emission glass. Although, with underground parking for three cars at the house, and for another six below the guest house/office, this is hardly an exemplar for environmentally conscious design, its embrace of the desert landscape is a pleasing contrast to the over-watered lawns of nearby Phoenix and is part of a growing water conservation movement in the region.

And though the response to the desert landscape is an idiosyncratic one that will not be to everybody's taste, it is a deliberate response, certainly to be preferred to the creeping mindless suburbanization that spreads out from far too many towns.

Above Local arid vegetation, 'tamed' by careful geometric arrangements, forms the xeriscaped garden, with a detached guest house/office behind.

JOSHUA TREE, CALIFORNIA, USA
JANET ARMSTRONG JOHNSTON

SACRED SANDS STRAWBALE B&B

Height above sea level
987.6m/3,238ft

Average annual rainfall
203.2mm/8in

Average high and low temperatures
43.33°C/110°F – 7.22°C/45°F

Below The rendered walls contrast with elements clad in rusting metal that deliberately evokes abandoned mine buildings.
Right Straw-bale construction.

Just 1.6 kilometers (1 mile) from the entrance to southeastern California's Joshua Tree National Park sits the Sacred Sands guest house, a small bed and breakfast place set in a dramatic landscape and built using sustainable techniques. The architect, local practitioner Janet Armstrong Johnston, is one of the founding members of the California Straw Building Association, and has used straw bales in the construction of this house.

One doesn't immediately associate straw with this high desert location. The 3,196 square kilometre (1,234 square mile) Joshua Tree National Park encompasses parts of not one but two deserts: the Colorado Desert and the Mojave Desert, the latter the home of the eponymous Joshua tree (*Yucca brevifolia*), which has a distinctive silhouette that looks fantastic photographed against the clear blue skies. But, in fact, the straw is Californian, if not from this precise area. The state produces nearly two million tons of rice a year, mainly in the Sacramento Valley. In 1992, the California Rice Straw Burning Reduction Act was passed, forcing rice farmers to find alternative methods of disposing of their straw waste. As part of an effort to help find those new markets, in 1995 the California State Guidelines for Straw Bale Structures were passed, and the following year the California Straw Building Association was formed by enthusiasts for the technique.

The site for this straw building is above a desert wash – a bed carved out by flood rainfall, which retains a small amount of dampness for a long time. Mountain lions have been seen crossing the road, and coyotes and other desert animals travel along the wash. The intention was to have a building that sat comfortably within this landscape, rather than being imposed upon it. Centred around a courtyard accessed from the common space and also from the kitchen, the building has two guest rooms, all with views and their own jacuzzis, plus private space for the owners.

Straw bales, which provide good insulation, also determine the aesthetic by creating thick walls, which here are coated with a clay plaster to further increase the thermal mass. Other parts of the building are timber-framed and are clad and roofed with profiled metal. This is deliberately allowed to rust, in an evocation of the abandoned mining buildings in the national park.

Above At first sight the interior offers conventional luxury, but the use of natural colours and the slight rounding to the window reveals betrays the use of unusual construction techniques.
Opposite Floor plan.
1. entrance; 2. kitchen;
3. bathroom; 4. laundry;
5. porch; 6. common room;
7. lounge; 8. guest room;
9. yoga bay; 10. private garden

In this extreme climate, it is not possible for the building to do all the work of providing comfort, so there are evaporative coolers (locally known as swamp coolers) which are an effective way of providing cooling in very dry environments, and propane wall heaters for the winter nights.

The straw for this building may have come from the other end of the state, but otherwise constructing the house was a truly local enterprise. The architect has a house in the same village, the contractor lives two minutes away in his own straw-bale house, the architect's husband helped out with the building, and so did the clients themselves. They had asked for 'desert funk' as a style and were satisfied that they had achieved it. And by importing building materials from one of the wettest parts of the state to one of the driest, they have ended up with a building that is eminently suited to its environment. Funky or what?

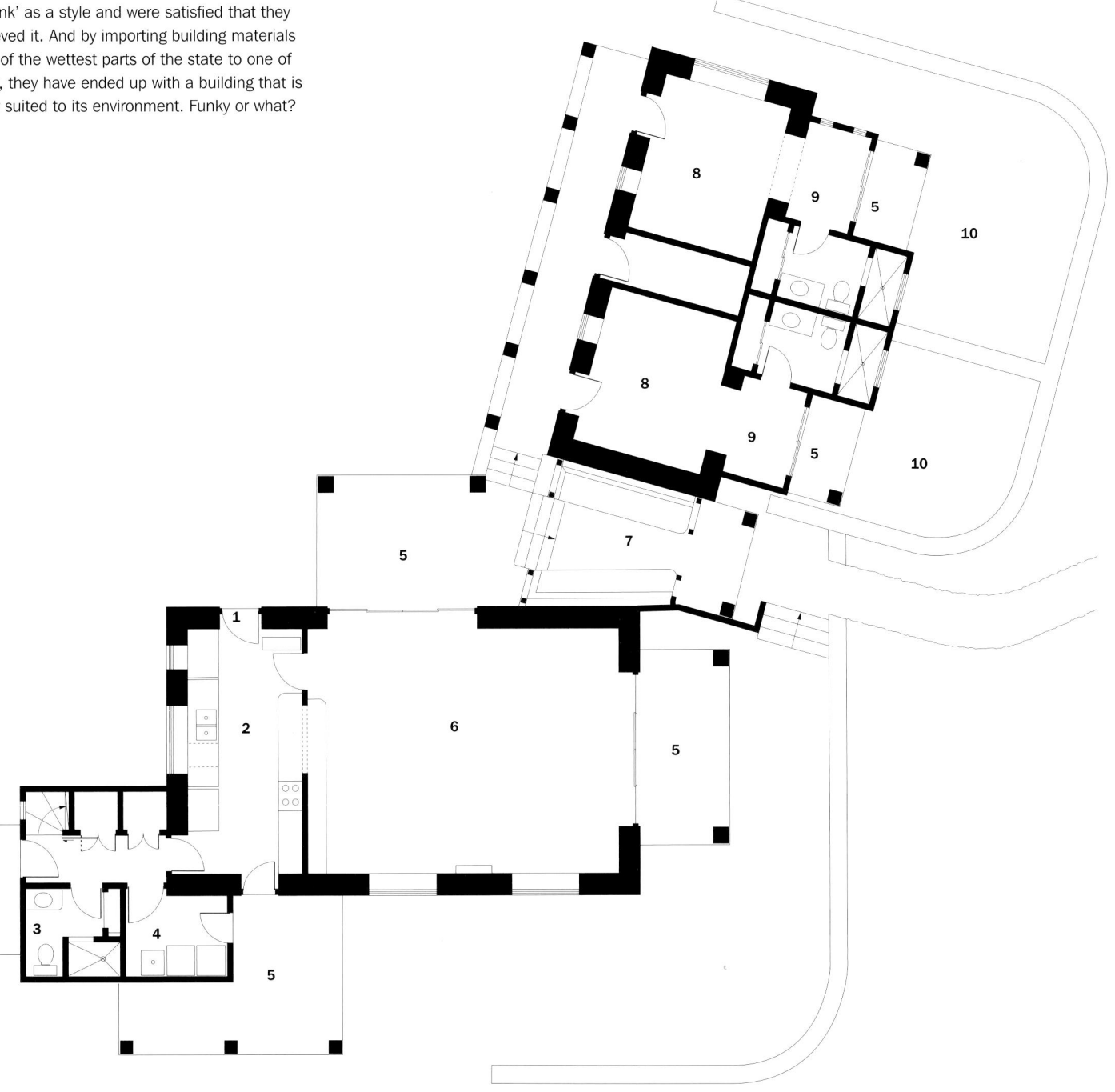

DJUGERARI, WESTERN AUSTRALIA
IREDALE PEDERSEN HOOK ARCHITECTS

WALMAJARRI COMMUNITY CENTRE

Height above sea level
280m/918ft

Average annual rainfall
540mm/21¼in

Average high and low temperatures
40.6ºC/105ºF – 10.7ºC/51ºF

Opposite The oversailing roof unifies the collection of buildings below.
Right Shade beneath the roof provides usable outdoor space.
Below Site plan. The seemingly random positioning of buildings provides key views of the landscape and sacred sites.

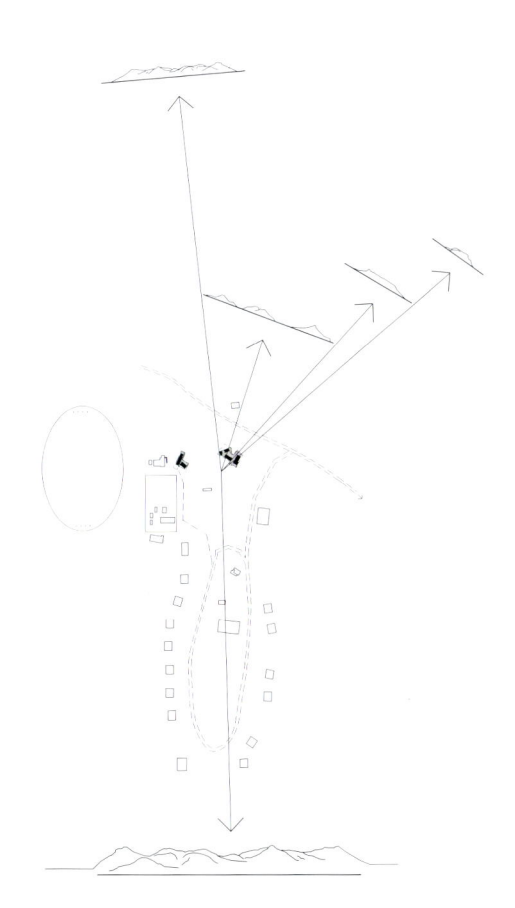

A cluster of buildings on a veranda, itself perched on dry red soil, seems to be informally arranged to the point of randomness. First impressions could be that the Perth-based architect, faced with such an expanse of space, spatial control and just dropped the buildings down with little consideration.

But this is not true at all. The relationship between the buildings is determined not by any formal positioning but by the views that they can afford of their surroundings. For although daunting and, in the immediate vicinity, very flat, this is not a featureless landscape. Djugerari, a tiny community with a population of just 80, sits on the edge of the Great Sandy Desert, one of the series of deserts that make up most of the western half of Australia. In one direction the buildings frame views of the sand hills of the desert. In the other, they look towards the mesas (broad, flat-topped elevations) that form the edge of the Fitzroy River valley.

Djugerari has become the focus for the Walmajarri, one of the groups of indigenous people who form most of the population in this part of the country. Originally nomadic desert dwellers, the Walmajarri became settled in the 1950s, working on cattle stations in the Fitzroy River valley. Djugerari now offers them a school, and this community centre with a meeting room, offices and training spaces. In deliberate links with the people's history, its views are of sacred places, including one that was the site of a massacre.

The materials for the building are simple and robust: a lightweight steel frame, largely corrugated metal cladding, and doors and windows sealed to keep out dust. Diesel generators power the air-conditioning system that will allow the building to be used all year round (summer temperatures can hit 48°C (118°F)) and is designed to be as efficient as possible. An oversailing roof both minimizes heat gain to the pavilions and allows maximum use of the outdoor space.

This is not iredale pedersen hook's only encounter with the desert. The practice, which characterizes its projects by their environment, is interested in the notion of edge conditions, and reacting to the essentially horizontal nature of most Australian landscapes.

In the Great Victoria Desert it uses a similar seeming informality, not once but repeatedly, in its Tjunjuntjara community houses for the Spinifex people. There, each house looks in the direction of the family members' specific sacred site, while also relating to a central community area where jaunty tented structures create circles of shade.

In Mardu Country, East Pilbara, Western Australia, the architect initially designed four semi-transportable houses, a project that expanded eventually to become 17 houses for six different communities. The aim was to produce houses that were simple and affordable to build but satisfied both climatic and social demands. Because up to 20 people typically end up using the infrastructure of each house, if not actually living in it, the architects came up with the concept of a 'house within a house'. The inner element consists of two fully enclosed pavilions on a prestressed concrete slab, with enclosure by corrugated coloured sheeting. An oversailing parasol roof provides shelter for the extended number of users, and helps keep the temperature down to bearable levels.

Far more formal-seeming, and with an entirely different demographic, is a simple overnight place that allows visitors to experience an Anthony Gormley installation as it is meant to be seen, at dawn and dusk. The work was created as part of the Perth International Arts Festival in 2002, but is actually 800 kilometres (497 miles) northwest of the city, on the edge of a huge salt lake. Called the Field House, the accommodation is a long building built from straw bales clad with plywood. It consists of a series of sleeping pods, all aligned to enjoy cooling breezes from the lake and offer optimum views of Gormley's work. Again, there is a large oversailing roof. Cooling here is far less technologically sophisticated than on the other buildings. The Field House functions like a 'Coolgardie safe', a system invented before the advent of refrigeration to keep food cool. It consisted of a storage box with hessian walls, kept constantly damp by a reservoir at the top. Water dripped down to wet the hessian, and evaporated, keeping the contents cool. Hessian curtains to the enclosure of the Field House act in the same way.

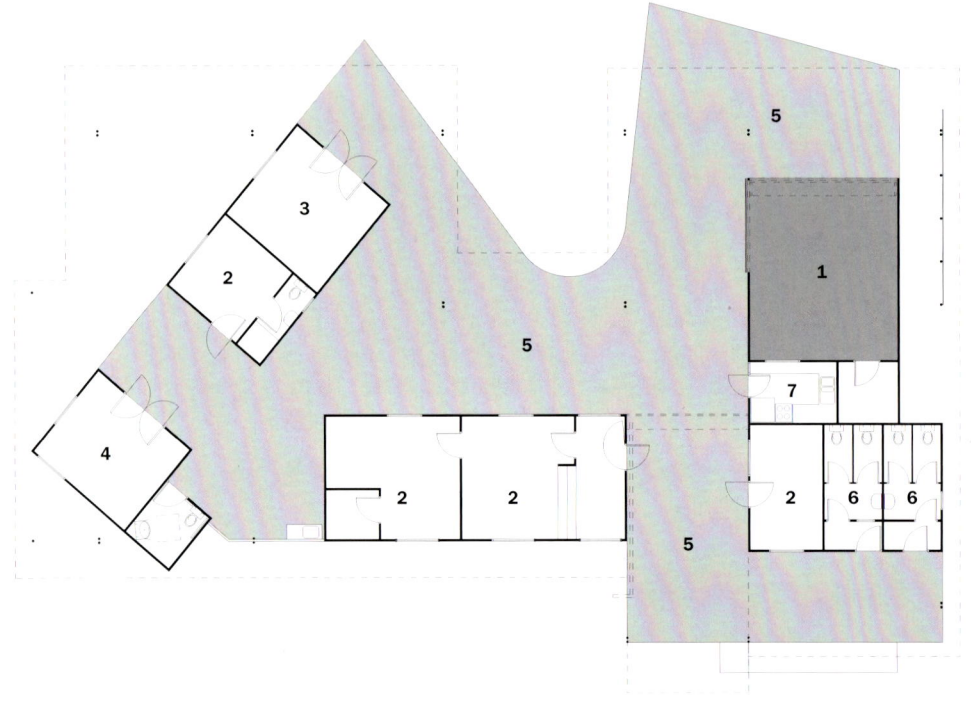

Above Children in one of the pavilions that sit under the roof.
Below Ground-floor plan.
1. meeting room; 2. office; 3. men's training; 4. women's training; 5. veranda; 6. WCs; 7. kitchen

Left Section
Below Doors and windows have been designed so that, when closed, they will keep out the desert dust.
Overleaf Views from the remote settlement include flat-topped mesas in the distance.

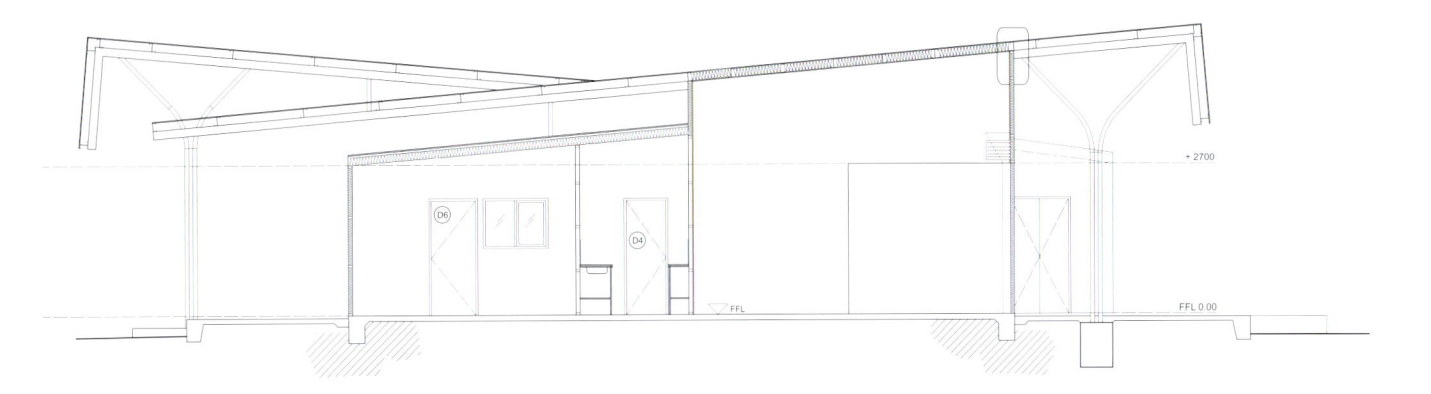

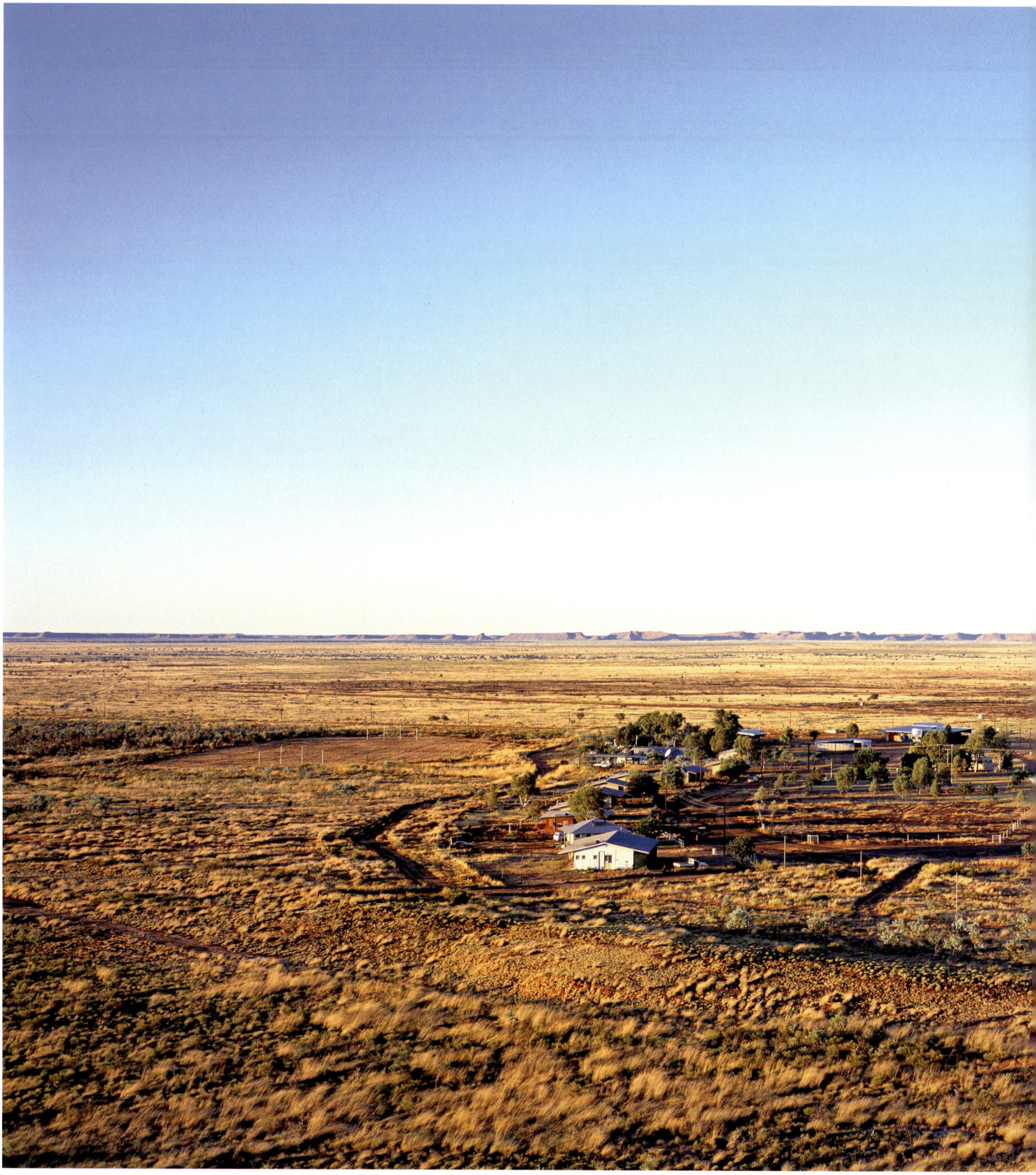

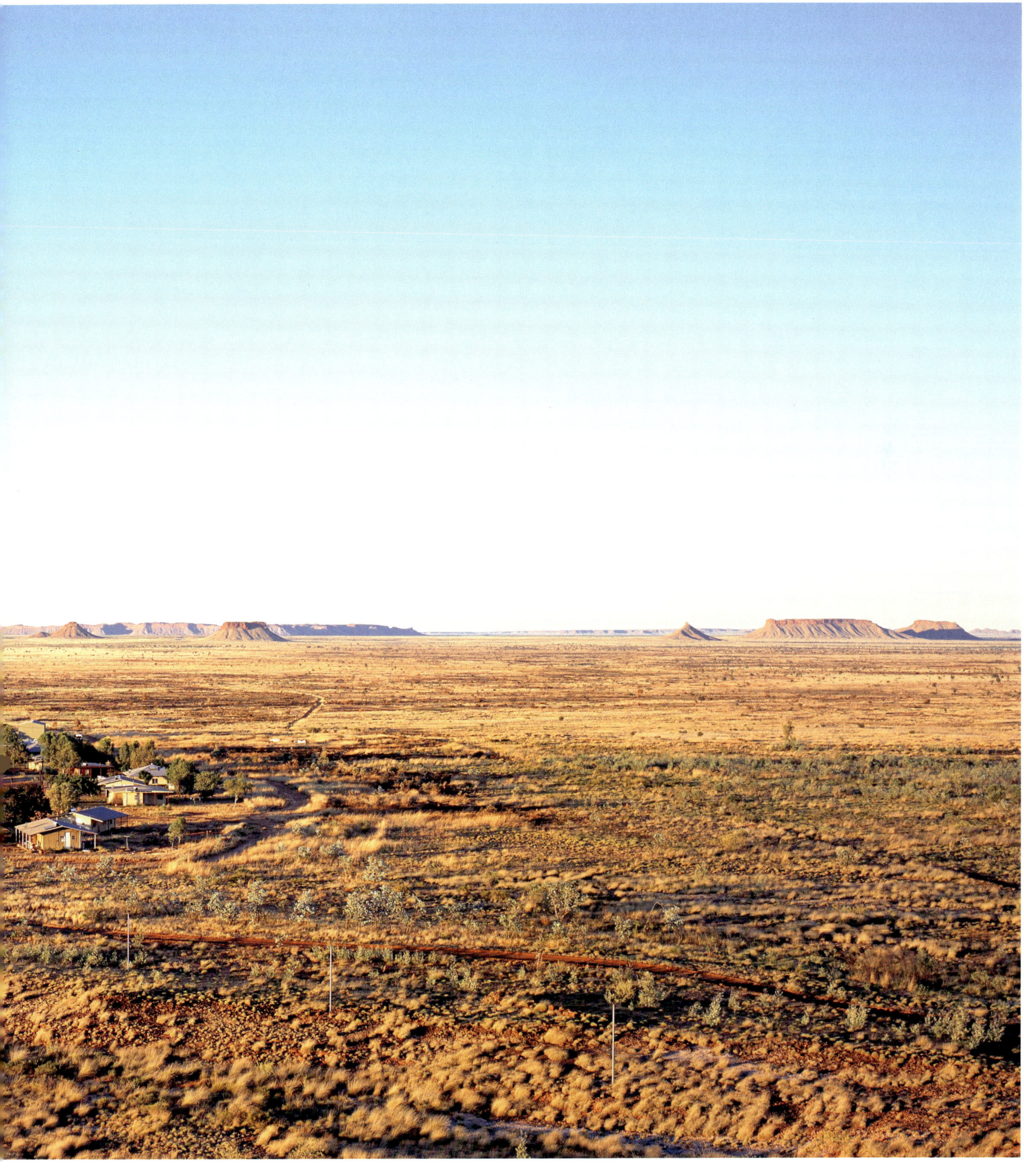

GANDO AND DANO, BURKINA FASO
DIÉBÉDO FRANCIS KÉRÉ

SCHOOL BUILDINGS

Height above sea level
Gando 308m/1,010ft
Dano 296m/971ft

Average annual rainfall
Gando 680mm/26¾in
Dano 680mm/26¾in

Average high and low temperatures
Gando 47ºC/116ºF – 15ºC/59ºF
Dano 47ºC/116ºF – 16ºC/60ºF

Opposite Built from earth blocks, the school at Gando has covered verandas separating the three classrooms.
Right The citation for the Aga Khan Award praised the school for 'laying the foundations of hope for the advancement of a people'.
Far right Inside the classrooms, mud blocks form both the walls and the ceilings.
Below Section

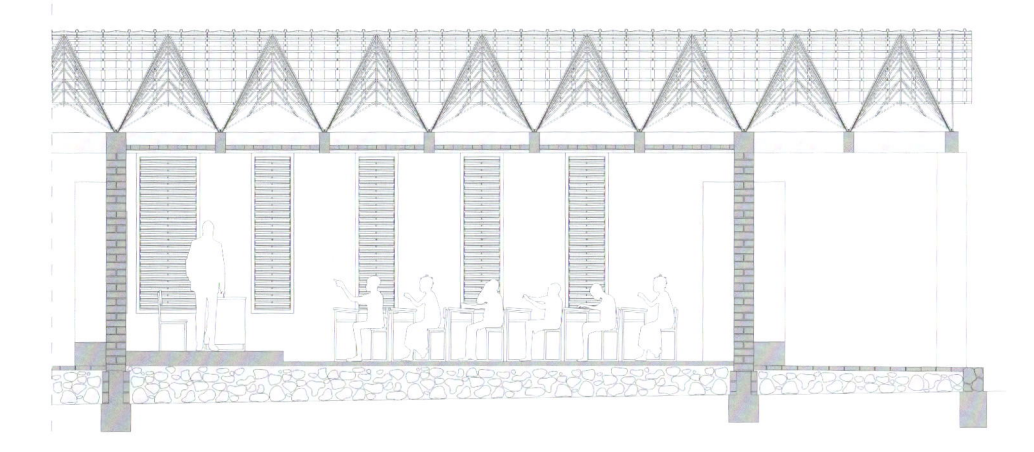

Burkina Faso is one of the poorest countries in the world, but one that is making enormous efforts to better itself. Levels of literacy, for example, while still far too low at only about 25 per cent, have doubled since 1990. Diébédo Francis Kéré epitomizes this move towards betterment, not only for the individual but also for the society. Trained as an architect in Berlin, he comes from the 3,000-strong village of Gando, which is about 200 kilometres (124 miles) from the capital Ouagadougou.

Kéré was the first person from Gando to study abroad, and he resolved to create a school for the village, setting up a fund-raising organization called Schulbausteine für Gando (Bricks for the Gando School) with German friends. The intention was not just to fund a school, but also to show what could be done with local materials to create sustainable, appropriate architecture and to transfer skills.

Burkina Faso has a dry and a wet season, the latter lasting about four months, and punishingly high temperatures. Shade and ventilation were therefore essential.

The three classrooms are arranged in a line, separated by covered outdoor areas that can be used either for teaching or for play. Stabilized compressed-earth blocks are used for the walls and also, supported on a grid of concrete beams and steel bars, for the ceiling. The high thermal mass of the blocks helps to moderate the temperature.

Also crucial is the low monopitched corrugated steel roof, supported on steel trusses. The space between the roof and the ceiling is used for ventilation, and the roof also projects to provide shade. It was necessary to build up the roof from relatively small elements, since the transport infrastructure meant that large items could not be brought in, and neither could a crane. The roof was therefore constructed from steel bars welded on site, with the sheeting laid on top on site. The architect taught local people to use a handsaw and a small welding machine.

The project won an Aga Khan Award for Architecture in 2004, an international award that aims to 'enhance the understanding and appreciation of Islamic culture as expressed through architecture'. In their citation, the judges called the project 'a structure of grace, warmth and sophistication, in sympathy with the local climate and culture. The practical and the poetic are fused. The primary school in Gando inspires pride and instils hope in its community, laying the foundations for the advancement of a people.'

Below left Shaded areas at the Dano school include a large gathering space.
Below centre Roofs at Dano undulate in both the horizontal and the vertical plane.
Far right The red and blue arrows illustrate environmental strategies for the Gando school (above) and Dano school (below).

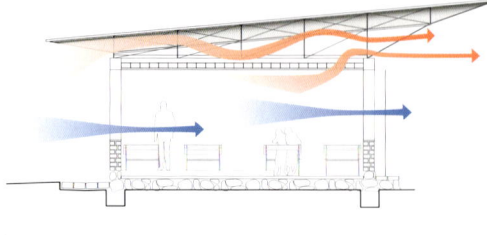

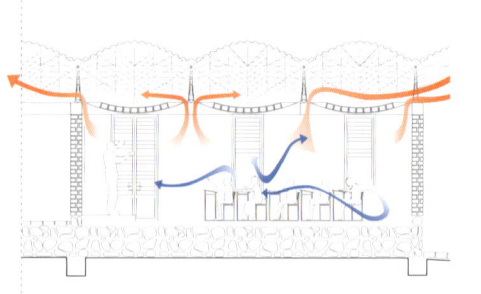

There are now more than 450 students at the school, and an extension was recently completed. In addition, Kéré has taken his ideas forward to another project 600 kilometres (373 miles) away, at Dano, capital of the province of Ioba. An extension to a school, for the Dreyer Foundation, it was built by young workers from Gando who Kéré had trained. This time the main building material was not compressed earth but local laterite brickstone, a product formed by the weathering of underlying rock. Since this stone is not particularly resistant to water, it was placed on a foundation layer of granite to enable it to endure the rainy season.

Again, shading and ventilation were paramount. The building is orientated east–west to reduce solar gain, and there are shutters and another oversailing roof, this time with a scalloped outline. Undulating in both the vertical and the horizontal plane, the roof assists rainwater run-off. As with the roof at Gando, it was built up from standard reinforcing bars on site. Among the shaded external spaces is an 'amphitheatre', a large gathering place for the students. The school also has slightly coffered suspended ceilings of timber and concrete.

There is an added confidence to this project, compared to the earlier one at Gando. Where the Gando school has the dignity of its utter simplicity, at Dano the architect, while still eager to use materials economically and appropriately, has also behaved more freely, with vaulted ceilings and variations in the colour of the shutters giving the building more personality. Internally, the shallow vaults of the suspended ceiling echo the regular arrangement of the desks. The level of control is impressive, and has an elegant austerity that would be deserving of applause on a project that had ten times the budget.

Below The structure at Dano was built up from small, easily transported elements, shown in this axonometric diagram.
Overleaf A base layer of granite protects the laterite brickstone in the rainy season.

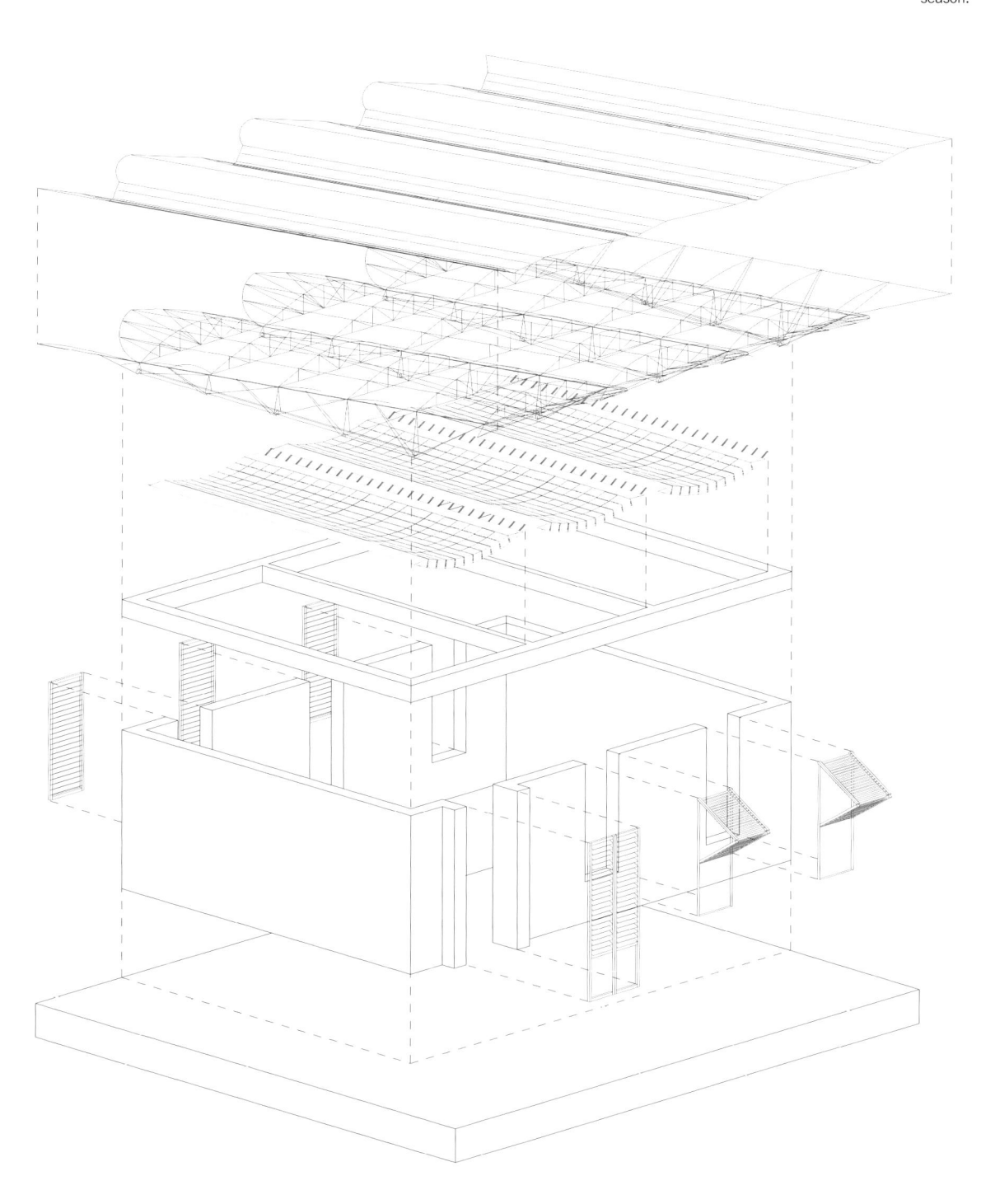

50 Extreme Architecture

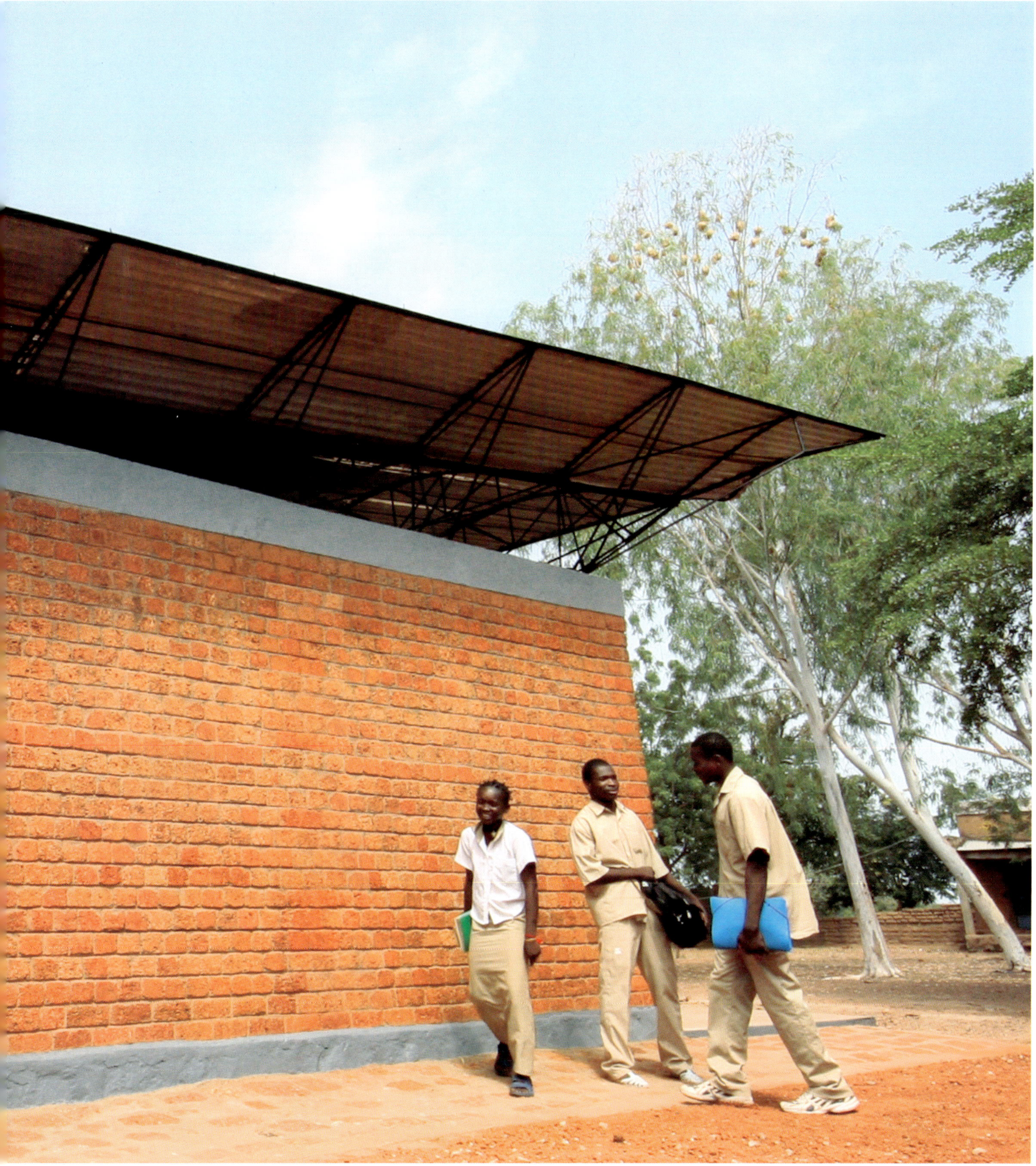

KOUDOUGOU, BURKINA FASO
LAURENT SÉCHAUD AND PIERRE JÉQUIER

CENTRAL MARKET

Height above sea level
290m/951ft

Average annual rainfall
728mm/28½in

Average high and low temperatures
40ºC/104ºF – 15ºC/59ºF

Above The central market is built on a repeating pattern, with the individuality coming from the animation that the sellers provide.
Opposite Shutters that close up the stalls at night act as awnings during the day.
Below Map of Koudougou showing the central market site (indicated by the red square on the left), and a proposed alternative (red square on the right) which the shopkeepers rejected.

If you go to Koudougou in Burkina Faso, you are likely to gravitate to the central market. First you will be impressed by just how busy it is, and then you may wonder when it was built. There is a great regularity and freshness to it that suggests it is relatively recent – it has not had time for all those accretions and ad hoc changes that come to any structure used by large numbers of people – and yet there is something seemingly timeless in the reddish mud blocks that have been used to build it. But then again, if you know anything about building traditions in Burkina Faso, you will know that those bricks have traditionally only been used for walls. Here they are used for roofs as well. What is going on?

What is going on is that this market is the product of a government programme to protect and promote the life of Burkina Faso's smaller towns, coupled with an aid programme from Switzerland.

Burkina Faso is a country undergoing transformation from an almost entirely rural population, through rapid urbanization. The pull has not just been to any town but to the capital Ouagadougou and to the second city, and former capital, Bobo-Dioulasso. To stem the exodus, not only from villages but also from the smaller towns, the government launched the Programme de Développement des Villes Moyennes (programme for the development of medium-sized towns) in 1990. Its aim was to strengthen the infrastructure of those mid-sized towns by providing elements such as markets, bus stations and slaughterhouses as a basis for sustainable development. This project has the backing of the Swiss Agency for Development and Cooperation (SDC).

As the country's third city, and situated only 75 kilometres (47 miles) west of the honeypot of Ouagadougou, Koudougou was a prime target for help. Revitalizing and rehousing the existing market was one of the key projects, and this has been achieved through a local committee, working with SDC architects Laurent Séchaud and Pierre Jéquier. As well as rehousing the market, by using mud bricks the project shows that there is a future for this traditional building material. It had been largely superseded by concrete-block construction, using imported materials. Similarly, straw roofs had been replaced by corrugated zinc sheets. The aim was to show that earth blocks could be used in sophisticated ways and that they have a better environmental performance than concrete – a real gain in this hot and, in the wet season, humid environment.

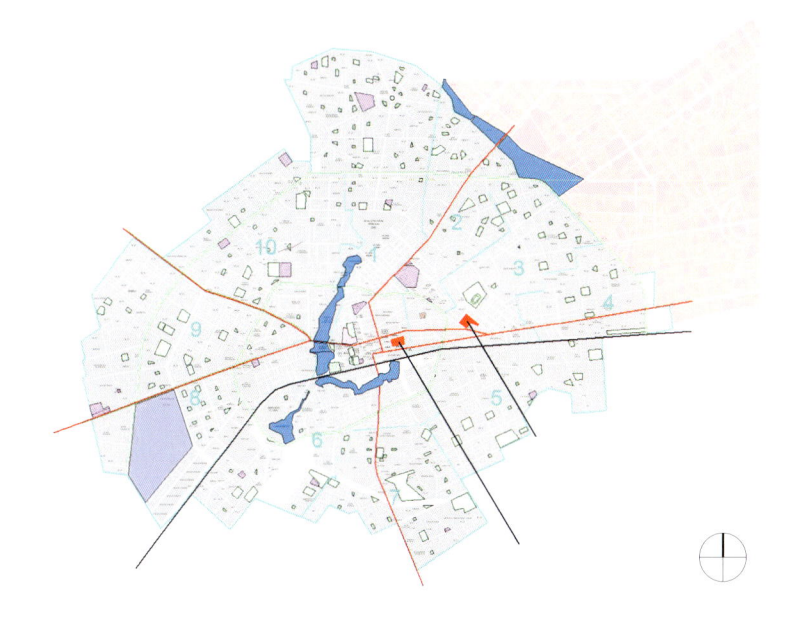

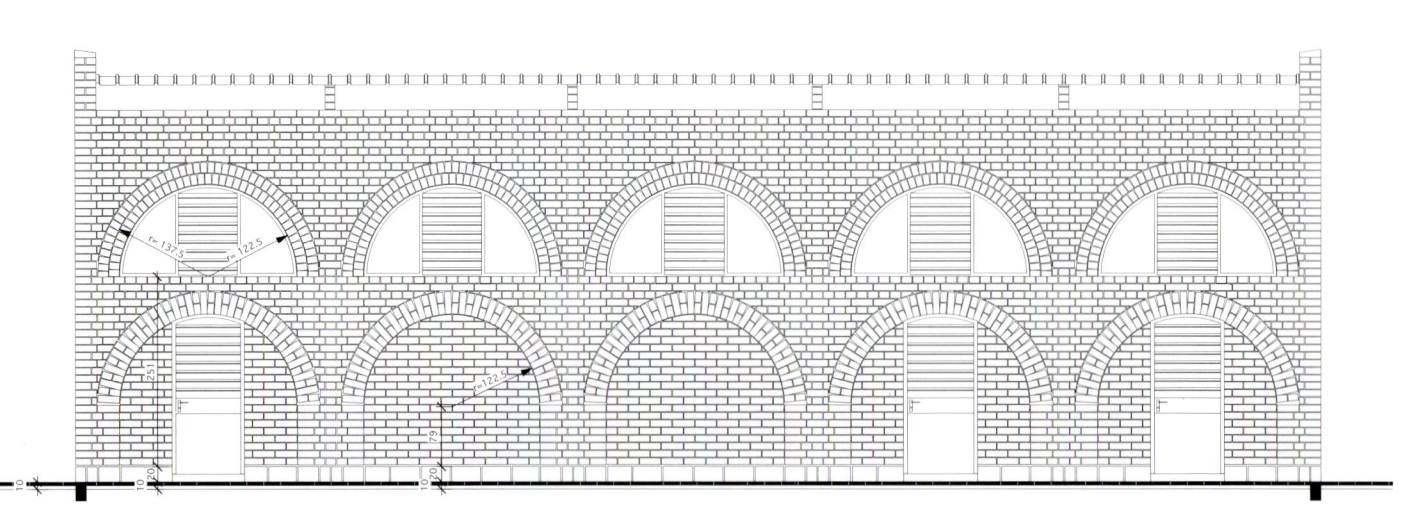

54 Extreme Architecture

Shopkeepers wanted to stay on their existing site, and it was therefore necessary to make the market very compact. In an area of just under 30,000 square metres (322,917 square feet), it accommodates 1,155 shops, 624 stalls and two administrative buildings.

The project started with the building of a prototype shop to test the design, and as a result several important modifications were made. The real construction took place in two phases. It used earth blocks, cut from a hillside only 2 kilometres (1.2 miles) away and employed in load-bearing walls 29.5 centimetres (12 inches) thick. The blocks were cast in hand presses on site, and made to the dimensions of either the load-bearing walls or narrower partition walls.

The central market is a rectangular area of vaulted domes, broken up by the open area surrounding an off-centre administration building. This area is surrounded by the shops, again on a regular grid, of different dimensions in each direction. On plan this could look oppressive, but it offers clear views and breezes. And there is a great tradition of building markets in this way – think, for instance, of the Grand Bazaar in Istanbul. The animation and variety comes from the people and the goods on display.

There are clever touches. For example, metal shutters close down the stalls at night but when open also act as awnings, providing shade. Vaults were built without using formwork, as timber is scarce in the country. Similarly, there was almost no timber used in the construction. There is, however, corrugated metal on the roofs to provide protection in the rainy season. By designing a gap between the domes and the metal roofs of about 35 centimetres (14 inches), more air can circulate.

This was a deliberately labour-intensive method of building, and also provided training. As a result of working on the project, 140 masons obtained certification in the techniques used.

Koudougou has ended up with a thriving market, in a dignified space that shows the value of traditional building techniques and has provided employment and training for local people. It is not surprising that in 2007 this project, like the Gando school in 2004, received a coveted Aga Khan Award for Architecture.

Above and top Workers learned new skills to build the vaulted construction.
Opposite top The market's vaulted domes form a rectangular grid.
Opposite bottom and this page, below Details of the vaulted mud-brick construction.

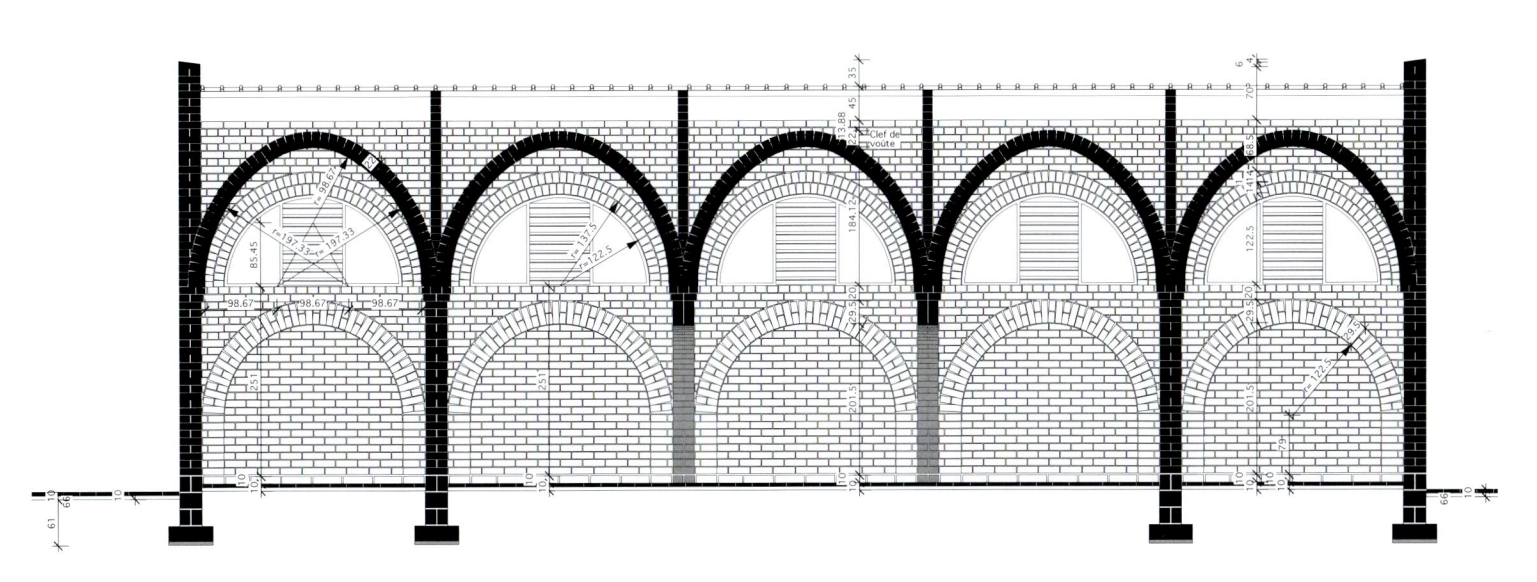

CHAPTER 2
COLD

Far left Explorer Captain Robert Falcon Scott in his hut at Cape Evans.
Left Hugh Broughton Architects has designed a summer Antarctic station for the Spanish, using the same modular approach as on the Halley VI Research Station.

There can be no worse conditions than those experienced by the earliest Antarctic explorers. When he wrote his tale of participating in Scott's doomed expedition of 1911, Apsley Cherry-Garrard was not using hyperbole when he called it *The Worst Journey in the World*.

Although the early explorers saw their huts as refuges from the terrible conditions outside, they would scarcely be considered acceptable today. Scott's hut at Cape Evans, still preserved today, is a prefabricated timber building, insulated with a quilt of seaweed. Unlike Shackleton's earlier hut, it was properly ventilated, and the insulation was adequate. And since it was heated with coal and lit with acetylene lamps it did not become as filthy as Shackleton's ill-ventilated hut, where seal blubber was burnt as fuel.

Scientists working in the Antarctic today enjoy vastly better conditions. Projects like Hugh Broughton's design for the British Antarctic Survey's Halley VI Research Station (see page 96) and his subsequent design for a Spanish station in the Antarctic are at the cutting edge, but all Antarctic stations offer comforts that would have been unthought of by those first explorers nearly a century ago: real warmth, clean clothes, decent food, safety, proper beds and even entertainment.

This does not mean that there are no hardships involved, although the stations are staffed by committed volunteers who tend to embrace these. In the polar winter, when it is endlessly dark, depression can set in. And however bad things get there is no chance to leave – it is only possible to fly people in and out during the relatively short polar summer. Although there are now electronic communications, there are no physical links with the outside world. If you haven't got it with you, or if it breaks, you have to make do. And any work that involves going outside takes an incredibly long time.

It is still necessary to be prepared for the unexpected. When Phil Wells of Hugh Broughton Architects was on site supervising the construction of Halley VI in February 2008, a sudden storm blocked up the entrance to his and several others' rooms and they had to camp out for a few days in other parts of the station – and that was in summer!

The Antarctic continent is so hostile that there has never been any permanent habitation, but people have lived, and continue to live, in very cold places. Anybody who has seen the Inuit film *Atanarjuat: The Fast Runner*, winner of Un Certain Regard in Cannes in 2001, will have had a fascinating insight into the traditional life of the Igloolik community of Nunavut in northern Canada. We see winter habitation in igloos made from snow blocks, and also the construction of a *qaggiq*, a large ceremonial igloo which has a roof of animal skins covering timber planks. In summer the Igloolik live in animal-hide tents, with a narwhal tusk as a tent pole.

Cold 57

Left A large ceremonial igloo, built of snow blocks by the Igloolik of northern Canada.
Below Visitors to the Abisko Ark Hotel in Sweden can combine ice fishing from inside their huts with views of the northern lights.
Opposite Houses in the Arctic are commonly built on stilts to avoid melting the permafrost below.

A less sophisticated structure was the *quinzhee* of the Athabaskan Native Americans from northwest Canada. More temporary than an igloo, this was hollowed out from a heap of snow, rather than being built up from snow blocks.

Life on the tundra was incomparably hard, but it has a romantic appeal that some like to imitate today. You can see that in the increasing popularity of ice hotels and bars (page 84) and in projects like the Abisko Ark Hotel in Sweden, 250 kilometres (155 miles) north of the Arctic Circle. Abisko is a meteorological curiosity, a place with almost permanently clear skies, so it offers one of the best opportunities for watching the aurora borealis (the northern lights).

The Abisko Ark Hotel combines this opportunity with another tradition from the Arctic Circle. In early spring it was customary for men to build huts on the ice, from which to fish. The hotel consists of well-insulated and heated huts placed on frozen Lake Tornetrask. Each sleeps three people, and beside each bed is a hole in the floor, which allows them to fish without getting out of bed!

Neither the Abisko Ark Hotel nor the ice hotels expect visitors to stay for more than one night, an indication of how far they are from our more usual expectations of civilized living. Whether we are talking about a hotel (a proper hotel) in a cold environment, or an arts or a university building, buildings in very cold places have several specific issues to contend with.

They need good insulation and top-rate construction if they are not to consume energy at a terrifying rate. Frequently, they need to be able to resist high winds and heavy snow loads, like the Echigo-Matsunoyama Museum of Natural Science in Japan (page 64) whose steel structure groans as it adjusts itself to the weight of snowfall. And they need to be architecturally very clever, as for most of the year they provide the only opportunity for people to gather. Sitting outside, meeting in the street or enjoying life on a piazza are rarely options in very cold places. If the buildings don't allow good interactions there is rarely a second chance.

Set against these difficult demands, though, is the fact that good buildings can be enormously appealing. Whether you are sitting inside the Delta Shelter in Washington state (page 60), dining at the Remota Hotel in Patagonia (page 70) or even working at the Amundsen-Scott station right on the South Pole (page 100), you will experience a primitive sense of pleasure in the notion of shelter. At these latitudes there is no nonsense about blending the inside and the outside. Inside is where you want to be, for a great deal of the time, and if you are in a place that is not only warm and dry but is also a great piece of architecture, you will feel very lucky indeed.

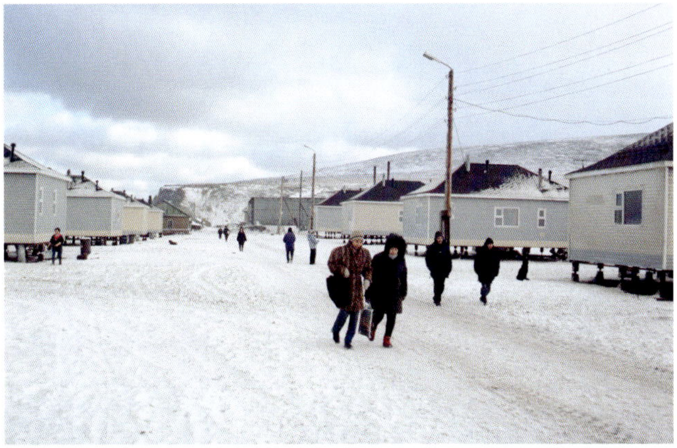

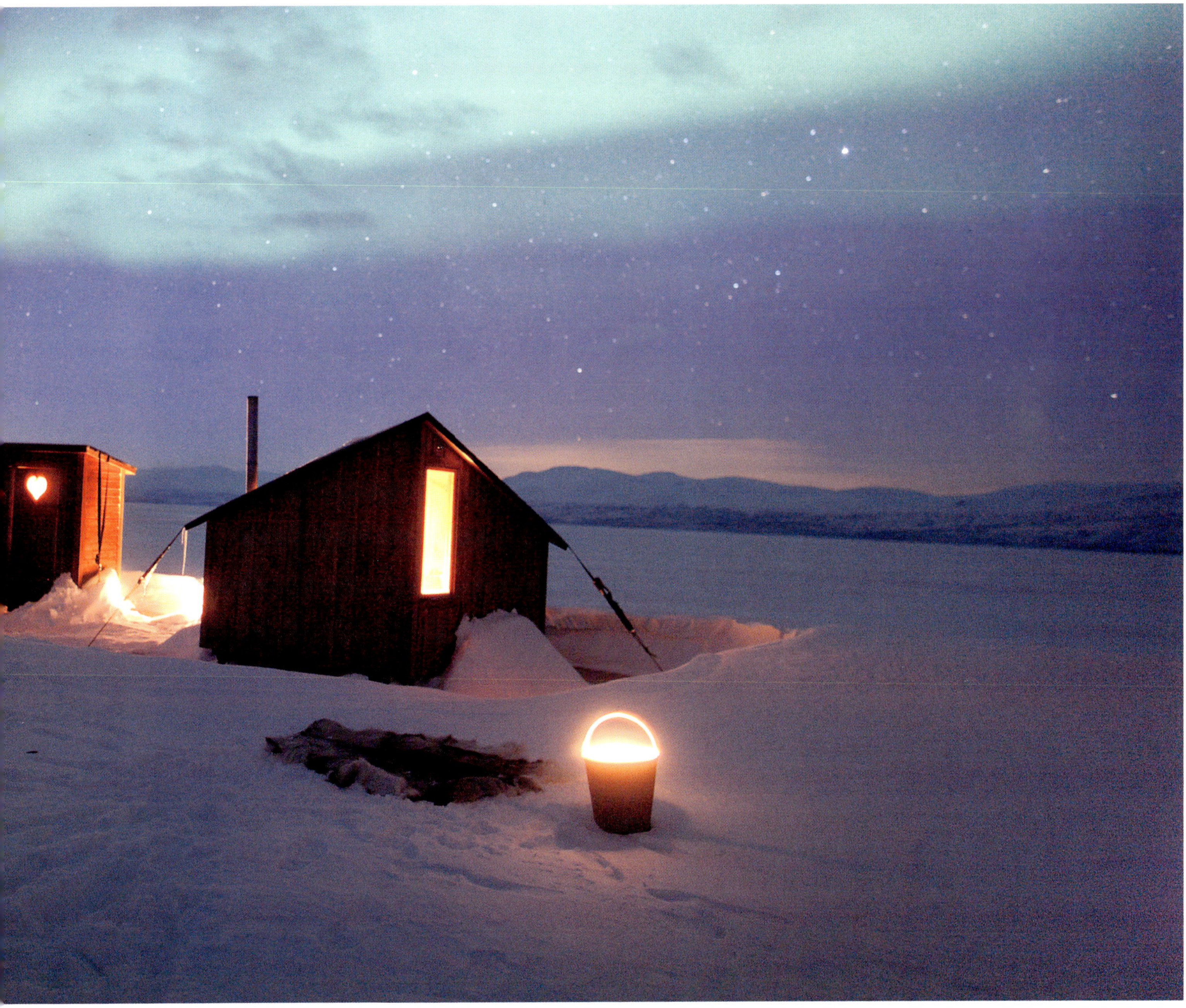

MAZAMA, WASHINGTON, USA
OLSON SUNDBERG KUNDIG ALLEN ARCHITECTS

DELTA SHELTER

Height above sea level
600m/1,967ft

Average annual rainfall
2568mm/22³⁄₅in

Average high and low temperatures
27.6°C/82°F – -9.7°C/14.5°F

Opposite However much it snows, the living accommodation in the Delta Shelter will sit above the snow.

Right From bottom: ground-, first- and second-floor plans: 1. storage; 2. bathroom; 3. guest bedroom; 4. master bedroom; 5. living room; 6. dining area; 7. kitchen

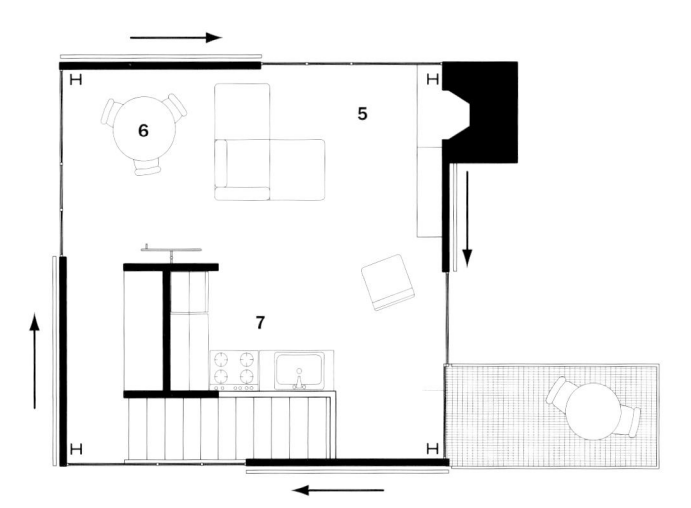

For three months of the year, the temperature in Mazama, a village on the eastern flank of the Cascade range of mountains, rarely rises above freezing, so a home constructed there needs to be snug. If it is to be used as a holiday house, it also needs to be secure during the time it is unoccupied.

But it is certainly not an environment for defensive architecture. Why choose to go there, if not to relish the scenery – the views of the mountains, the forests of Douglas fir and ponderosa pine – and its position on one of the world's longest cross-country skiing trails, which stretches 193 kilometres (120 miles) and runs directly through the village?

Olson Sundberg Kundig Allen Architects has dealt with this dilemma by designing a house that is lifted above the winter snows and spring floods, that makes the most of the views, and that can be made secure in a way that is intriguing rather than offensive.

The house stands on stilts, its two main storeys rising above a protected parking space, and a storage space that looks rather like a shipping container. On the higher levels glazing is extensive, with an oversailing roof that shades the top-level clerestory glazing. The first floor is occupied by bedrooms and bathrooms, leaving the top storey, with the very best views, for relaxation and eating. There are generous balconies for the good weather, again protected by the oversailing roof.

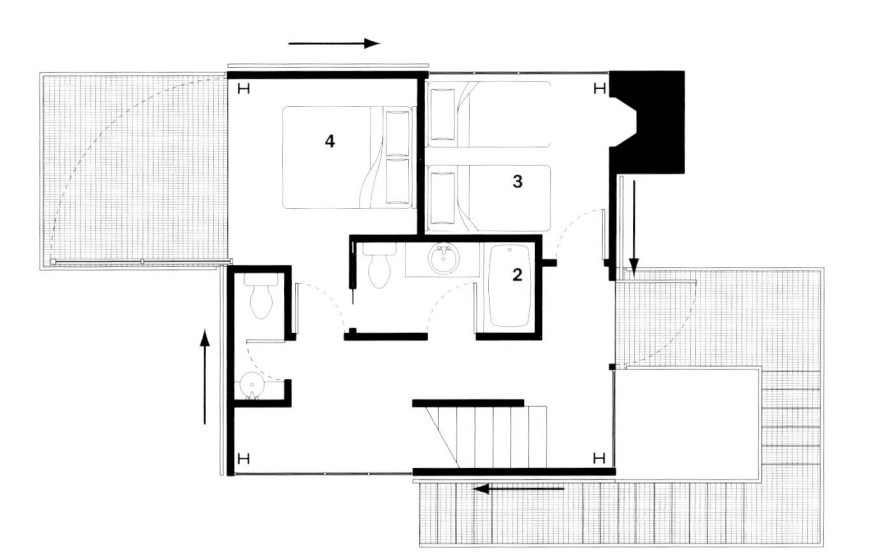

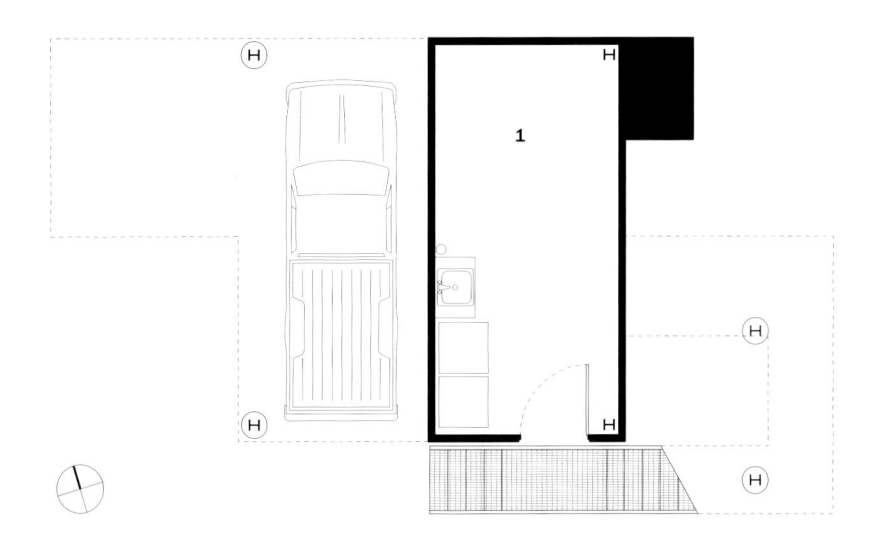

Choice of materials is key. The cladding is in weathering steel, which becomes a warm orangey colour and ultimately seems organic, blending with the spectrum of the trees. Full-height shutters of the same material slide across to close the building completely when it is empty or at night, turning it into an intriguing sculptural object, with only the clerestory glazing, too high to be accessible, still showing. For the occupants there must be enormous satisfaction in the fact that this glazing is closed mechanically, by turning an enormous ship's wheel.

Inside, finishes are simple but warm, in pale-coloured wood and frosted glass, with the slender frame of the structure expressed throughout. An industrial aesthetic kicks in again on the external stairs and the balconies, with metal-grid floors and simple mesh balustrades. The overall effect is to give this small building a sense of space, and there can be no greater pleasure than to sit, perched up among the trees, and watch the seasons change.

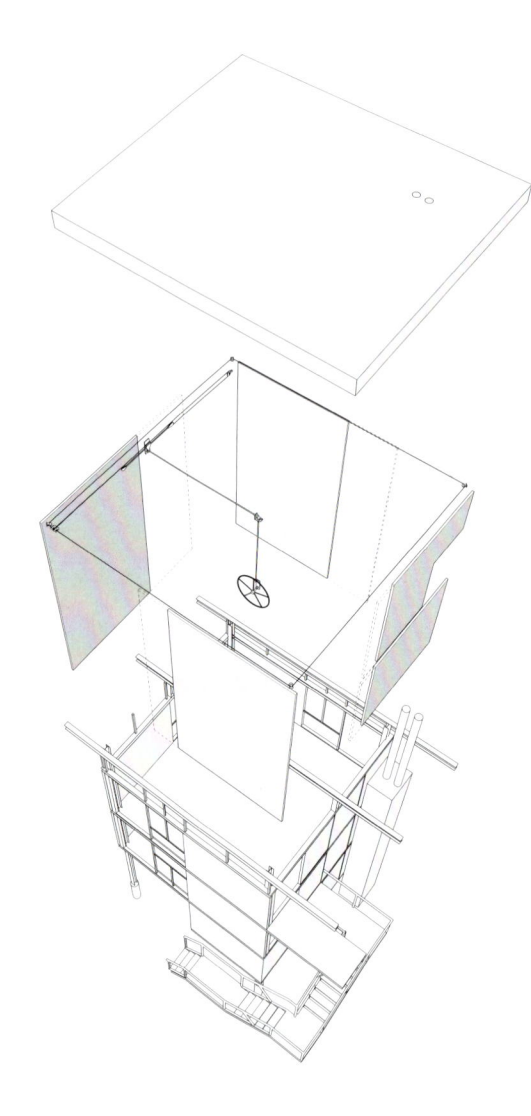

Opposite The slender steel frame is exposed inside the building. Views from the top floor are magnificent all through the year.
Above The building in open (left) and shut (right) modes.
Left Exploded drawing, showing the structural elements.
Bottom Drawings showing the mechanism (seen opposite) for closing and opening the shutters.

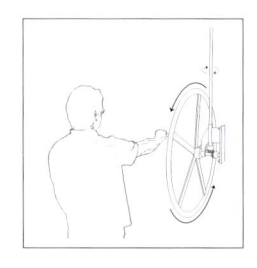

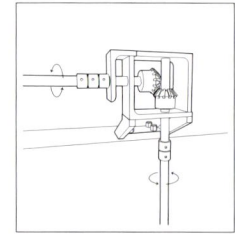

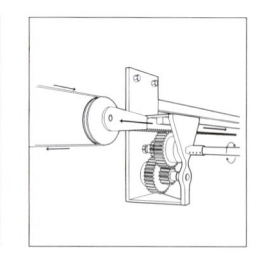

Cold 63

MATSUNOYAMA, NIIGATA, JAPAN
TAKAHARU + YUI TEZUKA

ECHIGO-MATSUNOYAMA MUSEUM OF NATURAL SCIENCE

Height above sea level
299m/981ft

Average annual rainfall
2,114.5mm/83¼in

Average high and low temperatures
27°C/80.6°F – 0.10°C/32°F

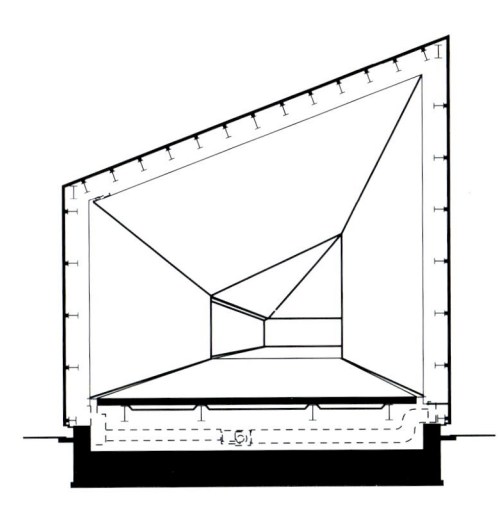

Approach the Museum of Natural Science in Niigata in the summer and you will find the experience both intriguing and confusing. The building sits on a small area of rising ground in a clearing in the conifer forest, and you can walk along a raised timber walkway, between the trees and rice fields, to the Cor-ten (pre-rusted) steel building. It is tough, it is uncompromising and it looks almost like a relic from some earlier industrial age. But was there ever heavy industry in such a spot, up on the spine of mountains that runs through the island of Honshu? And would it have had a pitched roof?

The industrial appearance of the museum is reinforced by the presence of an equally stern tower, with a lookout at the top. You can only reach the lookout by stairs as there is no lift. And there are no exhibits within the tower. True, the views are good, but they aren't bad from ground level either, looking over mountains and meadows. So if this really is a new building, why go to all the expense of building the tower?

But come back in the winter – if you can – and the reasons behind the architect's thinking will become clear. It snows here, a lot. With heavy falls and also drifting, snow can reach a depth of 7 metres (23 feet), a source of the area's fame, alongside its hot springs. So you certainly won't be tripping along those little timber walkways in winter, and it may be that the entire body of the building will be buried, with only the lookout tower protruding above the snow: it acts as both a beacon and the only way to see the outside world. From inside the museum itself, the build-up of snow is visible through large windows and, rather as if you were looking at a living example of a geologist's slice of rock, you can see the passages creatures have made through the snow – or even, if you are lucky, see a little animal pressed against the window as if on a specimen plate. These huge frameless windows are made not of glass, but of composite acrylic panes, up to 75 millimetres (3 inches) thick. This material and its thickness are necessary because of the enormous pressure the drifted snow can put on the building (up to 1,500 kilograms per square metre/about 330 pounds per square foot), and the need to resist this pressure is one of the reasons behind the surprising appearance of the museum. In addition, of course, there is the need to deal with the cold by maintaining an internal temperature that has to be considerably higher than that of the snow pressing up against the walls and windows.

Opposite The large windows are made from thick sheets of acrylic, to resist the snow.
Above left Section: the tough welded structure can resist the weight of winter snows. Air circulates between the structure and the plasterboard lining.
Above right In summer, the landscape is deceptively gentle.

Cold

Above The museum houses an impressive and beautifully displayed collection of butterflies.
Right The cafeteria has the grandiose title of Culinary Arts Experience.

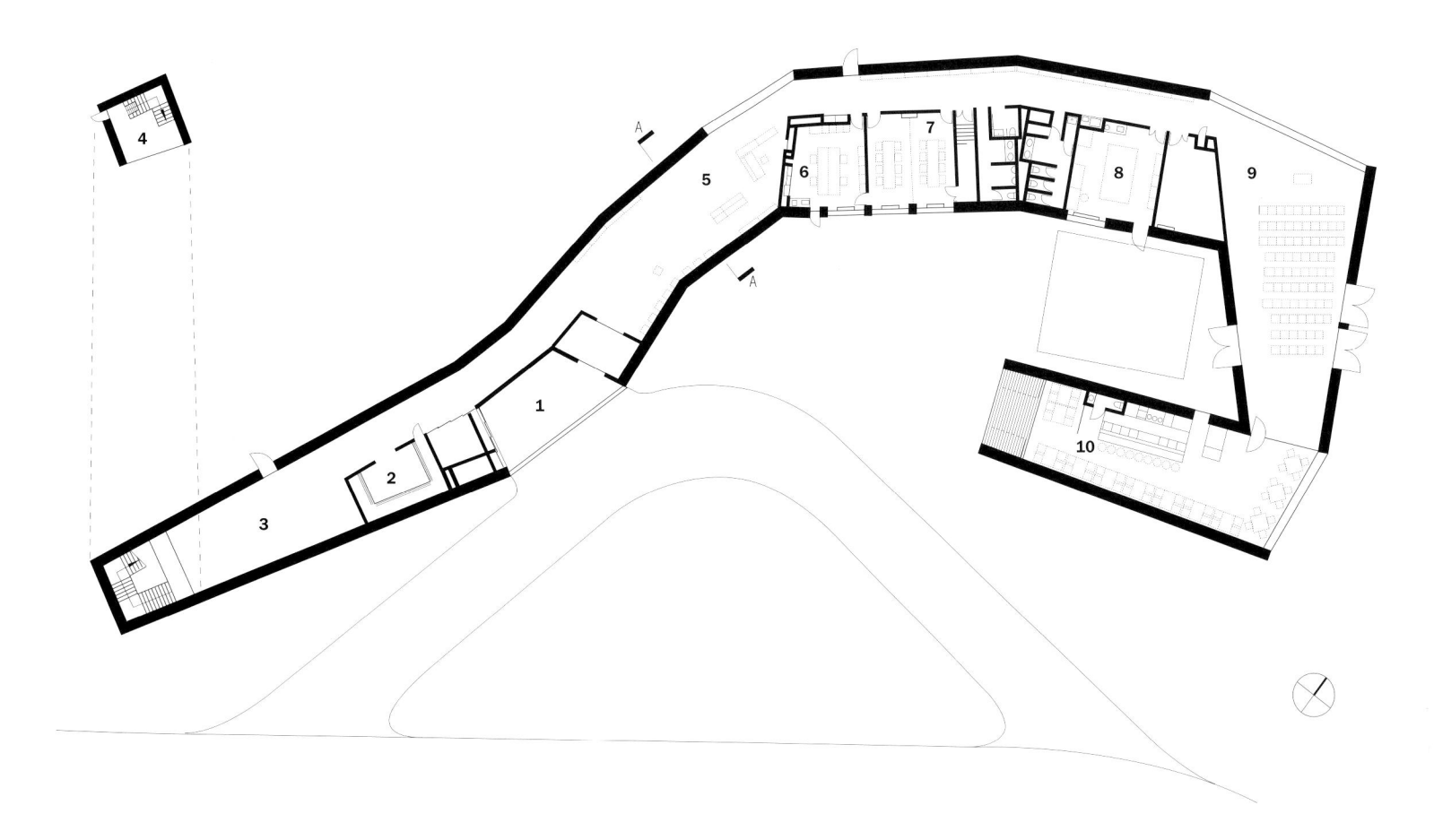

In plan, the building snakes across the landscape, creating shapes and views that are not rectilinear. Structurally, it is relatively simple, with a straightforward steel frame covered in the Cor-ten cladding, which was welded together on site like the boilerplate of a ship. Indeed, the thinking behind the construction is rather like that behind a submarine; here it resists the pressure of snow rather than water. The tower, of course, becomes a permanent periscope. Urethane insulation behind the Cor-ten helps to keep the building warm.

In contrast to the tough-looking outside, the interior has walls of white plasterboard, supported on a lightweight steel framework. Behind the walls is a cavity that is used for the circulation of warm air in winter. The air is injected through long grilles in the polished concrete floor and extracted through slots in the plasterboard at eaves level. Because the warm air passes behind the walls, floors and ceilings these also radiate heat. The system can be reversed in summer to circulate cooling fresh air.

There are galleries for displaying and interpreting natural history, including one with a special collection of butterflies, creatures that seem far too delicate to exist in the snowbound winter world. The building also has a lecture theatre and a 'culinary arts experience', aka a cafeteria.

In winter this is a museum that the visitor not only sees but also hears. Under the pressure of the snow, and as the structure expands and contracts with the changing temperature, the building groans – an indication both of the stresses that it has to withstand, and the extreme forces in this most aggressive of natural environments.

Above Ground-floor plan.
1. entrance; 2. Usuke Shiga Collection; 3. exhibition space; 4. viewing tower; 5. reception; 6. office; 7. meeting room; 8. laboratory; 9. Kyororo Hall; 10. Culinary Arts Experience
Overleaf In winter, much of the building is covered in snow with the tower protruding above it.

Extreme Architecture

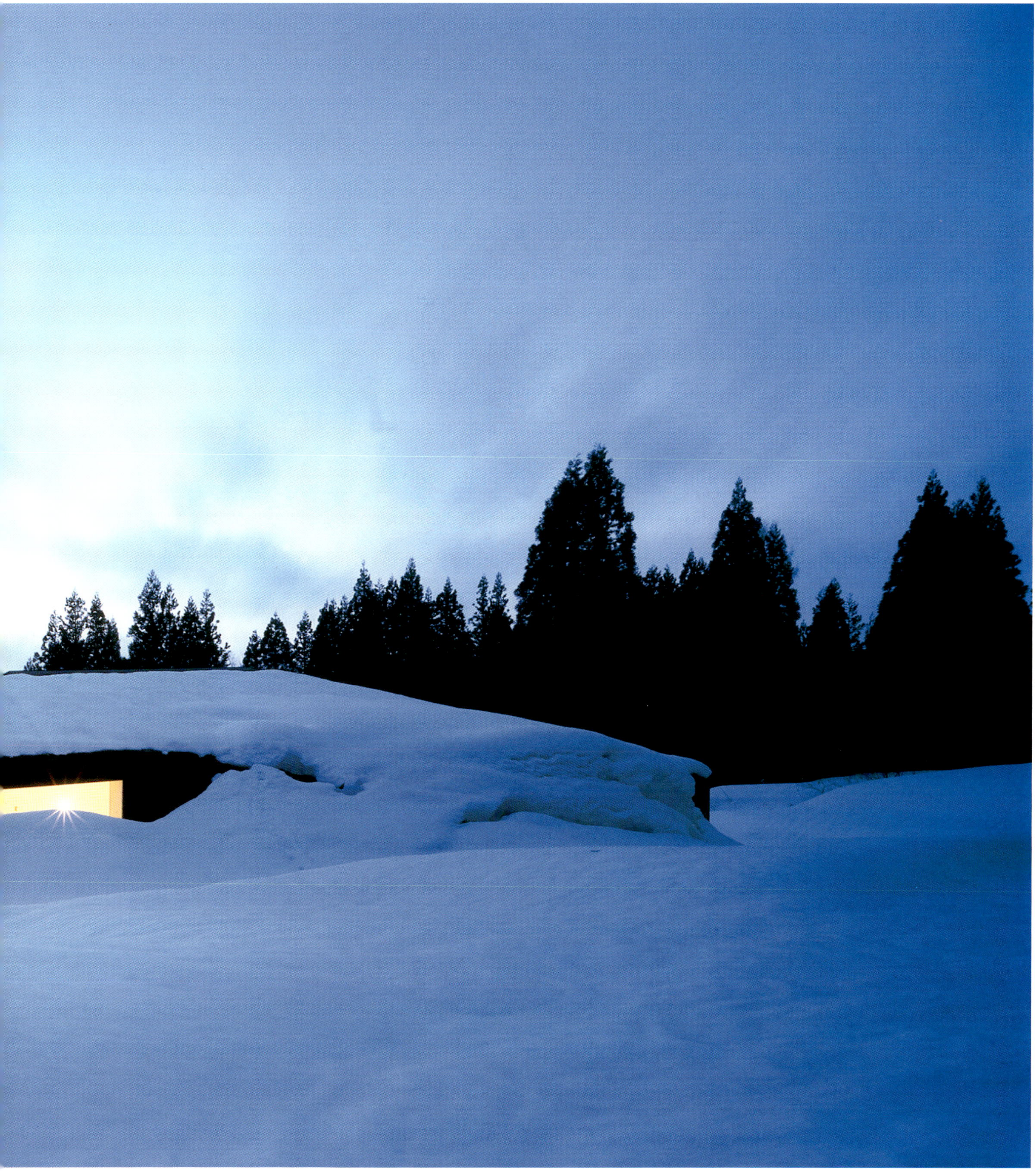

PUERTO NATALES, PATAGONIA, CHILE
GERMÁN DEL SOL

REMOTA HOTEL

▲ **Height above sea level**
10m/33feet

💧 **Average annual rainfall**
330mm/13in

🌡 **Average high and low temperatures**
29ºC/84ºF – 2.8ºC/37ºF

Opposite Set in the rugged far south of Chile, the hotel embraces the landscape rather than turning its back on it.

Right With their planted roofs, the buildings are as inconspicuous as possible.

There is at first a surprising austerity to the Remota Hotel in Patagonia. The landscape is extraordinary and unforgiving, so one might expect a hotel that exudes a cosy welcome. Instead, it is all straight lines and dark materials, built around a large courtyard designed not as a haven but as a showcase for the surrounding landscape.

This is a deliberate ploy by the architect, Germán del Sol, who is already known for two other hotels in breathtaking settings – one also in Patagonia and, at the other extreme of Chile's climate, another in the blazing dry heat of the Atacama Desert.

At the Remota he has drawn on the sheep-farming tradition of the area, mimicking not the main houses of the estancias but the barns used for drying the sheeps' hides and for other work that had to be carried out inside due to the hostility of the climate. Although Patagonia does not plumb incredibly low temperatures, it is often windy and wet.

The name of the hotel (remota means remote) is appropriate. It is 1.5 kilometres (1 mile) from the fishing village of Puerto Natales, which is itself three hours drive (in good weather) from Punta Arenas, and vies with Ushuaia in Argentina for the title of the most southerly city in the world. Approaching the hotel from a distance at dawn or dusk, its severity is immediately moderated by the sight of the glowing interior lights, which give a hint of the luxury – restrained, Modernist luxury, but luxury nonetheless – contained within.

There are three main buildings in the hotel, and these are arranged around the courtyard, leaving the fourth side closed by an agricultural-looking fence that allows views to the magnificent mountainous Torres del Paine nature reserve, one of the main reasons for visiting the area. The three-storey central building, with reception, restaurant, and a glazed conservatory on the top, is the tallest and sits at the back of the site. Along each side, running down to the water, are the bedroom blocks, joined to each other by covered passages that cross the courtyard. A third passage, leading to a separate sauna and swimming pool block, is open to the sky.

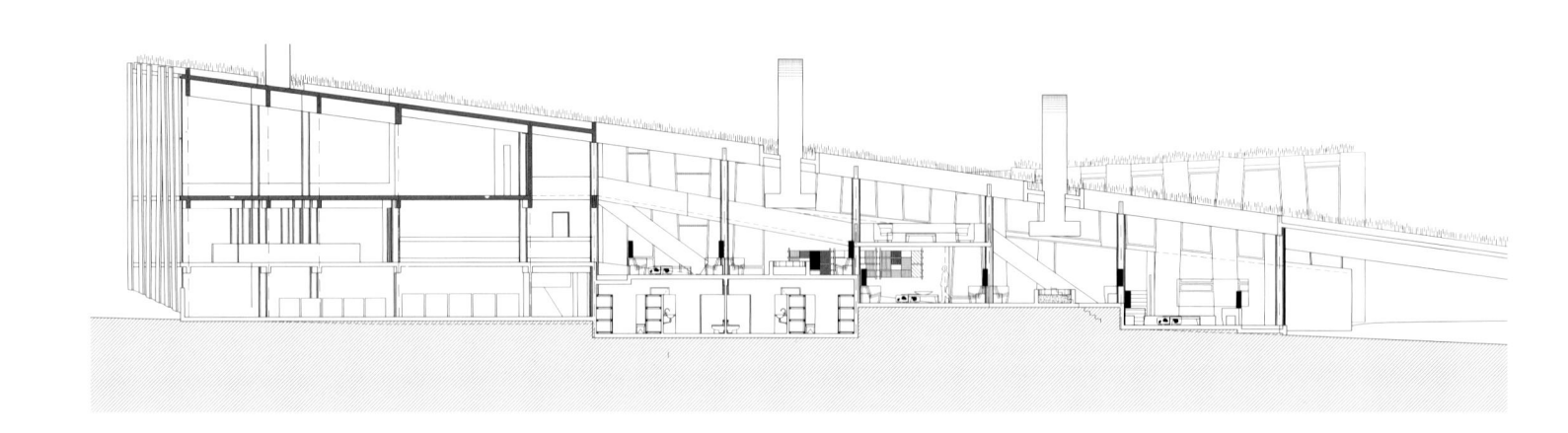

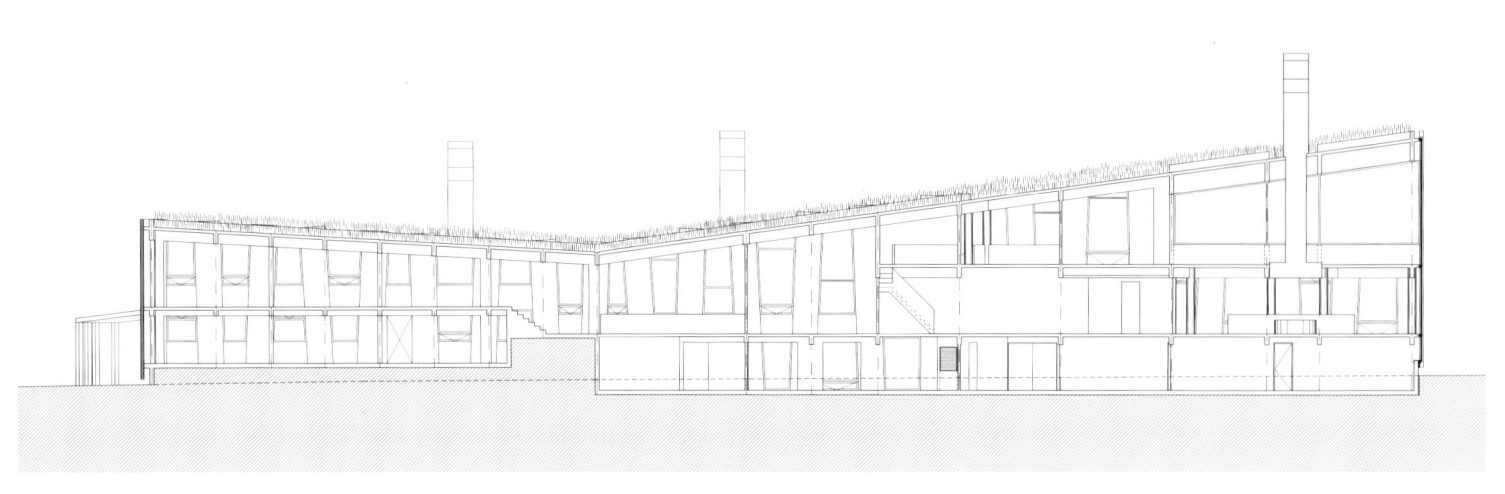

Above Sections.

Structurally, the buildings are made of concrete, to provide acoustic and fire separation. The roof was completed before the cladding, to give some shelter to the workers and the site. The cladding is waterproof plywood panels, with 30 centimetres (12 inches) of polyurethane insulation between them. On the outside the panels are coated with a synthetic asphalt to waterproof them, and the asphalt is in turn covered in a fine black gravel to protect it from ultraviolet radiation.

Large double-glazed windows bring the rapidly changing light into the hotel. Internally there is a great deal of exposed concrete, along with small areas of brightly coloured textiles and local fabric artefacts used as decoration. Slat timber ceilings hang below the concrete soffits. The architect commissioned local craftsmen to make furniture from large pieces of dead lenga wood, a native beech tree.

Another key element is the lighting. Germán del Sol has used low-energy bulbs throughout, but enclosed them in custom-designed yellow tubular shades to give a warmer hue.

But however good the interior design, in all but the foulest weather the visitor's attention will be directed outwards. The courtyard helps with this as it contains some large, seemingly random boulders, and otherwise is covered with local vegetation – mostly grasses – which extends over the roofs of the buildings. Having come to stay in a hotel that is far more welcoming than they may initially have anticipated, visitors are then seduced to leave it for the natural splendours that first drew them there.

Below Low-energy light bulbs encased in tubular shades are one of the careful touches that make the deliberately austere interior welcoming.

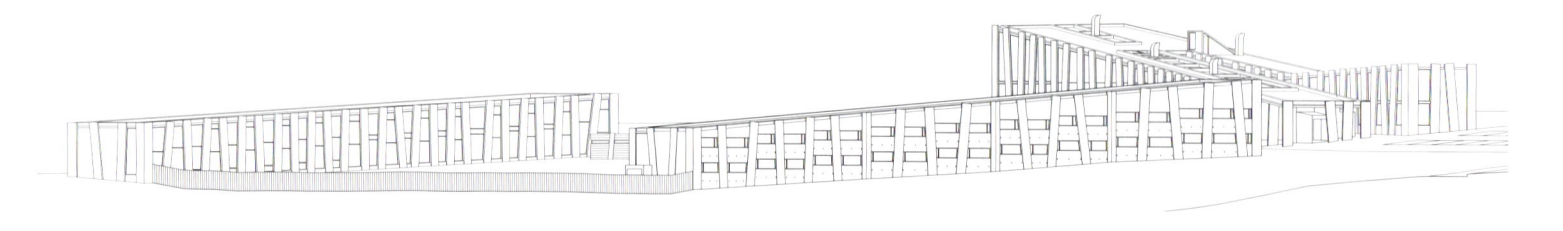

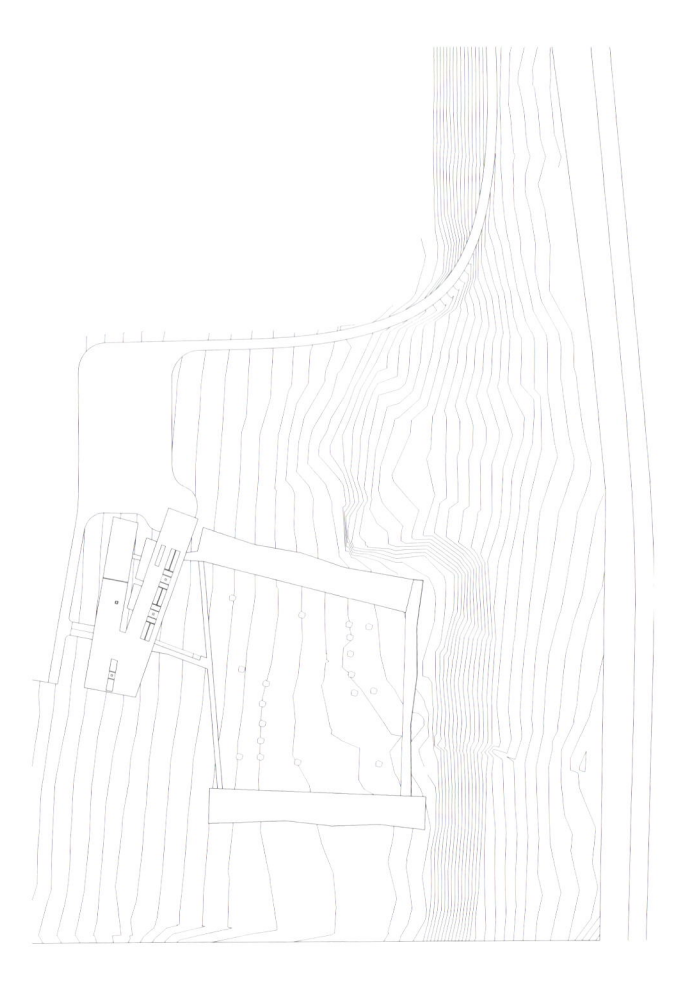

Top Elevations
Above Site plan: the main building and the two longs arms of accommodation embrace a section of landscape.
Opposite The buildings have large windows to maximize the views and are clad in plywood finished with synthetic asphalt and black gravel.

74 Extreme Architecture

Cold 75

LONGYEARBYEN, NORWAY
JARMUND/VIGSNÆS AS ARCHITECTS MNAL

SVALBARD SCIENCE CENTRE

Height above sea level
5m/16ft

Average annual rainfall
200mm/7⁶/₈in

Average high and low temperatures
6.2°C/43°F – -15.2°C/5°F

Opposite The science centre is the largest building on the remote island of Spitsbergen, and so an important gathering place.
Right Ground-floor plan, showing the mix of uses encompassed in the sprawling building.

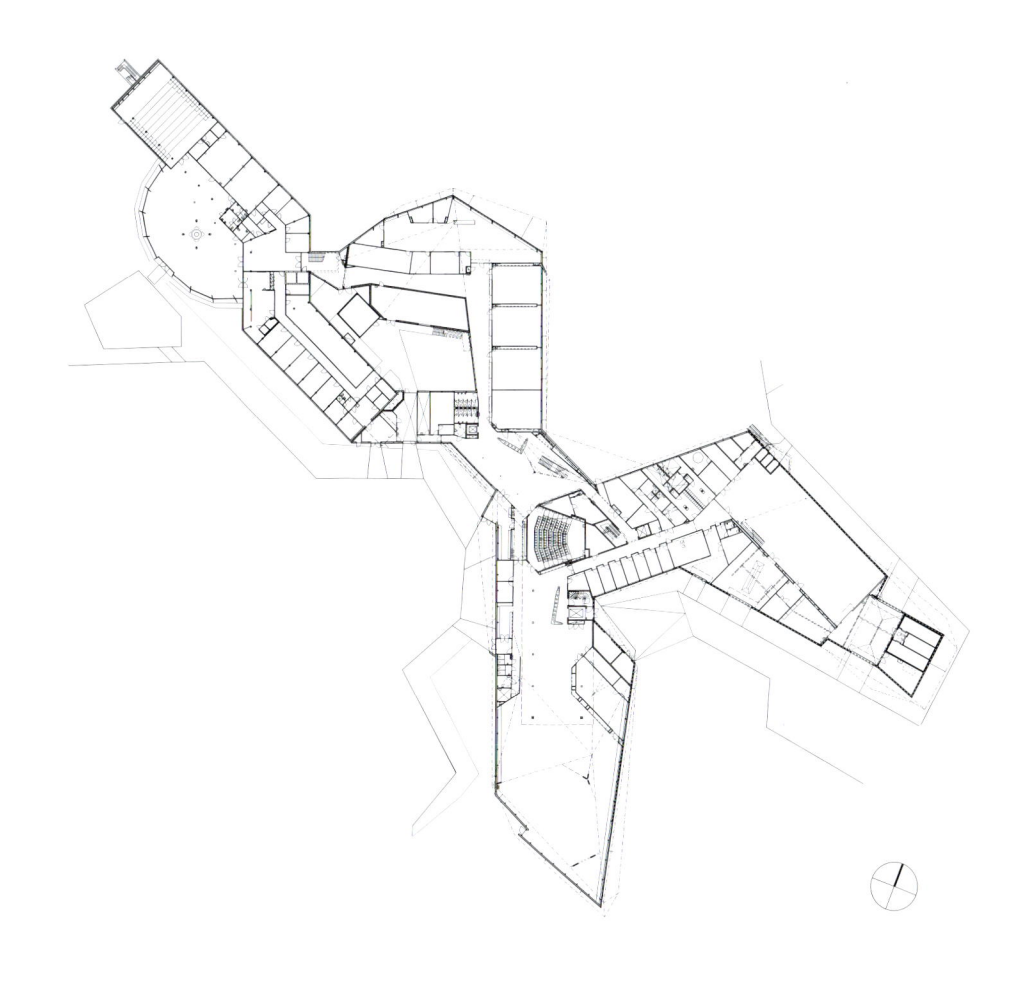

Longyearbyen really is a long way from everywhere. On the island of Spitsbergen, the largest of the Svalbard archipelago, 600 kilometres (373 miles) north of mainland Norway, it was first developed for coal mining. While mining still has an important role to play, so do tourism and research. The Svalbard Science Centre serves a conglomerate of four universities, and it both teaches and conducts research on specific Arctic-related subjects.

It certainly takes fortitude to live there. The polar night extends from the end of October to mid-February. On 20 February 2008, Norway's minister of research and higher education officially opened the new Aurora Observatory on a mountain above Longyearbyen. This was, reported the university's website, a cheerful occasion, with hot toddy and small bonfires compensating for the fact that it was snowing and the temperature was –35°C (–31°F).

In this environment, getting buildings right is essential, not only for performance but also as places of social interaction. Except in the height of summer, when temperatures can reach a dizzying 10°C (50°F), nobody is likely to stop and chat outdoors. Forget spatial planning, the spaces between buildings or concepts of city grids; buildings are places that you scuttle into from the unfriendly world outside. Longyearbyen does not have a cappuccino culture.

Look at the rather splayed plan of the building, and the oddly drunken angle of the internal walls, and it may seem as if this is a design by an architect who wanted to play – and why not? But, in fact, many elements that at first sight may seem gestural are actually purely practical. So, the building is raised above the ground – not out of some love affair with the history of piloti, but because it is essential not to melt the permafrost that provides the structural support.

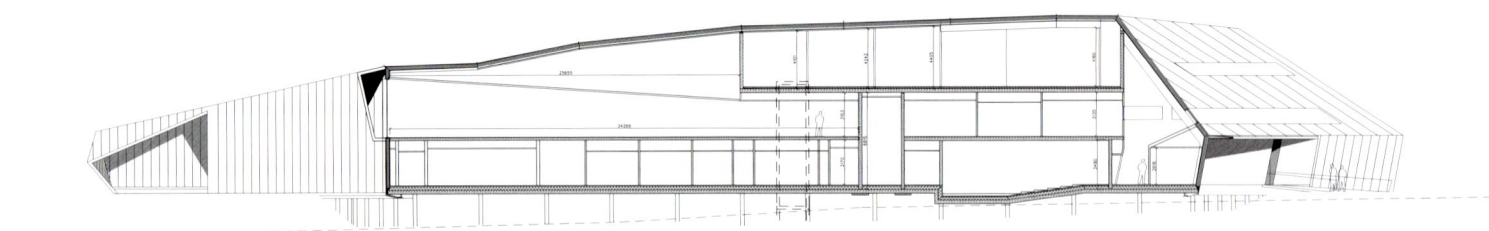

The structure is of timber, which provides a delightfully warm and welcoming interior, but this material was also chosen to avoid cold bridging. In a temperate climate, a cold bridge is an error, which may require the consumption of a little more fossil fuel; in Longyearbyen it would be a disaster. External cladding is in copper, a beautiful material that reflects the low-angled summer sun – and it is also workable at low temperatures, which greatly extended the construction season.

And all those odd angles? They were in large part chosen to prevent snow build-up at the entrances. But they also provide a wealth of interest internally, a variety of places not just for research and for teaching but also for chance encounters.

This is the largest building in Spitsbergen and so, for many who use it, the largest building they will encounter until their next, and relatively distant, visit to the mainland. Working at the science centre gives them the only opportunity to experience architectural richness and spatial experiment, and the architect is to be congratulated for giving it to them in a manner that is both so pleasurable and so logical.

Opposite top Section through the building, which is raised on columns to avoid melting the permafrost.
Opposite centre With scarcely a single right angle, a geometry generated by the need to avoid snow build-up at the entrances, the building has a dynamic interior with plenty of places for social interaction.
Opposite bottom The widespread use of timber gives a much-needed sensation of warmth as well as avoiding the risk of cold bridges.
Right Copper cladding reflects the low-angled sun.

SPITSBERGEN, NORWAY
PETER W. SØDERMANN/BARLINDHAUG CONSULT AS

SVALBARD GLOBAL SEED VAULT

Height above sea level
5m/16ft

Average annual rainfall
200mm/7⁶/₈in

Average high and low temperatures
6.2°C/43°F – -15.2°C/5°F

Not much grows on Spitsbergen, so it is ironic that this remote northerly island could be essential to safeguarding the future of the world's food supplies. A seed vault has been built here that provides a back-up to the world's gene vaults. Should their contents be lost, through mismanagement, political upheaval or natural disaster, there will always be a replacement available in the Svalbard seed vault. In this way the genome of the world's plants should be preserved, ensuring that, whatever appalling things we continue to do to our planet, nothing that may one day be essential to our survival will be lost irrevocably.

The way to preserve seeds indefinitely is to keep them cold, so this icy island was an obvious choice. Even here, refrigeration is needed to reach, and then to maintain, the desired storage temperature of −18°C (−0.4°F), but there is confidence that, should the refrigeration equipment fail, it would take many weeks before the temperature in the storage areas would rise to the −3°C (27°F) of the surrounding rock.

This planetary insurance policy is basically a set of giant vaults, bored into the rock of a hillside behind Longyearbyen airport and accessed by a tunnel driven largely through permafrost. There is a small administration office, just off the tunnel, that is heated to a higher temperature. With few people working in the facility, which will not be open to the public, this could have been seen as a purely engineering project, with little need to consider its public face.

But because of its global significance, and the great international interest that the project was attracting, a conscious decision was taken by the developer, Norwegian state company Statsbygg, to make a real statement with the portal of the building, the only element the public would see. Architect Peter W. Sødermann was appointed, working with consulting practice Barlindhaug Consult AS, and Public Art Norway set up a committee to appoint an artist to work on the portal. The Norwegian Dyveke Sanne was selected.

Opposite A fibre-optic artwork by Norwegian artist Dyveke Sanne enhances the enigmatic presence of the portal when viewed from above.
Above The portal, of concrete and steel, is designed to need minimal maintenance. Its geometry should ensure that snow is blown away.

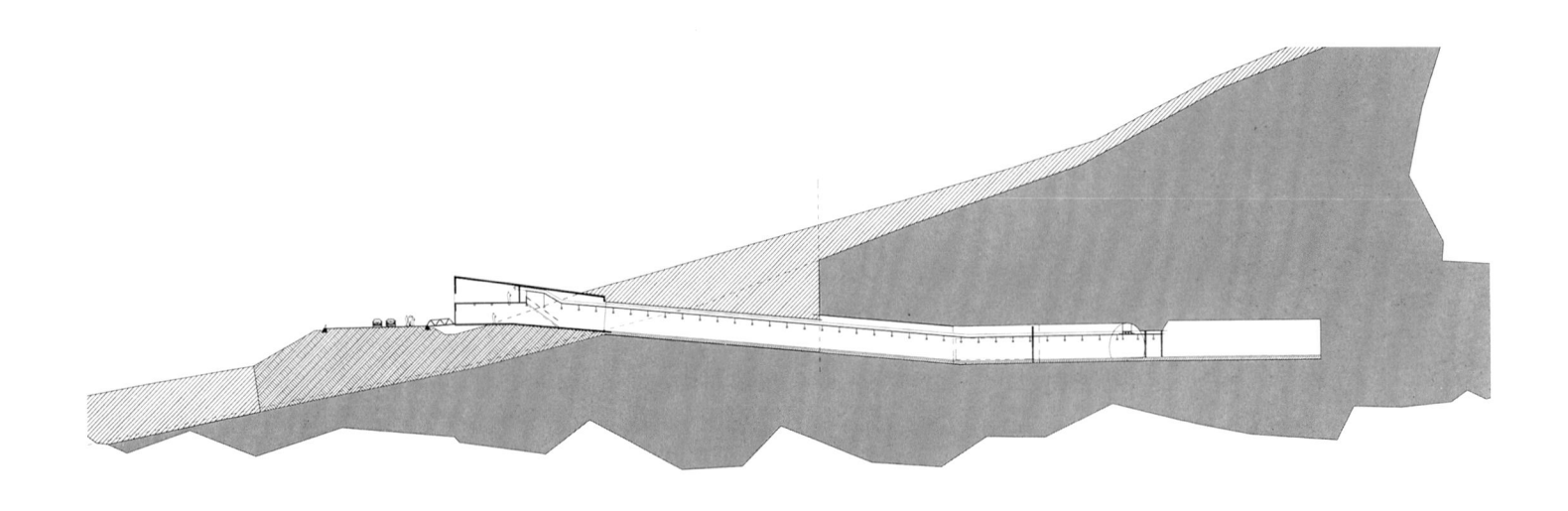

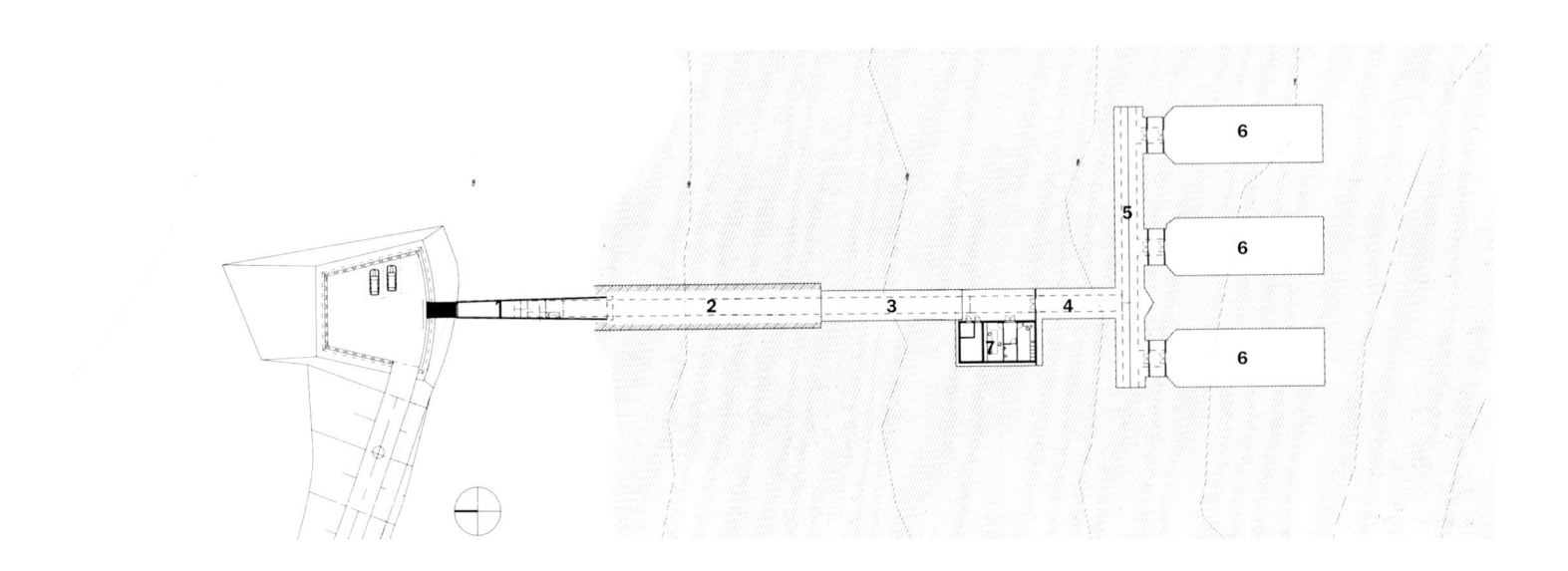

The portal is a simple, stark wedge protruding from the mountainside, its sharp form differentiating itself from the softer contours of nature around it. Sanne has contributed panels on the front and top of the wedge, forming a work called 'perpetual repercussion', a series of refractive elements housed behind safety glass and illuminated with fibre optics, to ensure that the building will be visible in daylight and also in the seemingly endless polar night.

Because the building will have minimal attendance, everything has been designed to be as maintenance-free as possible. So the design of the portal building, a smooth reinforced-concrete structure accessed across a steel bridge, is not only a clever piece of place-making, but has also been designed to prevent snowdrifts in front of the door. Because of the portal's projecting nature, and the smooth design of the entry area in front of it, the expectation is that snow will be swept away by the wind. Apart from the concrete, the main elements are a stainless-steel door and a ventilation grille above it. Above the grille sits the first of the two pieces of artwork.

Once through the portal, the visitor first travels down a steel tube, through the relatively unstable upper soil, and then through a tunnel blasted through the rock itself, to reach the three storage caverns sited off a final, transverse tunnel.

These caverns are 27 metres (89 feet) long and 9.5 metres (31 feet) wide, each taking five longitudinal runs of shelving. In total, the vault will have the capacity to store 4.5 million seed samples, twice the number of seed types currently held in all the world's gene banks.

At the opening in February 2008 the Norwegian prime minister, Jens Stoltenberg, said, 'This is a Noah's Ark for today, securing global diversity for future generations and, if crop species are lost in a global disaster, we can start all over again, here in Svalbard'.

It is a Noah's Ark that few will have the opportunity to enter, but exhibits, including a model, are going to the Svalbard Museum. Otherwise, visitors to the chilly hillside will have to make do with the intriguing sight of the forceful entrance, and the knowledge that there is something very special – and very cold – going on inside.

Opposite top Section showing the tunnel passing first through permafrost and then into rock.
Opposite bottom Plan: 1. portal building; 2. 'Svalbard tube', the steel tunnel section; 3. access tunnel; 4. rock tunnel; 5. transverse tunnel; 6. storage cavern; 7. administration area
Below The shelving can store 4.5 million seed samples in optimum conditions.

JUKKASJARVI, SWEDEN; SAINTE-CATHERINE-DE-LA-JACQUES-CARTIER, CANADA;
LONDON, UK; STOCKHOLM, SWEDEN
VARIOUS ARCHITECTS

ICE HOTELS AND BARS

Height above sea level
variable

Average annual rainfall
variable

Typical interior temperature
-5°C/23°F

Warmth and shelter are the first prerequisites for most of us when staying in a hotel, so the idea of an ice hotel may, at first, seem ridiculously perverse. But in the unending search for sensation and challenge it makes a mad kind of sense. In addition, ice is the most marvellous sculptural material and, given its transient nature, one knows that one can have an experience that only a relative few will share and that, after a single year, can never be repeated.

The first ice hotel, and still the best known, is redesigned and re-created every year at Jukkasjärvi, near Kiruna in the far north of Sweden. Its origin was almost accidental. Creating ice art is a popular winter activity in many countries, and in 1989 Japanese ice artists visited the area and put on an exhibition. In spring 1990, French artist Jannot Drid held an exhibition in a cylinder-shaped igloo in the area. One evening, when there were no rooms available in the town, some visitors asked permission to spend the night in the exhibition hall. They slept in sleeping bags on top of reindeer skins, and became the first guests of the 'hotel'.

Now the hotel is built every year, using ice from the nearby Torne River. It is typically open between December and April; the exact opening date varies, depending on when the ice forms. Although the design changes every year, it always includes fantastical bedrooms and a chapel. One year an open-air theatre was also created, with a performance of *Macbeth* in the local Sami language – a bone-chilling thought.

Opposite Entrance to Icehotel, Jukkasjärvi, Sweden. Although this is the 'original' ice hotel, it is redesigned every year.
This page Inside Icehotel, Jukkasjärvi, the designers re-create 'home comforts', although you need some pretty warm clothes to enjoy them.

Left Canada's Hôtel de Glace at Sainte-Catherine-de-la-Jacques-Cartier, Québec.
Below left Plan of the Hôtel de Glace, showing the scale and complexity of the complex, which includes a wedding chapel (top right of plan).
Below right Guests sleep on skins laid on beds of ice.

The idea has spread to other cold parts of the world, with ice hotels in Québec, Canada, and in Norway and Romania. Finland has a snow hotel within the monumental snow castle that it builds every year at Kemi on the Gulf of Bothnia.

In all these hotels the typical temperature is about −5°C (23°F), so thick mattresses, reindeer or other skins and warm sleeping bags are essential. The architecture tends to the rococo, with lots of carving to show that it can be done, and extravagant lighting effects. In almost all cases, guests spend only one night at an ice hotel as part of a longer stay in more conventional (and warmer) accommodation.

Another element ice hotels share is an the ice bar. This idea developed from the tradition of ice sculptures as centrepieces for banquets (swans have always been very popular). From this came the concept of ice bars for special occasions, with the bar structure made from ice. The degree to which a solid block of ice melts is relatively low for the duration of one evening.

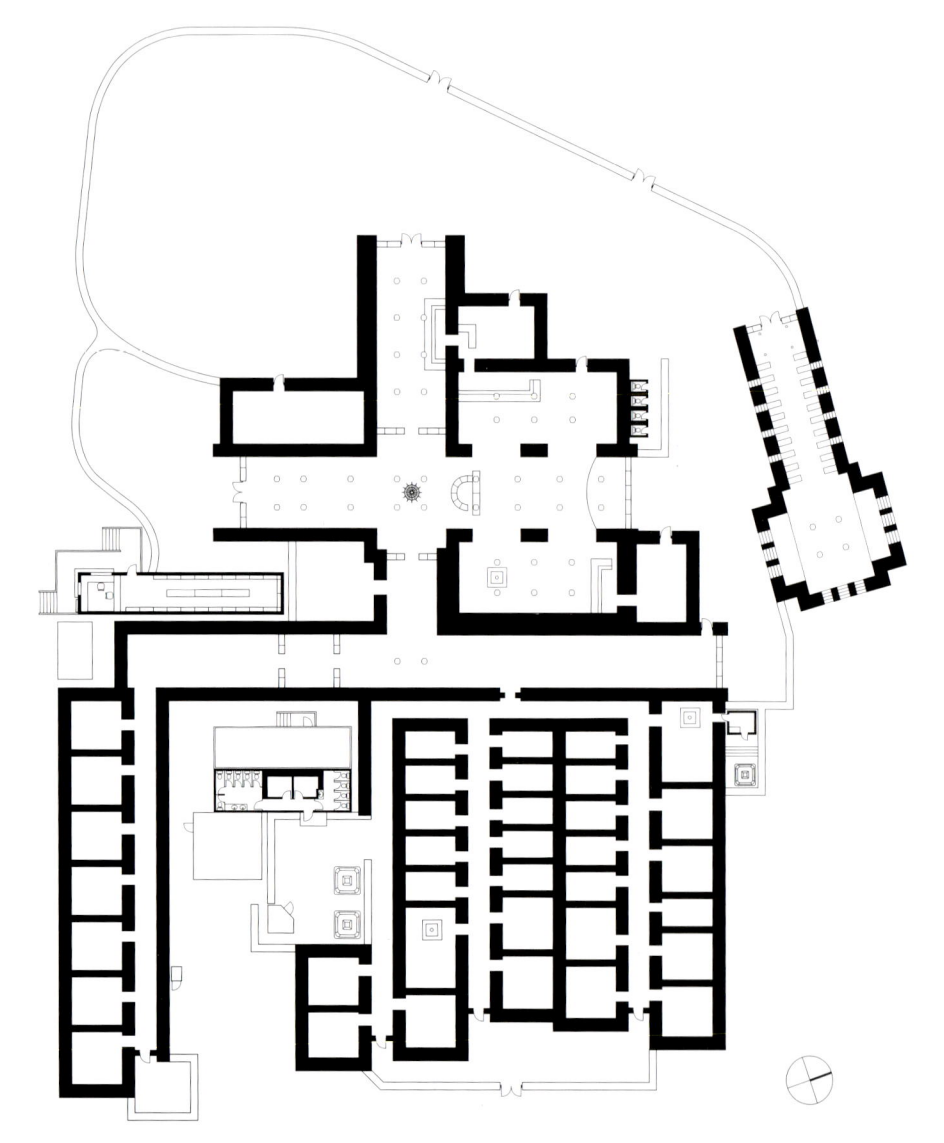

Left At the Hôtel de Glace even chandeliers and sculptures in the reception area and bar are made from ice.
Below Structural columns in the bar are carved from ice.

Left The Absolut IceBar in London's Mayfair.
Right Visitors to Stockholm's IceBar wear capes with fur hoods.

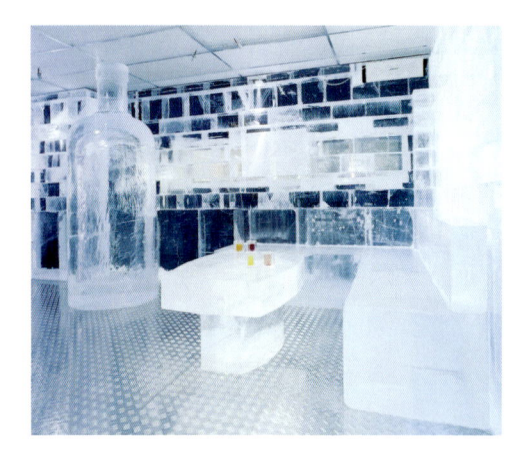

The idea was taken further with the creation of bars that occupied whole rooms, on a fairly permanent basis. The obvious drink in these places is vodka, which tastes at its best when heavily chilled. So London has its Absolut IceBar at Heddon Street in fashionable Mayfair. Unlike most other bars, you can't just drop in. Instead you have to book a 40-minute slot, and are given a thermal cape to wear while downing your vodka, which is served in glasses made of ice. The ice comes from the Torne River, the source used by Sweden's Icehotel.

There is another IceBar at the Nordic Sea Hotel in Stockholm, and Amsterdam has Xtracold. This was remodelled relatively recently with a sporting theme, including life-size sculptures of Dutch sporting heroes. One is Hein Vergeer, the former world champion skater, which seems appropriate, but the others are footballer Frank de Boer and kick-boxer Peter Aerts, which carries the underlying element of kitsch a little further.

One wonders how long this concept will survive in our warming world. Extreme cold may come to seem more exotic, but the concept of maintaining rooms as giant refrigerators will look less and less sustainable. Although, if we do want to experience those climatic extremes, it could be argued that sipping vodka in a metropolitan ice bar is actually more sustainable than flying to a distant destination. Cheers.

Cold 89

SESTRIERE, ITALY
CURATOR: LANCE FUNG

SNOW SHOW

Height above sea level
2,035m/6,677ft

Average rainfall January–February
40mm/1 1/2in

Average high & low temperatures January–February
7°C/44°F – -1°C/30°F

Opposite Yoko Ono and Arata Isozaki created a circular, high-walled maze called Penal Colony.
Right Penal Colony under construction, indicating the degree of technical effort required to create these ephemeral structures.

It gets quite nippy in the Alps in winter, but nothing like as cold as it does in Lapland. So when curator Lance Fung transferred his idea for a snow show from Lapland, where it ran successfully in 2003 and 2004, to Sestriere, 105 kilometres (65 miles) from Turin in the Italian Alps, he was faced with both an opportunity and a challenge.

The opportunity came from the fact that the show coincided with the Winter Olympics in Turin, which ran in February 2006, and that what had already been a celebration of an evanescent material – snow – could this time work with it in a form that was likely to vanish even more quickly. Opening a day or so before the Olympics, Fung's show ran to the end of March, with plenty of time for mutation through melting.

The 'challenge', which could be treated as a synonym for 'terror', was that it wouldn't be cold enough and the whole enterprise would melt before it was complete. Sestriere typically has 30 centimetres (12 inches) of snow on the ground in January and February, but although daily temperatures can be below −2°C (28°F), more often than not they are above 0°C (32°F) . With the unpredictability introduced by global warming, there wasn't much of a comfort factor. In an interview with Dominic Lutyens in the culture magazine *Spoon*, Fung said 'I'm sweating bullets. Who knows, we could have no snow?'

Cold | 91

Far left and left Projects were created to look pristine, but the process of melting was treated as part of the show, as with this work by Paola Pivi with Cliostraat, which created snow and fake-fur enclosures for trees. It is seen in its original form (far left) and during melting (left).

But he did get snow, and an acclaimed series of collaborations between artists and architects. It is this collaboration that made Fung's shows special. Many cold countries hold ice shows – those at Harbin in China and Sapporo in Japan are particularly well known – but although they can be mesmerizing displays of artistry, there is not a great deal of Art with a capital A. Fung felt that by bringing his artists and architects together to work in a medium that was in most cases unfamiliar to both, and where the architects' superior technical knowledge was largely irrelevant, they could collaborate on a level playing field.

And the collaborations at Sestriere were certainly impressive. Fung paired two Frenchmen, conceptual artist Daniel Buren and architect and product designer Patrick Bouchain, to produce a series of slatted-timber bench-like structures marching down the hillside, called Snowbeams. Their interest was in the way snow built up and then melted from the structures, and in the effect not just on the structures themselves but on their shadows.

American architects Tod Williams and Billie Tsien worked with Belgian-born artist Carsten Höller on a project called Slide Meeting, which was a kind of bunker penetrated by chutes for high-speed sliding. The Japanese pairing of Yoko Ono and Arata Isozaki created a circular high-walled maze called Penal Colony.

Italian artist Paola Pivi collaborated with Turin-based art and architecture practice Cliostraat on building enclosures that both celebrated and protected trees, and decorated the enclosures with stripes of brightly coloured artificial fur. Britain's architectural superstar Norman Foster worked with Spanish artist Jaume Plensa on a piece called Where Are You?, which took the form of a dial engraved with the GPS coordinates of Foster's London office.

Right Slide Meeting by architects Tod Williams and Billie Tsien, working with artist Carsten Höller, was a bunker penetrated by slide chutes.
Below Daniel Buren and Patrick Bouchain used a timber-slatted structure to create Snowbeams.

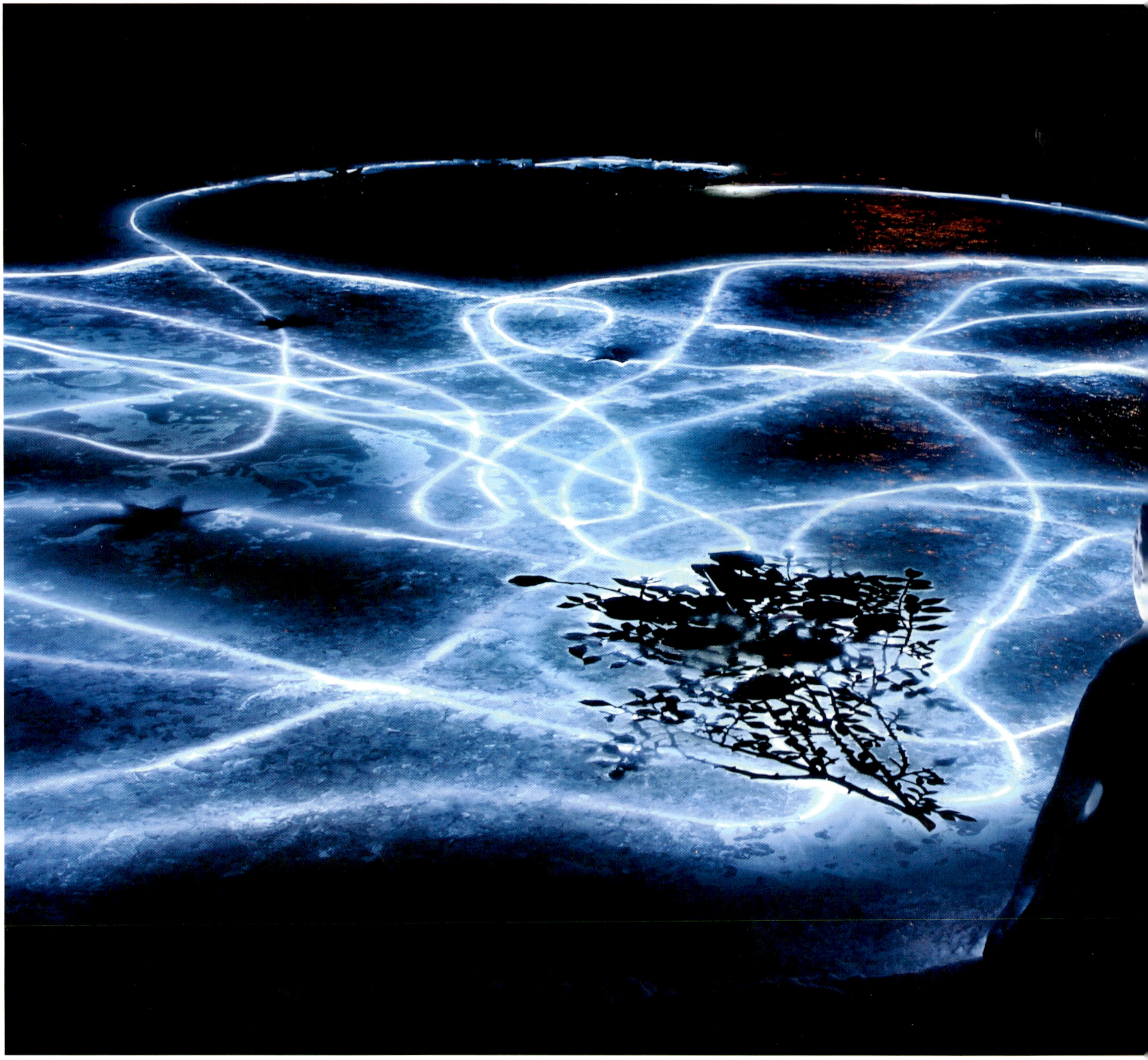

And finally, American academic and theoretical architect Lebbeus Woods and American feminist artist Kiki Smith produced probably the most poetic piece of all. Called Looking Glass, it consisted of a mirror-like sheet of ice containing fibre-optic cables that created traces like the palimpsests of passing skaters, all overseen by a female form sculpted in snow.

How do you top such an exhibition? If you are Fung, you don't, but wisely move on to the next thing. Having toyed with the idea of an exhibition called Sink, that would have taken place entirely under water, he chose to curate a large-scale exhibition alongside the 2008 Olympics in Beijing and to be the curator of the 2008 art biennale in Santa Fe in the southwest United States. But with the Sestriere show carefully documented at www.thesnowshow.com, from first ideas through realization, completion and melting, it will never quite disappear.

Above Where Are You? was a collaboration between Norman Foster and Jaume Plensa, based on the GPS coordinates of Foster's London office.
Opposite Looking Glass by Lebbeus Woods and Kiki Smith had a female form looking into a frozen pool containing fibre-optic traces.

ANTARCTICA
HUGH BROUGHTON ARCHITECTS

HALLEY VI ANTARCTIC RESEARCH STATION

Height above sea level
20m/65½ft (ice shelf 150m/492ft)

Average annual snowfall
1m/3ft 9in

Average high and low temperatures
4.5°C/40°F – -55.3°C/-66.6°F

Opposite The line of blue modules, with a red social model, will be a beacon in the featureless wastes in this part of the Antarctic.
Left A typical module. The prefabricated modules are relocatable, and can be jacked up above the build-up of snow.
Below Longitudinal section through an accommodation module, with social spaces at the ends.

The Antarctic is such a tough environment that until recently the role of the architect in designing buildings there has been treated very much as a subsidiary one – the crucial factors were dealing with logistics and the cold and dark.

This changed, however, with the appointment of British-based Hugh Broughton Architects to design Halley VI, the latest station for the British Antarctic Survey (BAS). Broughton won an international competition, beating 85 other entrants despite, or perhaps because of, having no experience of working in such an extreme environment.

Admittedly Broughton is working with a vastly experienced engineer, Faber Maunsell, but he brings a freshness of approach to the environment that has allowed some imaginative thinking while not discounting the technical demands of designing and building for survival in such a bleak environment.

'One of the key reasons that we won,' said Broughton, 'was because of the interior design.' He has reacted against the previous rather fusty cosiness that made the interiors of previous stations look something like a cross between a students' union and an old people's home, while at the same time giving consideration to creating spaces for different kinds of interaction and for privacy – essential when small groups of people are cooped up together for such a long time. In summer there is a population of 52, which shrinks to only 16 in winter.

Broughton has also brought an original approach to some of the problems that bedevil this particular location. Sitting on the Brunt Ice Shelf, Halley is the most southerly of the BAS's stations, and is in an ideal position both for science, as it lies within the auroral zone, and for ease of servicing. But the 150 metre (492 foot) thick Brunt Ice Shelf moves at 400 metres (1,312 feet) a year towards the sea, with the seaward sections calving (breaking off). In addition, there is snowfall of typically 1 metre (3 feet) a year, which builds up to bury the stations. For this reason, BAS is now building its sixth Halley station – the first was completed in 1956. Halley III and IV were designed as buried stations, but were soon crushed by the ice. Halley V is on stilts, but has to be jacked up every year, a task that occupies 40 people for several days. In contrast, with Broughton's design, a bulldozer driver and two other people will spend just two to three weeks each year jacking up the legs.

The key to Broughton's design is that it is both modular and relocatable. Using modules makes the construction repeatable, and if more facilities are needed in the future these can be added easily. With the exception of one social module, all the others are similar in form. Two modules are separated from the rest by a bridge. There are two reasons for this. One is that this requires the scientists to go out of doors every day, which is considered to be good for their mental health. The other is that, in the case of a fire on the station, these two modules will be protected and all the staff will be able to live in them until they can be taken off the station. There are six blue modules (there were ten in the original design, before value engineering), with the social module a bright red – an echo of the colours of the Union flag. In a landscape that on an overcast day can be entirely devoid of colour, Halley VI will be an uncompromising feature – if not the only feature – in the landscape.

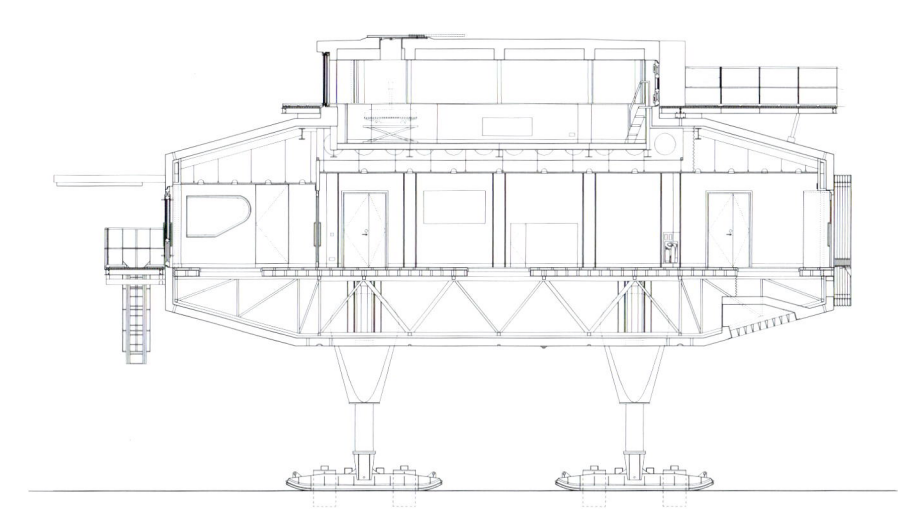

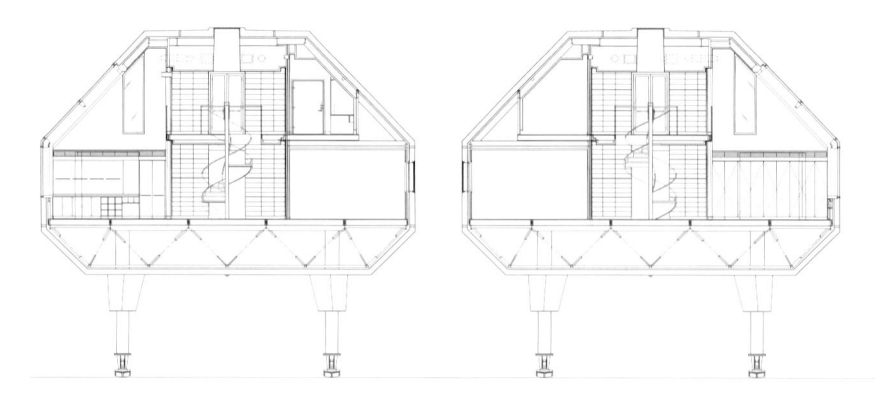

The fact that the modules are relocatable, travelling on giant skis, is essential both to the construction process, and to the station's longevity. As the ice shelf shifts, it will be possible to move the station further inland before it is in danger of being lost. Halley VI has a design life of 20 years, at least twice that of any previous station. Broughton says science runs in five-year programmes, and he hopes the science, rather than problems with the building, will be the only impediment to the lifespan of the station.

The modules are in a continuous line, side-on to the prevailing wind, to minimize snow build-up. This means there is effectively a single very long corridor – something that could both smack depressingly of an institution and be very disorientating. Broughton has tackled this by making each module unique internally, with its own colour palette. There are four pairs of bedrooms in each living module, each sleeping one person in the winter and two in the summer. With lavatories and a shower at one end, there is a social space at the other with a couple of chairs where people can stop and chat informally.

On Halley V all the bedrooms are separated by plywood, and Broughton was keen to make the acoustic separation better. His modular design for Halley VI, with the use of pods for the bedrooms as well as the bathrooms, is a great improvement. The walls are of Fermacell, a hard sound-absorbent material. Boards on the walls will allow residents to pin up pictures, personalizing their space.

The large social module is open plan, and has a dining room and bar. Upstairs is a large observation window, positioned to allow views of the aurora australis, the magnificent southern lights seen in winter, which offer some compensation for the unending darkness. Again, the idea of this module is that it offers a range of spaces, so that people can withdraw for quieter activities.

The steel-framed modules consist of an elevated space frame on four hydraulically operated steel legs. They have lots of bracing because of the very high winds they will encounter. Originally the plan was to clad the modules with timber SIPs (structural insulated panels), using aluminium overcladding. This is the tried and tested method for Antarctic stations and, as Broughton says, 'In Antarctica tried and tested is a good way forward'. But at a review with senior people from BAS, and also from the French Antarctic team who had recently completed a station at New Concordia, 'We had a major turning point'. The French suggested that Broughton should consider a GRP (glass-reinforced polymer) system that they had used. 'We realized that there were a number of benefits,' said Broughton. The lower GRP layer would act as a barrier in its own right, and remove the need for a vapour barrier. The outer GRP layer could be painted in the factory, so removing the need for a separate finishing process. GRP has a good fire performance, and it could be treated in the factory to reduce its electrostatic conduction, which is both unpleasant for residents and can interfere with scientific experiments. There was no doubt about the material's performance at low temperatures, since it is used for cryogenic experiments down to –250°C (–418°F) (a temperature that makes the Antarctic look positively balmy) and will also be used on the planned new lunar space shuttle.

The project was let in packages, with the key fabrication done in South Africa, prior to shipping to the Antarctic. The ship carrying all the components arrived in the Antarctic at Christmas 2007 and, during a ten-week period, the units were assembled to be weathertight next to Halley V.

Assembly was due to be completed during the summer season of 2009, and the modules will then be dragged 15 kilometres (9 miles) inland to the Halley VI site. As the ice shelf weakens, they will move again.

Opposite top Transverse sections through the social module.
Top Assembly of a module in the Antarctic during the summer season 2007–2008.
Left Cutaway image of the social module, which is on two levels and provides both large social spaces and room for withdrawal and contemplation.

Cold 99

SOUTH POLE, ANTARCTICA
FERRARO CHOI AND ASSOCIATES

AMUNDSEN-SCOTT SOUTH POLE STATION

Height above sea level
2,657.6m/8,719ft

Average annual snowfall
200m/7⁶/sin

Average high and low temperatures
-13.6ºC/7ºF – -82.8ºC/-117ºF

Opposite The station sits on the 3.2 kilometre (2 mile) thick ice shelf at the South Pole.
Right The previous station had key buildings sheltered by a geodesic dome.

What can an architect based in Honolulu, Hawaii, understand about the South Pole? Rather a lot, actually, if that architect is Ferraro Choi who has just finished the new Amundsen-Scott South Pole station, which is described as 'one of the most technological and sophisticated structures ever built at the South Pole'. This is surely an understatement. It must be the most sophisticated, and certainly improves conditions significantly for the relatively large numbers of people who work at the pole: 154 in the three-month summer season and 50 in winter.

The previous station, completed in 1975, was largely underground and included a geodesic dome covering a number of individual buildings. It may have seemed an exciting, futuristic project when first completed, but the reality was that the dome sheltered a collection of undistinguished buildings scattered around like an icy shanty town. Access to the dome was via a tunnel, people had to put on outdoor clothes to move from one element to another, and they couldn't really see out. And that was before snow build-up began and elements started to distort and break.

Snow excavation is a regular user of manpower and fuel in the Antarctic – because it is so cold, the snow never melts. Buildings too often prevent it being blown away, so each year's snowfall accumulates on top of that from the previous year. The architect has taken a dual approach to dealing with this on the new station. First is the physical form. The building is on stilts with a profile like an aeroplane wing facing into the prevailing wind. Just as with an aeroplane wing, the wind speed below the 'wing' increases, leading to a reduction in pressure. On an aeroplane, this Venturi effect is what provides uplift; on the polar station, it creates scour, reducing build-up of snow beneath the station. But since this only means a reduction, not a total elimination, of snow build-up the station has also been designed so that it can be jacked up in 25 centimetre (10 inch) increments.

The U-shaped building in fact consists of a number of linked modules, since the 3.2 kilometre (2 mile) thick glacier on which it sits moves laterally by about 10 metres (33 feet) each year (which means the marker for the South Pole constantly has to be moved). Any differential movement will be taken up by the links between the modules.

The buildings are also insulated to five times the level specified in building codes in the United States – both for comfort and, again, to reduce fuel use.

The architect had to design the frames and cladding of the building in modular elements that could be brought in by the only available transport – ski-equipped LC-130 Hercules cargo aircraft that make the three-hour journey from the US McMurdo base on the edge of the Antarctic continent (weather permitting).

Construction took a total of 12 years, with the official opening of the station in January 2008. Now the scientists, who carry out work that is only possible in the very clean atmosphere of the Antarctic where humidity is zero, can enjoy a wide range of luxuries and necessities. These include a NASA-designed plant-growth chamber for producing fresh food, improved computer power and communications, a gym, an infirmary and, best of all, windows out of which the scientists can look at the inhospitable but extraordinary environment that surrounds them – and perhaps think gratefully about the architect in faraway Honolulu.

Opposite Section through the new station (left) and the buried tunnels (right).
Below The new station is to the top right of the picture. On the left is the geodesic dome of the previous station, with buried tunnels behind it.
Below left Plan showing the new station (top right) and the previous station (bottom left).

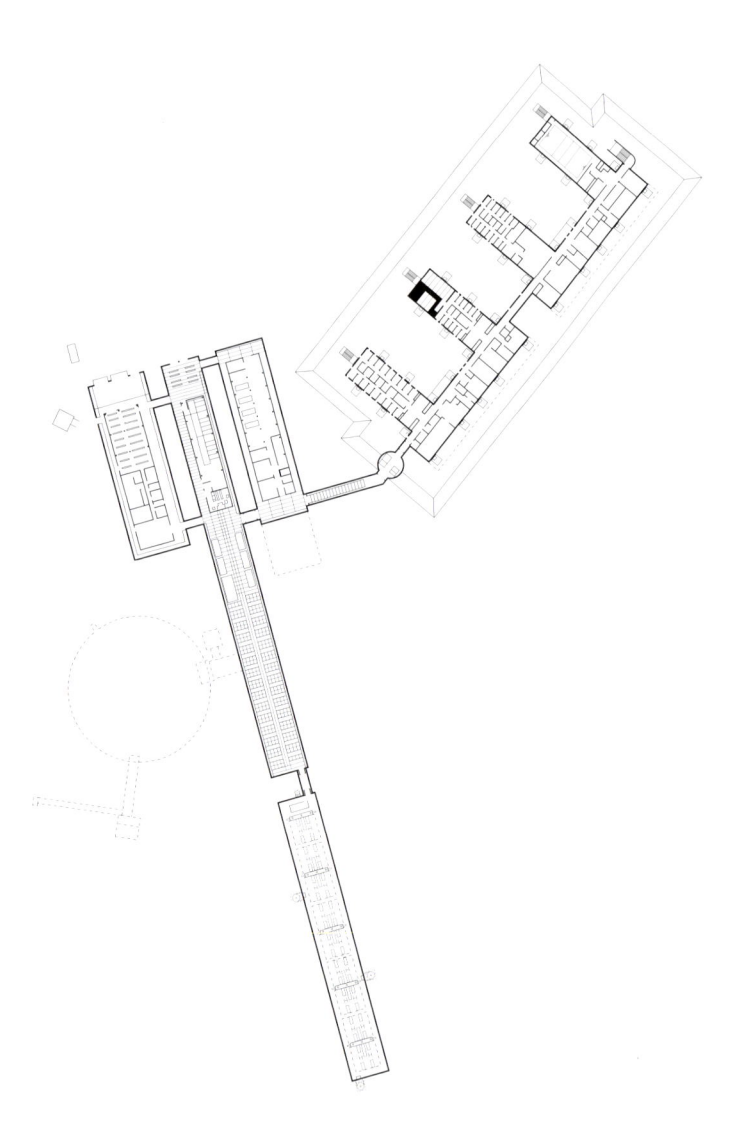

Cold 103

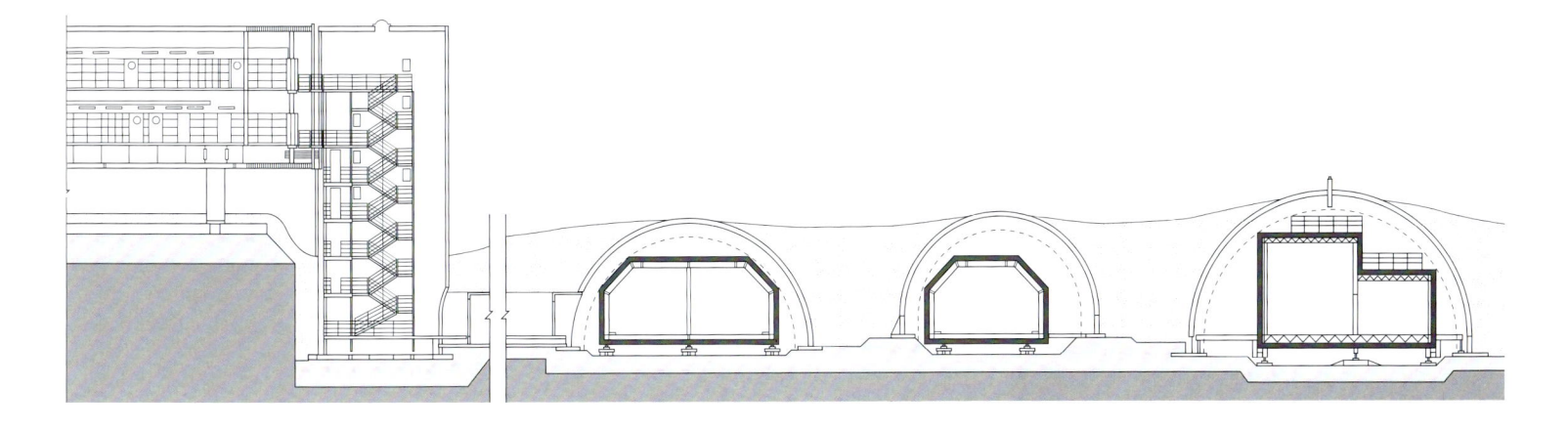

CHAPTER 3
HIGH

Left Foster + Partners has remodelled the Dolder Grand Hotel in Zurich, Switzerland, and added new wings, to bring it up to twenty-first-century standards of luxury.
Below left Proposals by Heinz Julen and Üeli Lehmann for a steel and glass pyramid on top of Switzerland's Klein Matterhorn have caused outrage.

Why do we want to build on mountains? Traditional settlements have been at lower levels, where the climate was less extreme and the soil more fertile. Even the Alps, the mountains set at the centre of Europe and containing important routes across the continent, were for centuries only settled in the valleys and on the lowest slopes.

Early Alpine travellers also stuck to the valleys, with the first explorers of the peaks being H.B. de Saussure and the Benedictine monk Placidus Spescha, both at the end of the eighteenth century. The nineteenth century was seen as the 'golden age of Alpinism', brought to a close when Edward Whymper ascended the Matterhorn, one of the last unconquered peaks, in 1865.

Where intrepid travellers led the way, the less intrepid and then mass tourism followed. In the *Guardian* newspaper's travel awards in 2007 and 2008, readers voted Switzerland, at the heart of the Alps, as their most popular European travel destination.

If the projects on the pages that follow are predominantly, although not entirely, Alpine, that is because of the Alps' unique properties. The climate is relatively benign, historic routes make the area accessible, it is in the centre of an affluent part of the world where the holiday habit developed earliest, and the mountains, although high enough for grandeur, are small enough to offer constantly changing views.

Left Zaha Hadid Architects' Bergisel Ski Jump in Austria was one of the first incursions by a signature architect into Alpine design. **Opposite right** Salginatobel Bridge in Switzerland, designed by Robert Maillart, was completed in 1930. **Opposite far right** The glass-bottomed Grand Canyon Skywalk in Arizona.

For all these reasons, the Alps became the earliest and most popular centre of mountain tourism. First they were summer resorts, then, with the growth of skiing, winter resorts and now, with increasing world affluence, they are reinventing themselves as all-year-round destinations and seeking to squeeze more money out of the market by offering increasing luxury and diversion.

So, in 2008, Foster + Partners completed the entire remodelling of the Dolder Grand Hotel in Zurich, maintaining the fabric from the original building of 1899, but bringing it up to the standards that luxury travellers demand today – travellers such as those who would stay in Mario Botta's Tschuggen Bergoase Spa in Arosa (see page 144). That spa could be seen as a continuation of a trend set by Peter Zumthor's Thermal Baths at Vals, completed in 1996. But whereas the Vals building, by the most Alpine of architects, is hugely admired, it is not pitching itself at the level of luxury that Botta and others are offering.

There is a danger that this relatively small area (192,000 square kilometres/74,132 square miles) could become swamped, and the very diversity of flora and fauna that visitors admire could be damaged. The World Wildlife Fund, the global conservation organization, writes that: 'The construction of ski runs causes irreparable damage to the landscape. The increasing use of snow cannons sets off additional problems by their use of water, energy and chemical and biological additives. Tourism is also a strong driving force behind urbanization: tourist buildings and the growing number of inhabitants with their need for space and infrastructure make for more extended settlements even in relatively remote areas. Large tourist resorts present an area consumption rate that is far bigger than that of a non-tourist community.

'The worst indirect tourism-related threat is the increase in motor traffic, especially in remote and sensitive elevated areas.'

Realization of the threat has led to controversy over a proposal to build a 117 metre (384 foot) high steel and glass pyramid on top of the Klein Matterhorn in Switzerland. Designed by artist Heinz Julen and architect Üeli Lehmann, this would take the peak above the magic figure of 4,000 metres (13,123 feet). Already the highest sightseeing place in Europe accessible by cable car, the Klein Matterhorn offers magnificent panoramas. It would get the highest hotel and conference centre in the world, 100 metres (328 feet) above the Hotel Everest View in Nepal. The building would be pressurized to counteract the effects of altitude.

With several other projects on key mountain tops proposed, including one by Switzerland's most famous practice, Herzog & de Meuron, the Klein Matterhorn has become a focus for protest against the desecration and commercialization of the landscape.

Part of the drive towards increasing commercialization of the Alps comes from the fact that, with declining snowfalls through global warming, income from winter sports is likely to fall. But at the moment this means not that attention is being diverted away from these facilities, but that resorts are competing with each other ever more fiercely.

Just as there is a market for increasingly luxurious spa hotels, so the means of transporting skiers up mountains are becoming increasingly sophisticated. Projects such as the Carmenna Chairlift Stations in Arosa, Switzerland (page 126) and the Galzigbahn Base Terminal in Austria (page 132) show that with careful design such buildings can enhance rather than deface a mountain.

Similarly, the significant input of architects into ski jumps is relatively recent. m2r's Ski Jump at Vogtland in Germany (page 136) captures all the excitement of the sport, exceeding in drama Zaha Hadid's Bergisel Ski Jump, built in 2002 for five times the cost. Almost too solid, Hadid's solution was perhaps the slightly uncomfortable reaction of a non-skier to what seemed a difficult brief.

But she excelled with the cable railway stations leading out from Innsbruck in Austria (page 122), which celebrate the joy of travelling into the mountains. This too is in a great tradition of exciting transport in the Alps. Most dramatic of all is the Jungfraujoch Railway, opened in 1912, which tunnels up through the Eiger, that most treacherous of mountains, with a stop at a viewing platform, and carries on to the top of the Jungfrau mountain.

Swiss bridges such as Robert Maillart's springing concrete Salginatobel Bridge, completed in 1930, and Jurg Conzett's 2005 Traversina Footbridge of larch and steel cables slung across a steep-sided valley, not only enhance their environment, but also offer magnificent views. This desire to enjoy views has led to projects such as the Aurland Lookout in Norway (page 108) and the glass-bottomed Grand Canyon Skywalk that projects out 1,219 metres (4,000 feet) over one of America's greatest pieces of landscape.

Whether in the Alps or beyond, all the projects in this chapter share a delight in views and in space; a sense of being 'on top of the world'. It seems appropriate, then, that the last of them, Manned Cloud (page 152), should be one that really is above everything – a proposal that allows you to look down on the earth from an airship. It offers a travelling experience as different from using a budget airline as a luxury Alpine spa hotel is from a basic mountain refuge.

SOGN OG FJORDANE, NORWAY
TODD SAUNDERS AND TOMMIE WILHELMSEN

AURLAND LOOKOUT

Height above sea level
640m/2,100ft

Average annual rainfall
2,400mm/94½in

Average high and low temperatures
20°C/68°F – -20°C/-4°F

Opposite The lookout makes the most of a drop of 600 metres (nearly 2,000 feet).
Above left Set on a winding road, the project includes not only the lookout itself but also a parking area, pedestrian path and toilet facilities.
Above right The laminated-wood cladding to the sides of the ramp fits well with the surrounding trees.

The word 'lookout' takes on a double meaning at the Aurland lookout at Sogn og Fjordane on Norway's west coast. You certainly can look out to see one of the most dramatic views offered in a country famed for its fabulous scenery. But, if of a nervous disposition, you may also want to 'look out' for a sensation of vertigo.

This is the safety-aware twenty-first century, and of course every care has been taken to ensure that people wandering out from their cars to enjoy the view won't plunge down the mountainside. But, equally, the architects have done all they can to foster the impression that this is exactly what may happen. Projecting over a drop of 600 metres (1,969 feet), this diving-board-like structure, perched among the treetops, flies out horizontally and then curves back on itself for support in the rock of the mountain. The visitor walks along the timber platform towards – well, seemingly towards nothing. In fact, a glazed balustrade terminates the walkway, providing perfect security alongside the illusion of danger.

Tommie Wilhelmsen has written: 'I have been there a few times and have seen people that will not walk along the ramp. Or, they walk out confidently only to slow down before the edge, and then slowly put their hands on the rail. It is meant to be scary, but the structure and glass are very safe.'

What is so pleasing about this structure, in addition to the vertiginous thrill, is its feeling of simplicity and utter rightness. What other solution could there have been? And like many such seemingly simple solutions, it took a good deal of talent and ingenuity to achieve.

The architecture practice won a design competition run in 2002 by the Norwegian Highways Department (Statens Vegvesen) which was worried that this unspoilt beauty could be the victim of its own splendour – attracting visitors who would, in turn, destroy the magnificence they had come to admire by littering the landscape with parked cars. Neither is just stopping to gawp a particularly safe thing to do on such tortuous roads.

The winning solution therefore comprises not just this dramatic structure, which has been likened to a a ski jum as well as a diving board, but also a parking area set down from the road that can accommodate ten cars and two coaches (this is remote Norway, where notions of overcrowding are a little different from those in a major European metropolis). Set just below the road, this parking area then connects to the lookout by a pedestrian path.

Left The lookout is angled to give visitors the sensation that they could step out into the void.
Below From top: plan and section of the ramp.
Bottom The structure viewed from underneath.

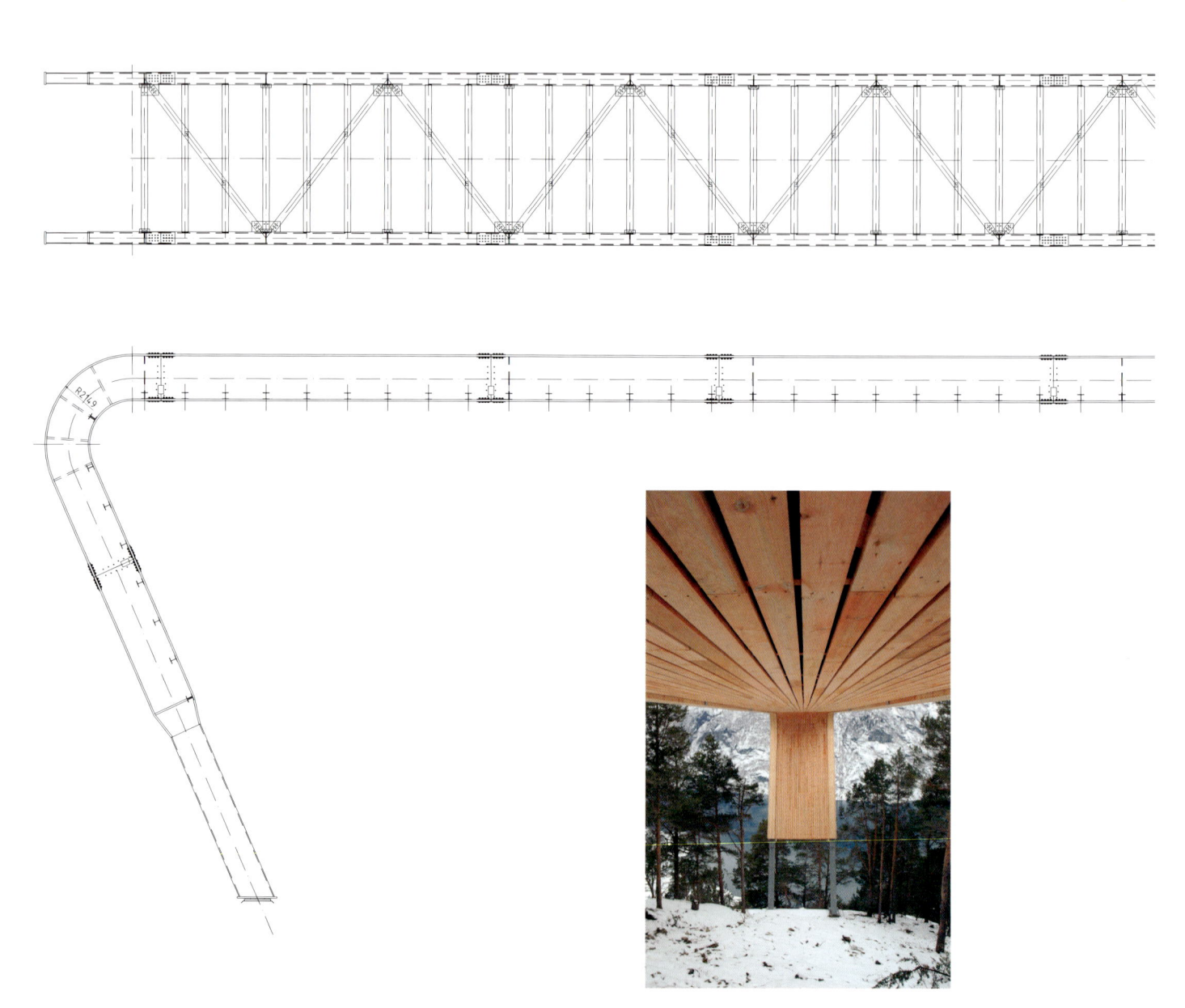

110 Extreme Architecture

The lookout itself is a steel-framed structure 4.2 metres (13 feet 9 inches) wide, 33.6 metres (110 feet 3 inches) long, and with a height of 13.5 metres (44 feet 3 inches). There are two concrete foundations. The upper one, at the level of the ramp, is U-shaped and bolted into the mountainside beneath the road by nine tension bolts. This is the ramp that has to withstand most of the lateral wind forces. The lower foundation supports the legs of the lookout, fixed into the rock with two bolts.

The steel framework was built up in relatively small sections, as these were all that could be transported along the winding roads. It is at the bend back at the end of the ramp that the greatest stresses are experienced, and from there back to the road a criss-cross grid of steel spans between the two sides.

Cladding of the ramp and of a part of the 'return' support is in pressure-treated pine, intended to turn grey over time. Laminated wood is used for the sides. Saunders & Wilhelmsen took care wherever possible to conceal joints and fixings. This elegant consideration gives a sense of deliberation to the way the steel legs protrude from the timber cladding, a reminder that this is very much a manufactured and engineered object and not just part of the landscape. At the parking area there are WC blocks, of concrete with a rubberized finish and timber cladding. Walls on the fjord side are glazed, a first glimpse of what is to come for those of a nervous disposition.

The lookout is not a year-round attraction, as the roads become impassable in the winter. But for the summer months it certainly enhances rather than detracts from the experience of nature. The only concern must be that it is such a landmark in its own right that some time fairly soon that car park may need extending.

Above Even the WCs offer dramatic views.

STAVANGER, NORWAY
ARKITEKTFIRMA HELEN & HARD

PREKESTOLHYTTA

Height above sea level at base
280m/918ft

Average annual rainfall
2300mm/90½in

Average high and low temperatures
26°C/78°F – -16°C/3°F

Prekestolen, or Pulpit Rock, is one of the most dramatic natural tourist attractions near to Stavanger in the south of Norway. A column of rock rising to more than 600 metres (2,000 feet) above sea level, it is topped with a nearly flat slab offering a magnificent view of Lysefiord. Astonishingly, accessing it is relatively easy, and it has become a popular day trip from Stavanger, with a path that takes about two hours to climb.

However, reaching the path involves first a boat ride and then either a bus or a car journey, so the Stavanger Turistforening (tourist association) decided to build a mountain lodge with 28 bedrooms and a restaurant/café at the base of the walk, in Refsvatnet. It appointed local architect Helen & Hard, based in Stavanger, who has come up with a building almost entirely in timber that adapts the old typology of timber cabins. Built of solid timber elements, the building is kinked to make the most of the views over the fjord, and to avoid a large rock on the site.

Although the temperatures experienced are, for Norway, relatively temperate, rarely dropping below −10ºC (14ºF) in winter and with only about 50 centimetres (1.6 feet) of snow, there are other climatic difficulties: wind and rain. The key to making a timber building durable in such circumstances is ventilation, so beneath the pitched roof (essential for rain run-off and to avoid snow build-up) there is a ventilation space, and there are ventilation outlets in the roof ridge.

The solid timber cross walls are made up of five layers: a central load-bearing layer with the elements aligned vertically, sandwiched between two panels oriented diagonally and, on the outside, a final layer of panels oriented horizontally.

In the sleeping areas, the solidity of this construction is maintained to provide sound insulation, whereas in the open spaces it is cut away to provide a more spacious feel. Through some clever use of geometry, the architect has managed to create the large spans needed in public areas, such as the café, from a system that is more usually adopted for cellular structures.

One of the main modulating elements of the construction is the contrast between privacy and openness. At 1,114 square metres (11,991 square feet), the lodge is much bigger than any of the mountain huts from which it draws its ancestry, and so some variation is essential.

With sleeping accommodation on the upper two levels and, on one half of the building, some at ground level as well, the sleeping areas are defined by the relatively small window openings in the overhanging roof that covers all but the ground floor. For the ground-floor bedrooms, vertical timber cladding provides a similar function.

Opposite Sloping timber cladding gives a sense of privacy to the sleeping areas.
Above Prekestolhytta provides access for walkers to the dramatic Pulpit Rock, which rises almost vertically from the fjord.

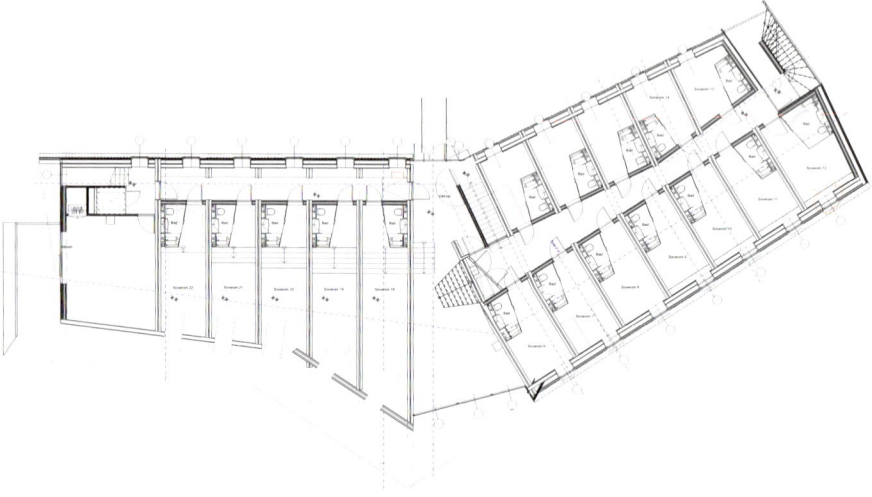

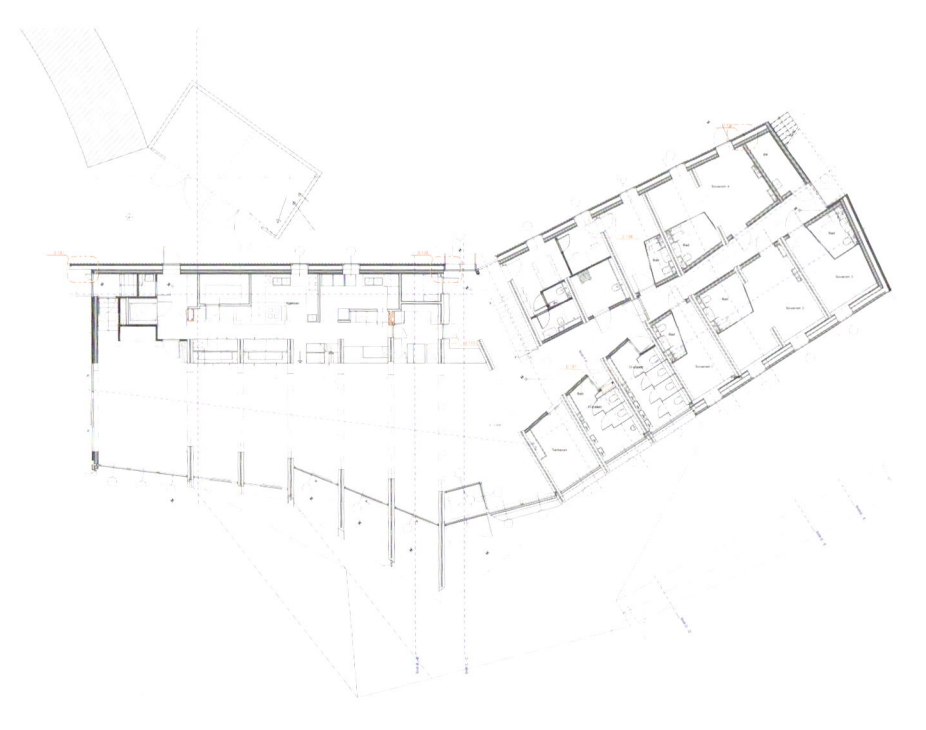

Top left Parts of the solid timber structure are cut away to create the more open communal spaces. **Above** Ground- and first-floor plans show the contrast between the cellular sleeping areas and more open communal accommodation.

114 Extreme Architecture

Below Section through the building.
Bottom Entrance to the building is via a highly glazed space placed at its central 'knuckle'.

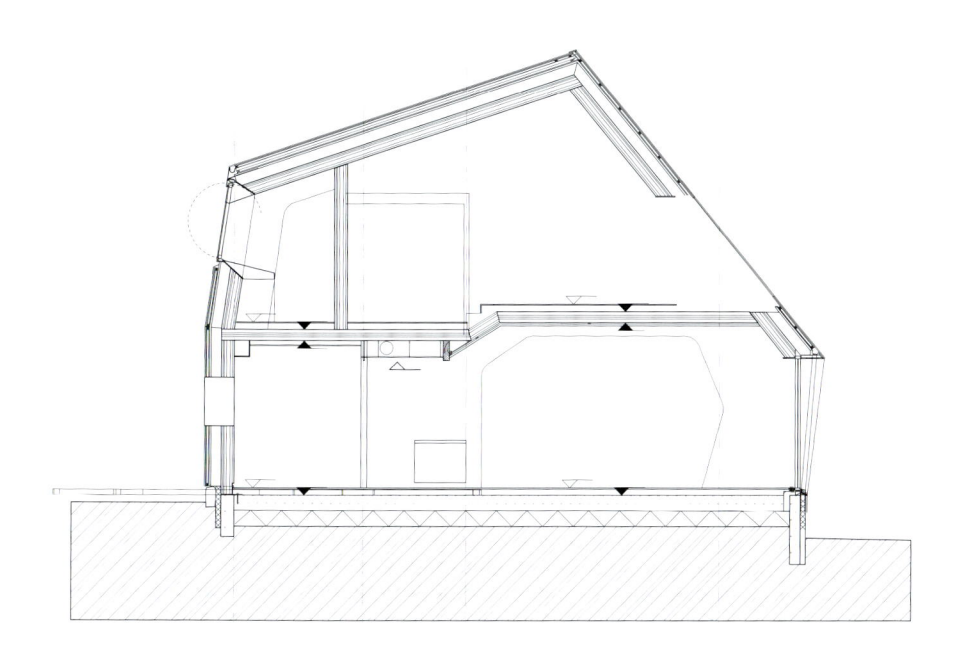

In contrast, the public spaces, on the side of the building facing the fjord, are much more open. The entrance space in the 'knuckle' between the two wings is fully glazed, and there is extensive glazing to the other public areas, with overhangs to provide some protected sitting out.

The overall effect on users of the building is of exposure to the timber construction, of planes and slopes that make the rooms interesting and welcoming without being quaint. From the outside, this is not a beautiful building, but it is a well-considered one that makes its environmental credentials fairly obvious (it uses geothermal heating). It offers fabulous views combined with a sense of shelter. And if it looks just a little grounded and solid, the nervous who will shortly be amazed by the vertiginous drop at Pulpit Rock are likely to remember it fondly for that very reason.

HEMSEDAL, NORWAY
DIV.A ARKITEKTER AS

MOUNTAIN LODGE

Height above sea level
1000m/3,280ft

Average annual rainfall
975mm/38^{3}/sin

Average high and low temperatures
29ºC/84ºF – -35ºC/-31ºF

Even the snow seems to respect the rigour of the mountain lodge designed by div.A for and by the firm's founders, Henriette Salvesen and Christopher Adams, in Hemsedal, southern Norway.

The simple, flat-roofed rectangular form is topped in the winter by a neat line of snow – this may be a place to be surrounded by nature and to enjoy it, but it certainly makes no concessions to any of the more chaotic aspects of the natural world. Every element is carefully considered and beautifully executed, yet it provides what is traditionally wanted from a skiing house: simple but comfortable bedrooms with great views, spaces for conviviality and hospitality, and a couple of well-appointed bathrooms.

It is not in a remote place. Hemsedal is Norway's second-largest ski resort, and the new house, built in an area recently designated for development, has plenty of neighbours. Its altitude gives it excellent skiing, available from the front door, and the angle of the house, a simple bar facing almost due south and downhill, offers delightful and almost uninterrupted views, as well as maximizing solar gain.

The arrangement of the house is linear, with an entrance at one end and a change in level moving up from the living area to the eating space. This is achieved with four steps running the full depth of the building, adding to the sense of enclosure of the living space while simultaneously enlarging it, with cushions placed on the steps. Beyond the open-plan cooking and dining space, again running the full depth of the house, is a double-loaded corridor, with bedrooms on the south side – three small ones each with a double bed, and a bunk above, and a master bedroom at the end – enjoying the best views. Bathrooms, a sauna and a spa room are on the north side.

Opposite It is possible to ski virtually to the front door of the house.
Top left Seen from behind, the house presents a blank face to the chilly north.
Above Fixed louvres provide shading and privacy to the bedrooms, which are set back to provide a sitting-out space.

The architect describes the building as a timber box placed inside a concrete frame. Externally the concrete is only really visible on the relatively small ends of the building. On the front, south-facing façade, oak clads the main frame and is also used on the louvres that provide both privacy and solar shading to the windows. Both the entrance and adjoining garage, and bedrooms, are set back from the building line, and their external walls are clad in black-stained spruce so that they recede from view. At the rear the house is virtually 'blind' with just a shallow row of windows set at ceiling level. Above this is a narrow strip of oak cladding; below it, more black-stained spruce.

This hyper-rational use of materials becomes even more straightforward internally. Oak is used on horizontal surfaces – floors and ceilings, and the steps between the living and dining area – whereas vertical surfaces are clad in black-stained spruce or black MDF. Unless, that is, the concrete is exposed, as it is most dramatically on the wall between the entrance hall and the living space, which incorporates the fireplace. This is beautifully finished concrete, with all the fixing marks from the shuttering anally regular, but it is something of a subversion of the cosy idea of the fireplace as the focus of such a house in the chilly months. As if in recognition of this, the sofas in the living room are arranged at right angles to the fireplace instead of, as one might expect, looking towards it.

Cupboards are built along the rear wall running the length of the sitting area and the kitchen. These act as book shelves in the sitting area and morph into kitchen cupboards. A relatively high top in the seating area becomes, with the change of level, a kitchen work surface. This horizontal surface is, of course, in oak, with black MDF used for the fronts of the cupboards.

The generous use of timber, at least externally, was a planning constraint for the area, and one that the architect has embraced with great intelligence. With the exception of the exposed concrete, which is a highlight rather than dominant, the palette is extremely conventional. Yet this is a building designed in an uncompromising manner that, while not precluding a sense of warmth, does drive out any nostalgic attachment to the past. It is this, perhaps, that made the building something of a cause célèbre in Norway as it struggled to achieve planning permission. It is certainly what makes it such an admirable piece of work.

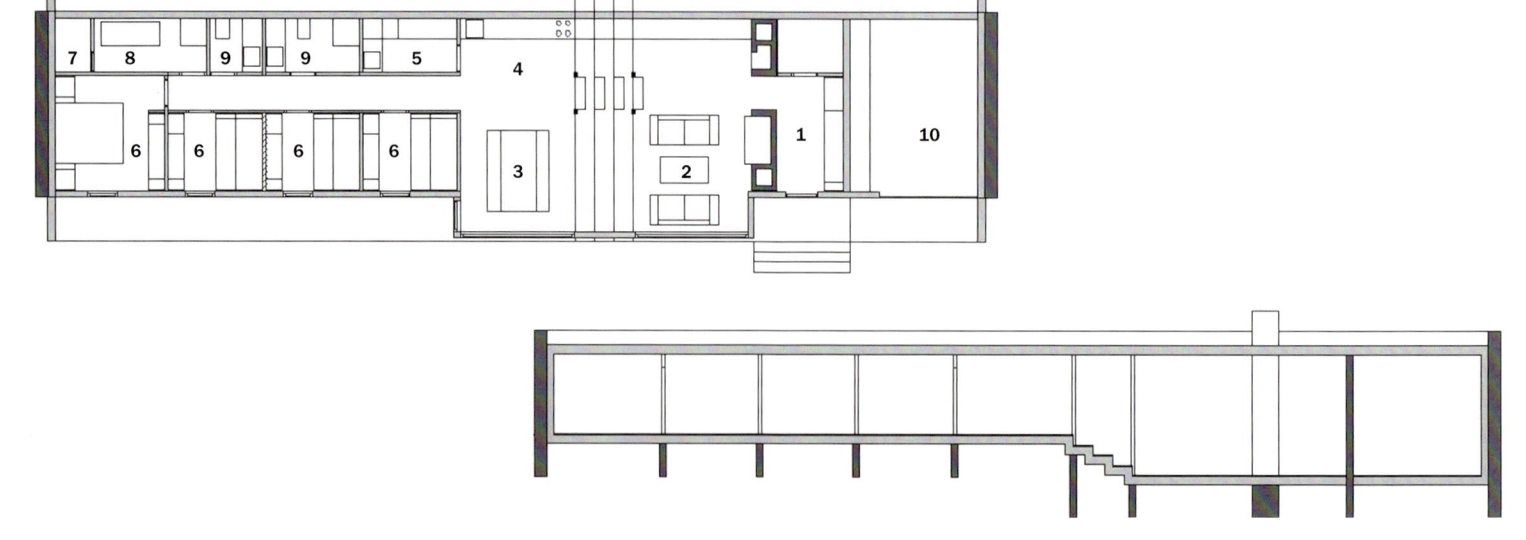

Opposite top Four steps provide a change of level between the living area (to the right) and the kitchen (to the left). Storage is set against the back wall.
Opposite centre Plan: 1. entrance; 2. living area; 3. eating space; 4. kitchen; 5. pantry; 6. bedroom; 7. sauna; 8. spa room; 9. bathroom; 10. garage/storage.
Opposite bottom Long section through the house, showing the change in level.
Right The wall beside the main entrance is one of the few places where concrete is exposed.

ARCHITECTURE AND VISION

SNOWCRYSTALS

Height above sea level
2,190m/7,185ft

Average annual rainfall
330mm/13in

Average high and low temperatures
29°C/84°F – -8°C/17°F

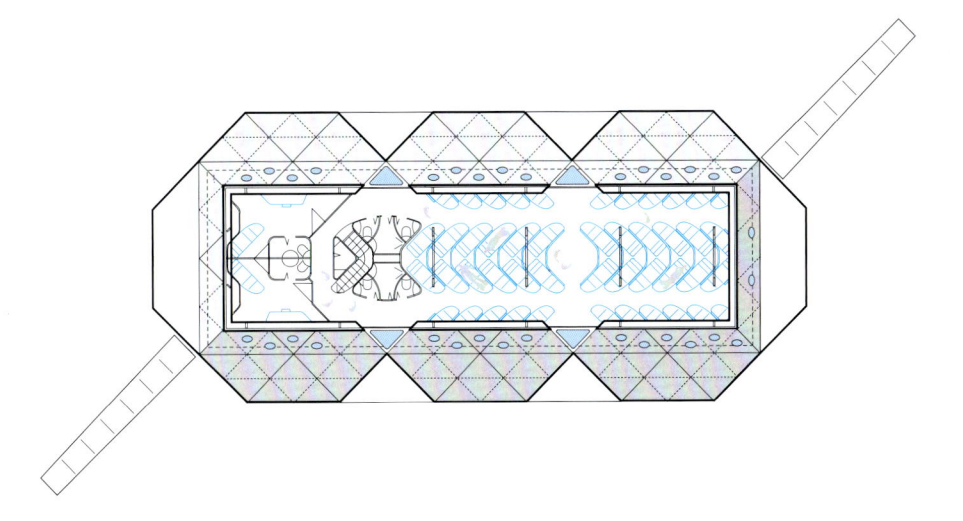

Architects ranging from Le Corbusier's collaborator Charlotte Perriand to the pioneer of compact architecture, Richard Horden, have been intrigued by the idea of developing a lightweight structure that can be installed easily on a mountainside. The latest practice to embrace this concept is Architecture and Vision, which designed a modular mountain hut to be built in California.

The Swiss-Italian duo worked with David Nixon of Altus Architects in Los Angeles, one of the original founders of London-based Future Systems, who has, like the partners of Architecture and Vision, concentrated much of his energy on architecture for space.

Like Richard Horden's SkiHaus, the SnowCrystals hut is designed to be brought to site by helicopter from an assembly point a couple of miles away. (Perriand would doubtless have loved this technology, too, but in 1929 had to settle for old-fashioned manpower.) Called SnowCrystals, it echoes the hexagonal geometry of snowflakes and is a lightweight and self-sufficient solution, powered by solar-powered batteries and hydropower. All grey and black water will be recycled or collected.

The hut is built up from a lightweight steel frame assembled on site and supported on minimal foundations. The appropriate cladding can be chosen for the site, from a high-tech white finish to a more rustic use of timber.

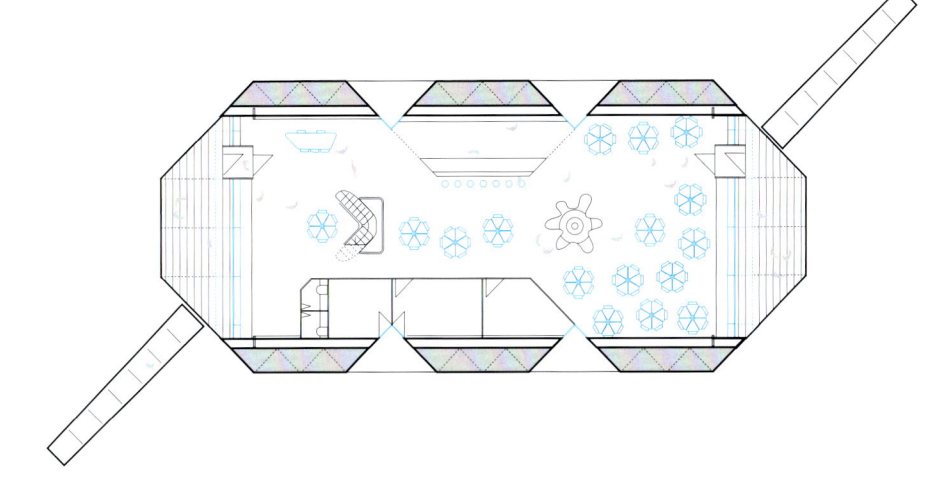

The basic design consists of three-dimensional hexagonal elements joined together and accessed by ramps, with the lower floor an open living space, served by large inclined windows. Above is a much more enclosed dormitory, with small holes in the cladding above allowing views of the stars. The building will offer visitors a kind of compact luxury, which the architects say is inspired by their work on first-class airline interiors.

The architects calculate that it would take six people three weeks to erect one of the modules which, fully equipped, would weigh 18,000 kilograms (40,000 pounds). Free of the infrastructure of the towns and of the sentimental associations of much ski architecture, SnowCrystals offers a radical alternative form of accommodation that is both forward-looking and more in touch with nature. It reflects the preoccupations of its designers in terms of ease of assembly and independence, while definitely being suited to the aesthetic of life on earth.

Opposite Visualizations showing SnowCrystals with tiny openings for stargazing, and solar panels on top.
Above Plans showing the more enclosed upper deck and the open main deck.

INNSBRUCK, AUSTRIA
ZAHA HADID ARCHITECTS

NORDPARK CABLE RAILWAY

Height above sea level
574m/1,883ft

Average annual rainfall
856mm/33¾in

Average high and low temperatures
14.3°C/58°F – 3.8°C/38°F

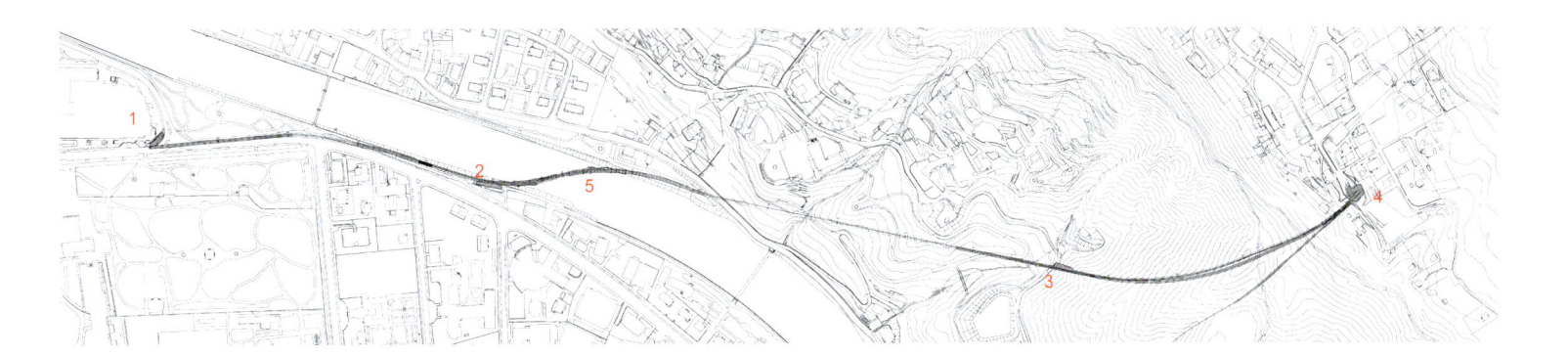

Opposite Doubly curved glass canopies were technically demanding, but create a relaxed ambience and have an affinity with the surrounding snowy mountains.
Top Map of the cable railway. 1. Congress; 2. Löwenhaus; 3. Alpenzoo; 4. Hungerburg; 5. new bridge over the river Inn

Above Löwenhaus station sits beside the River Inn. To the right of the station you can see the inclined concrete pylons that support the cable-stayed bridge.
Below Section through Löwenhaus station.

Few journeys can be more exciting than one that starts underground and ends on top of a mountain. This is the experience that is offered by Zaha Hadid Architects' Nordpark Cable Railway, which takes travellers from a station in the centre of Innsbruck on a journey of 1.8 kilometres (1 mile) up the Nordkette mountain. From the last station, at Hungerburg, which is 288 metres (945 feet) above the starting point, you can take a cable car to the top of the Seeberg mountain, ready to start skiing.

There are two clues that decrease the surprise of the journey, while not diminishing the excitement. The first is the city of Innsbruck itself. One of Europe's oldest ski centres, Innsbruck is visibly surrounded by mountains, so it would not take a genius to guess where one was going. The other clue comes from the design of the stations themselves. All part of a family, they each have a distinct identity as Hadid has responded to both the topography and the constraints of space. At Congress, the well-detailed but simple concrete entrance is topped by a white glass canopy that curves down at the edges like a suspended slice of melting slow. Where else can the railway be leading but to the mountains?

This organic white canopy is the leitmotif of all the stations. From Congress, the line goes through a tunnel to Löwenhaus station beside the River Inn. This station is above ground, cocooned by a more extreme 'melting' hat. From there, the railway continues across the river on a steel cable-stayed bridge, with the cables supported by slightly inclined round concrete pylons.

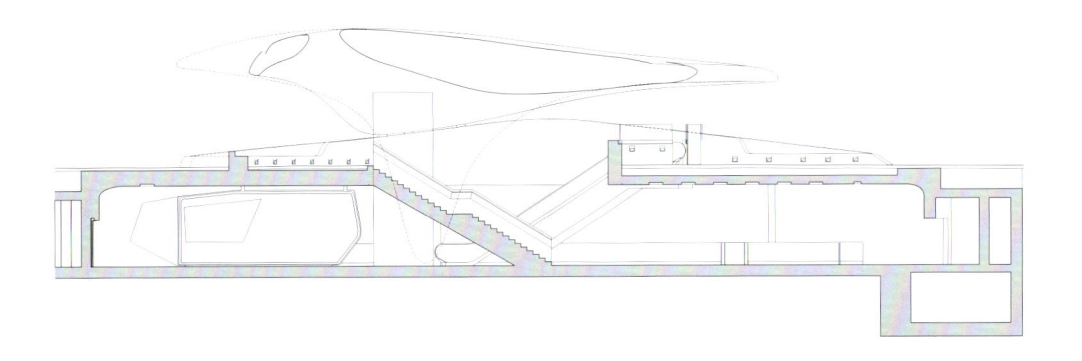

High 123

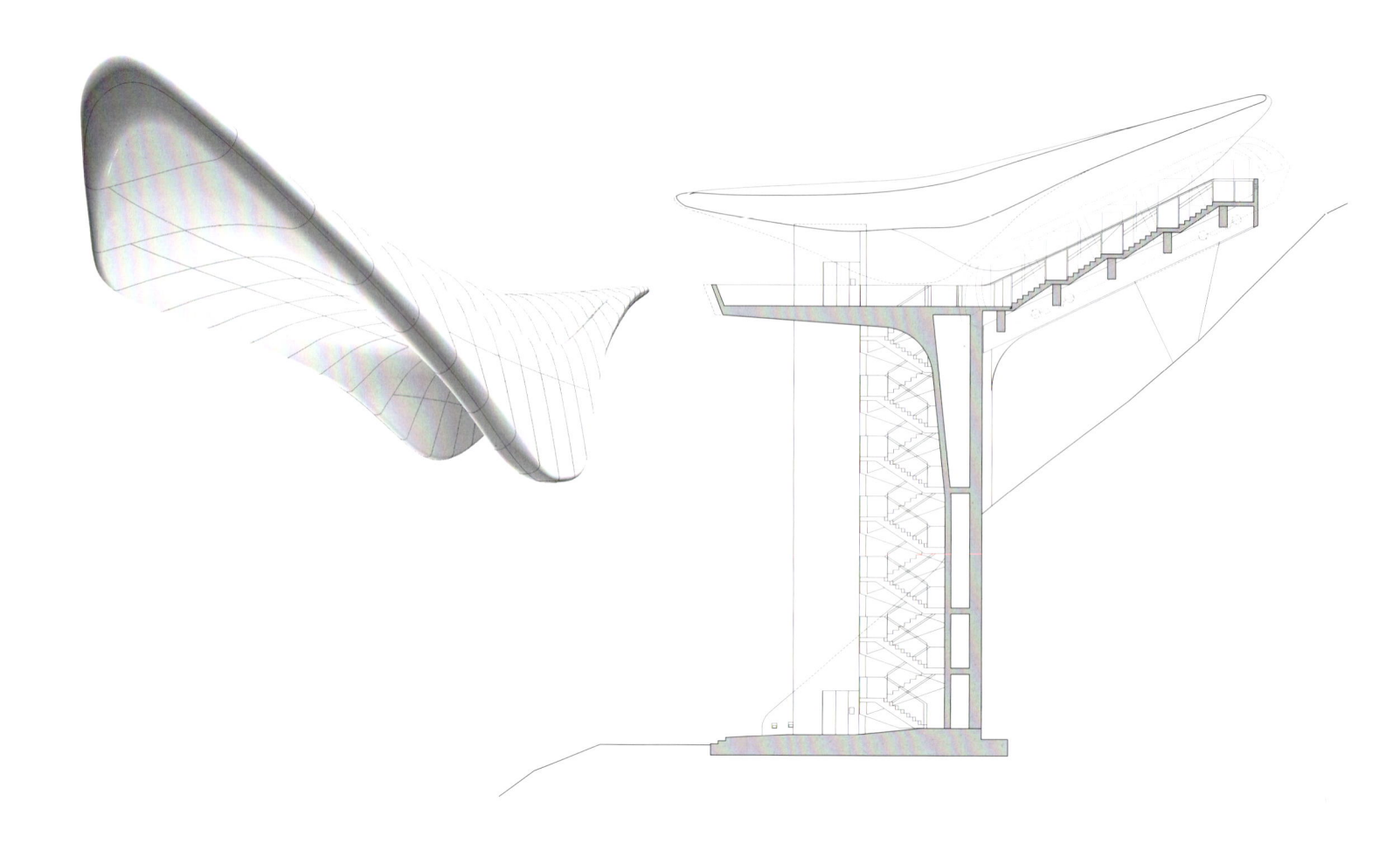

Then the drama really kicks in, as the line climbs steeply along the side of the Nordkette mountain to Alpenzoo station, cut in between stands of fir trees. Because the land slopes even more steeply here than the rail track itself, the city side of the station is suspended far above the ground, with a glazed stair tower descending from the cantilevered concrete structure. At the last station, Hungerburg, instead of a single canopy there is a double one, anchored in the centre, and looking like a white bird prepared to take flight into the mountains whose form it echoes.

As always with Hadid's architecture, advanced technology underlies the achievement – in this case the use of CNC milling and thermoforming to achieve the double curvature of the glass canopies. And yet there is a kind of effortlessness in the results that few of Hadid's other buildings have.

Her architecture is a million miles away from the cosy Gemütlichkeit image that is nearly synonymous with Austrian skiing, but it is not the first time that Hadid has made an assault on this status quo – and been welcomed for it. Her concrete ski jump on Bergisel mountain, overlooking Innsbruck and completed in 2002, won the Gold Medal for Design from the International Olympic Committee in 2005. Now with the rail line, which joins the city even more intimately to the mountains around it, it is as if she has been slightly overwhelmed by the grandeur that surrounds her. She has not lost her touch, her skill, or her imagination, but seems to have accepted that however glorious the results, her architecture cannot dominate the magnificent scenery. The result is the first architecture she has created that, while not alien to her other output, does not immediately shout the name of its creator – and is all the better for it.

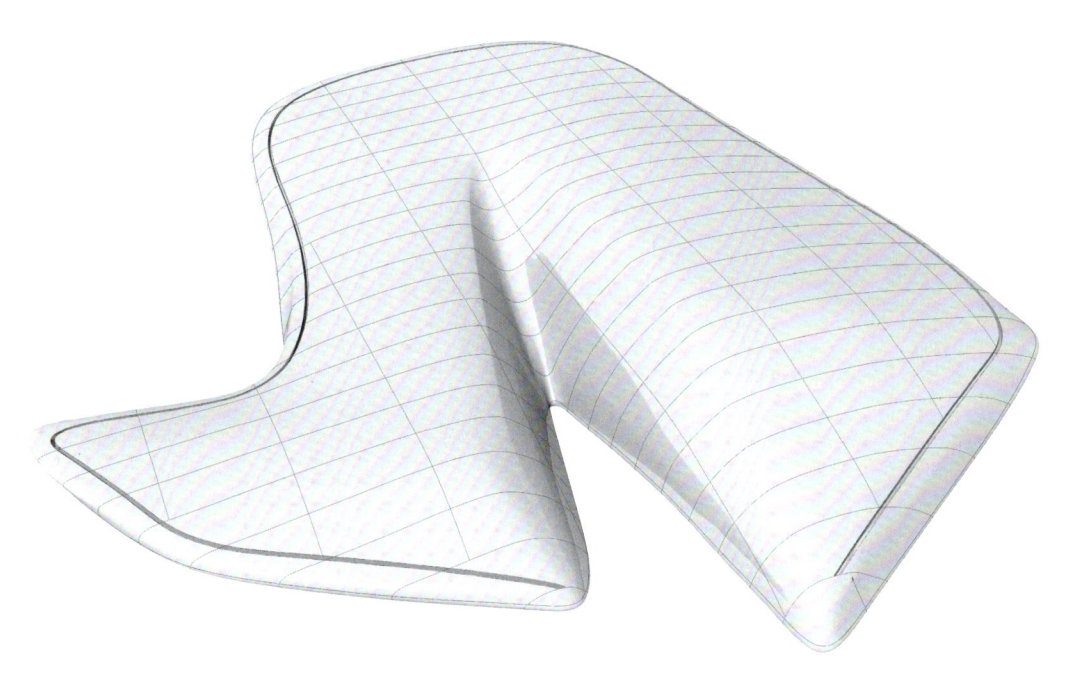

Opposite page CAD drawing (top left), section (right) and photograph (bottom) of Alpenzoo station, which sits on a steeply sloping site. **Above** Hungerburg, which has a double-winged roof, is the mountain terminus. **Left** CAD drawing of Hungerburg roof.

AROSA, SWITZERLAND
BEARTH & DEPLAZES ARCHITEKTEN

CARMENNA CHAIRLIFT STATIONS

Height above sea level
valley 1,905m/6,250ft; top of lift 2515m/8,251ft

Average annual rainfall
1,335mm/52½in

Average high and low temperatures
18°C/65°F – -12.1°C/10°F

Opposite The base station, clad in front in polycarbonate panels, echoes the form of the mountains.
Above Seen from behind, the lowest station is dominated by a glowing orange maw.
Below Section through the base station, showing the space for 'parking' chairlifts.

Skiing has never been so chic. The Carmenna Chairlift, rising above the village of Arosa in Switzerland, bursts out of an orange-coloured, womb-like space, halts at a dramatic bridging structure clad inside in bright yellow, and finishes its journey on top of the mountain in a building that, although solid, wittily reinterprets the tent that an intrepid traveller might pitch, as well as echoing the shapes of the surrounding peaks.

One of the highest ski resorts in Europe, at 1,739 metres (5,705 feet), Arosa is in a lovely situation, 160 kilometres (99 miles) southeast of Zurich, set around and above Lake Obersee. While most of it is a harmonious, although traditional, collection of Swiss buildings, there is also the show-stopping Tschuggen Bergoase Spa designed by Mario Botta (see page 144). Bearth & Deplazes practises a less muscular architecture than Botta, but has not eschewed drama.

This is an area prone to avalanches, which took out two previous chairlifts on the route, so the current four-person chairlifts need to be well protected. The largest of the three stations is the lowest one, since it has to accommodate the cables, technical equipment and storage for the chairs. It is also the most complex in shape, presenting the village with a minor Alpine landscape of irregular peaks. The village-facing façade is in vertical strips of polycarbonate sheeting, and the building's roof is covered in grass – in winter, of course, itself clad in snow. This means that at all seasons the roof blends into the landscape.

So far, so restrained, but once inside the lift building one finds oneself in a space clad in timber panels painted a bright orange colour. To add to the drama, the control room juts out into this space as a translucent half-circle, raised slightly above ground level. If you look back to the lift station from the mountainside, you see nothing of the structure at all; just a brightly lit orange maw opening in the hillside.

Above The intermediate station is painted a yellowy-green colour inside.
Right From the intermediate station, there is access to skiing and views.
Below Section through the top station.
Overleaf The top station evokes the image of a remote tent.

The top station, running parallel to the ridge of the mountain, is a simple ridge-tent-shaped form with the peak of the ridge leaning forward as if to embrace the arriving chairs. Externally it is clad with profiled metal sheeting, with a glazed end to admit light and offer tantalizing views. Inside, timber panels are painted in a bright, greeny-yellow colour. This colour is used again on the intermediate station, which is more of a tunnel-like structure, as the chairs pass straight through it.

The area around Arosa is a bowl that offers skiing that extends over a relatively restricted area, but with plenty of challenging runs plus opportunities to go off-piste. The Carmenna Chairlift is only one of a number, and the dedicated skier will doubtless choose to travel in different directions on different days. But for those concerned with style, and the drama of travel, going up in the Carmenna chairlift and – dare one suggest it? – even coming down again the same way, will certainly offer a most elegant and fulfilling experience.

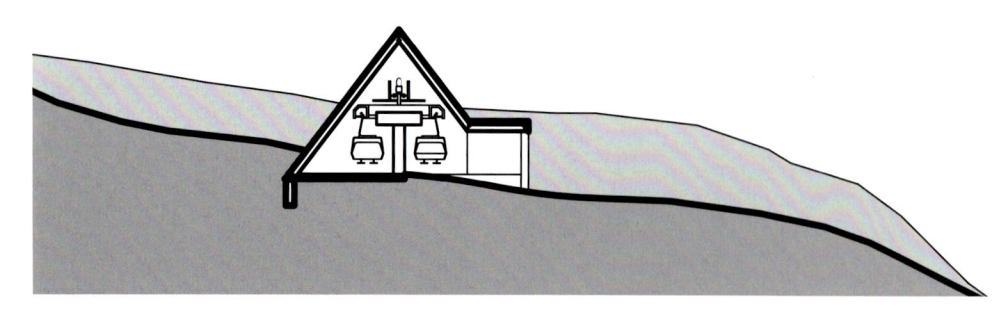

Extreme Architecture

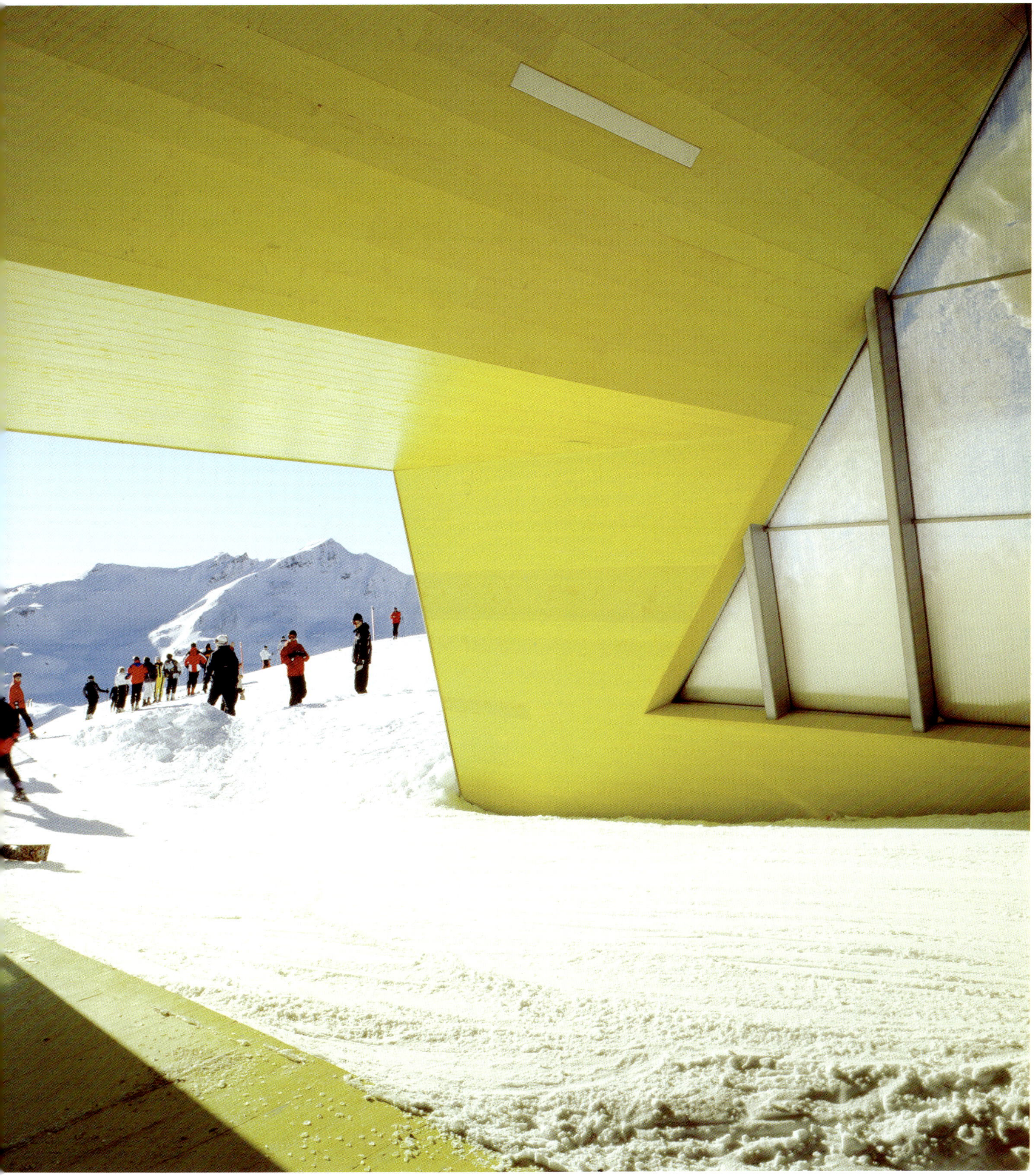

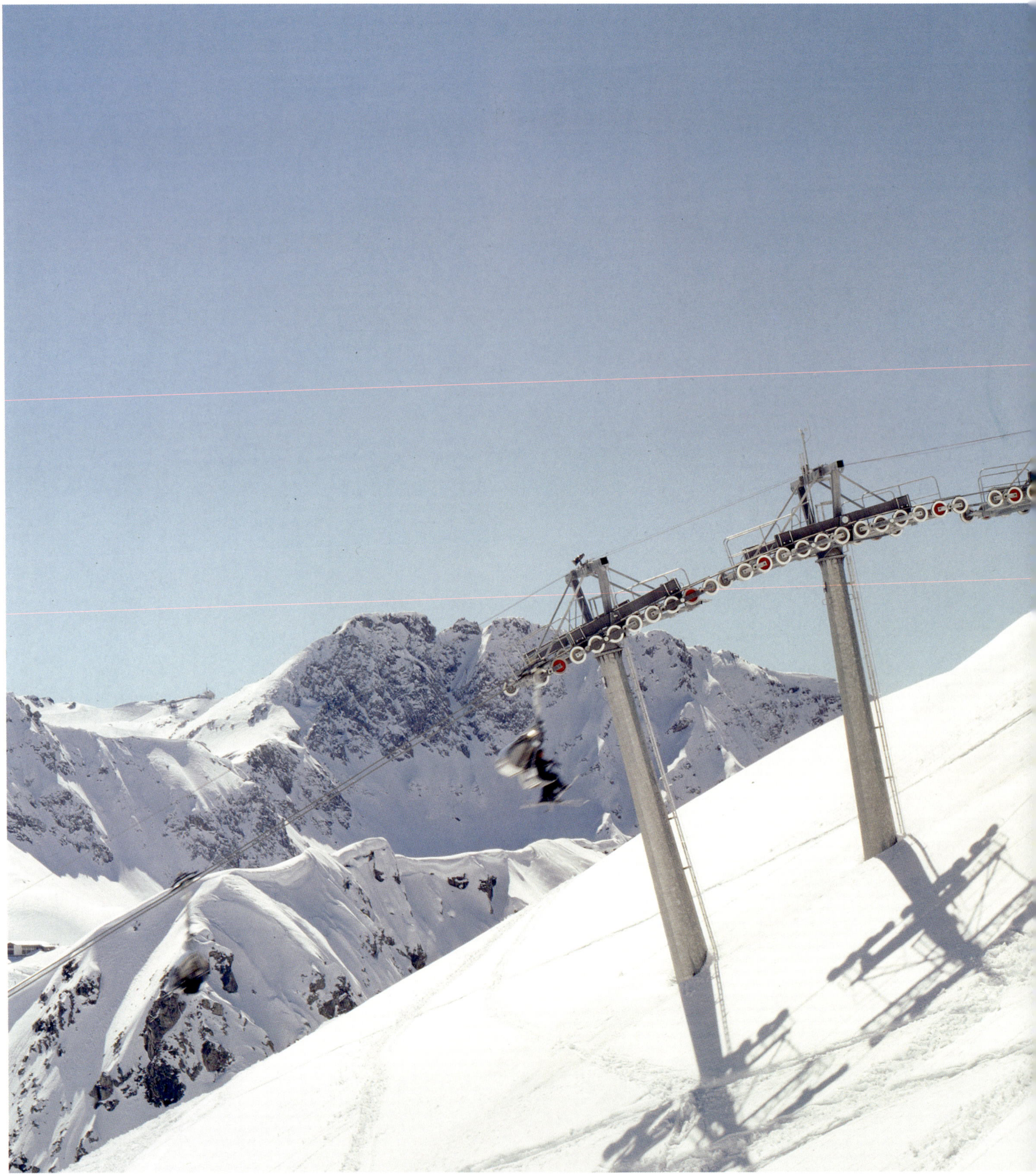

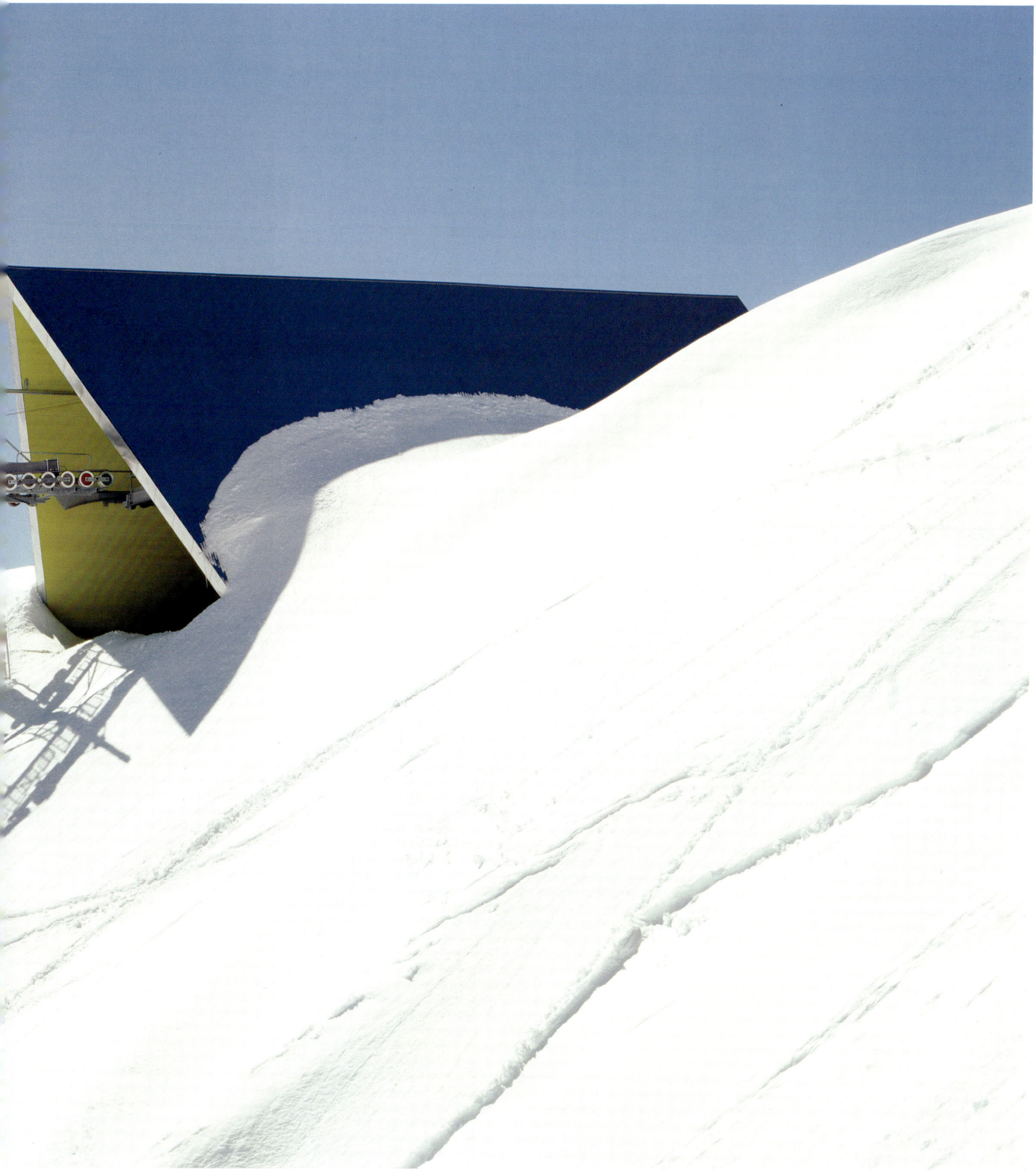

ST ANTON AM ARLBERG, AUSTRIA
DRIENDL*ARCHITECTS

GALZIGBAHN

Height above sea level
1,300m/4,265ft

Average annual rainfall
1275 litres per m2/c.336 gallons per ft2

Average high and low temperatures
11ºC/52ºF – -0.2ºC/32ºF

Opposite Pairs of wires exit from the rear of the station. This Funitel technology allows cable cars to operate in higher winds than was previously possible.
Right Giant Ferris wheels bring the cars down to ground level.
Below From left: lower- and upper-floor plans. The staircase is only for emergency access.

Architecture as a celebration of engineering can rarely have worked so well as at this cable car station which is vaguely reminiscent of the shovel used for opencast coal mining. The sight of the giant wheels turning within this glazed enclosure is so hypnotic that it is hard to work out what is more enticing – to enter one of the rather bug-eyed gondolas and go for the ride up the mountain, or stay on the ground and watch, for far longer than one originally intended, the simple drama of the wheels going round.

It is appropriate that St Anton am Arlberg should be the site for such a futuristic ski lift, as it has always been a pioneer of mountain transport. Opened in 1937, the Galzigbahn (which takes visitors up the Galzig mountain above St Anton) became, along with Davos and St Moritz in Switzerland, one of the first cable cars to be used primarily by winter visitors – in the early days of this technology summer traffic usually dominated. In its first year, the Galzigbahn carried nearly 60,000 visitors in its 30-person cars.

In 1964 it was upgraded, raising the hourly carrying capacity to 700, but with the increasing popularity of winter sports this too became inadequate. Even with the addition of a chairlift in 1990 capacity was insufficient, resulting in long queues. In addition, the staircase up to the station was difficult to negotiate.

Factors like this can have a devastating effect on the success of a town's tourism, especially now that guidebooks are supplemented by so much information available on the Internet. So finding a solution was essential.

The town plumped for a Funitel solution. This is a relatively new, but proven, technology that hangs cable cars from pairs of wires. It can operate in higher winds than conventional gondolas suspended from single wires (at St Anton, at wind speeds above 100 kilometres (62 miles) per hour), because two wires provide more stability than one; and it is also a fast way of transporting a lot of people, since rapidly moving cable cars can be spaced closer together.

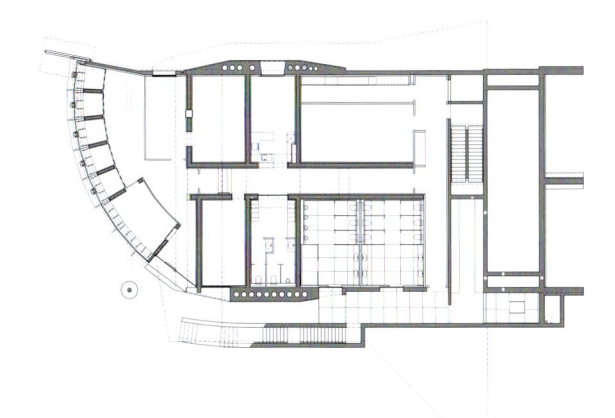

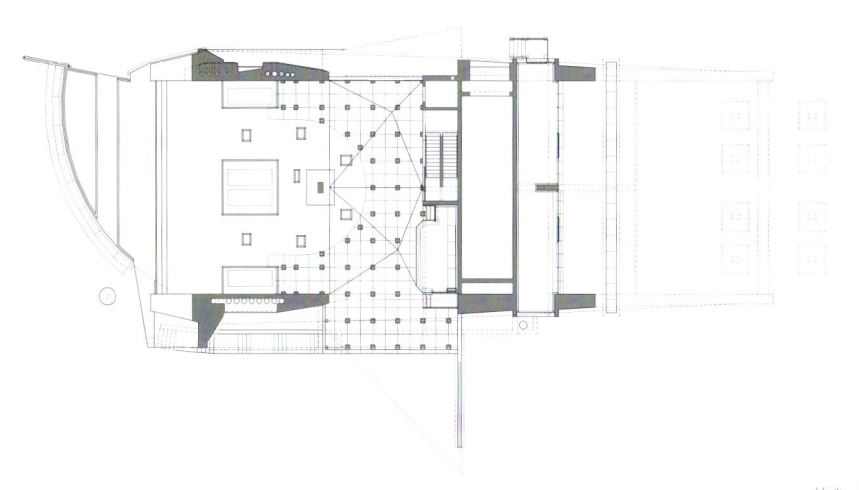

High 133

Left An elegant external truss supports the glazed 'hood' so that no internal supports are needed.
Opposite top Structural drawings of the glazed roof (left) and concrete base (right).
Opposite bottom The projecting hood provides shelter for customers using the ticket booths.

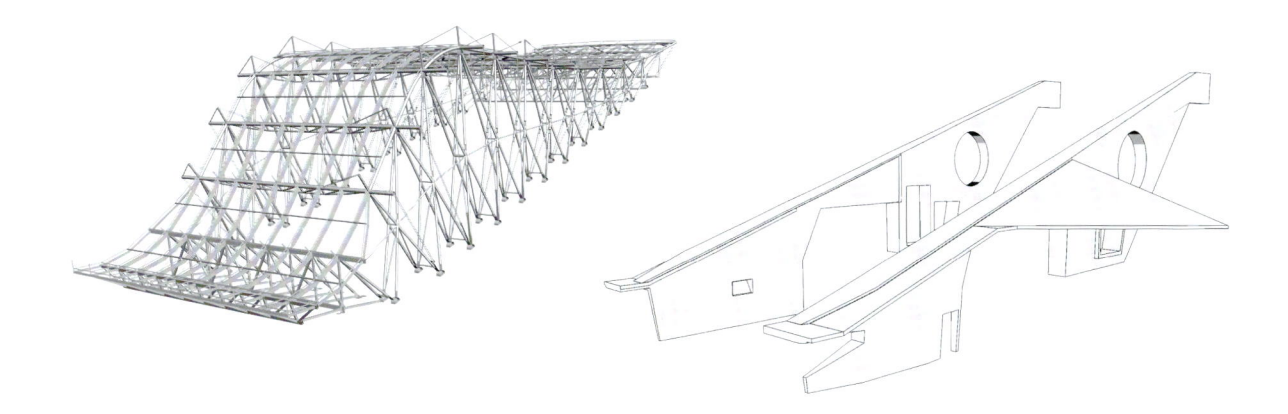

Because the speed of travel is faster than that at which people would feel happy mounting or dismounting, at the stations the cars are transferred from the cables to a wheel that slows them down. The innovation at St Anton was to use Ferris wheels that bring the cars down to ground level, so that passengers do not have to climb a staircase. With 28 gondolas each carrying 24 passengers at a speed of 7.5 metres (25 feet) per second, and rapid embarkation, the Galzigbahn can now carry up to 4,000 passengers an hour.

In theory this technological achievement could have been accompanied by a mundane building, but fortunately the design of the station was awarded to Georg Driendl, who has risen to the challenge with a building of steel, glass and concrete that both celebrates the technology and is eminently practical. The concrete base rises above the ground in a triangular form, pointing up the mountain. A massive circular opening at either side enhances the industrial feeling, as if a giant spindle could be inserted through it.

Above this massive base sits a glazed hood, supported entirely by an external filigree truss, so that there is no internal structure. This hood projects forward into a peak that shelters the ticket offices and their users, making the whole experience of using the station as easy as possible. Passengers walk into the station, enter their cable car, which is carried up on the Ferris wheel to engage with the cables, and shoot out upwards from a glazed overhang at the back of the building. In what better way could a day's skiing begin?

VOGTLAND ARENA, KLINGENTHAL, GERMANY
M2R-ARCHITECTURE

SKI JUMP AND JUDGES' TOWER

Height above sea level
850m/2,788ft

Average annual rainfall
820mm/32in

Average high and low temperatures
15.5°C/60°F – -2°C/28°F

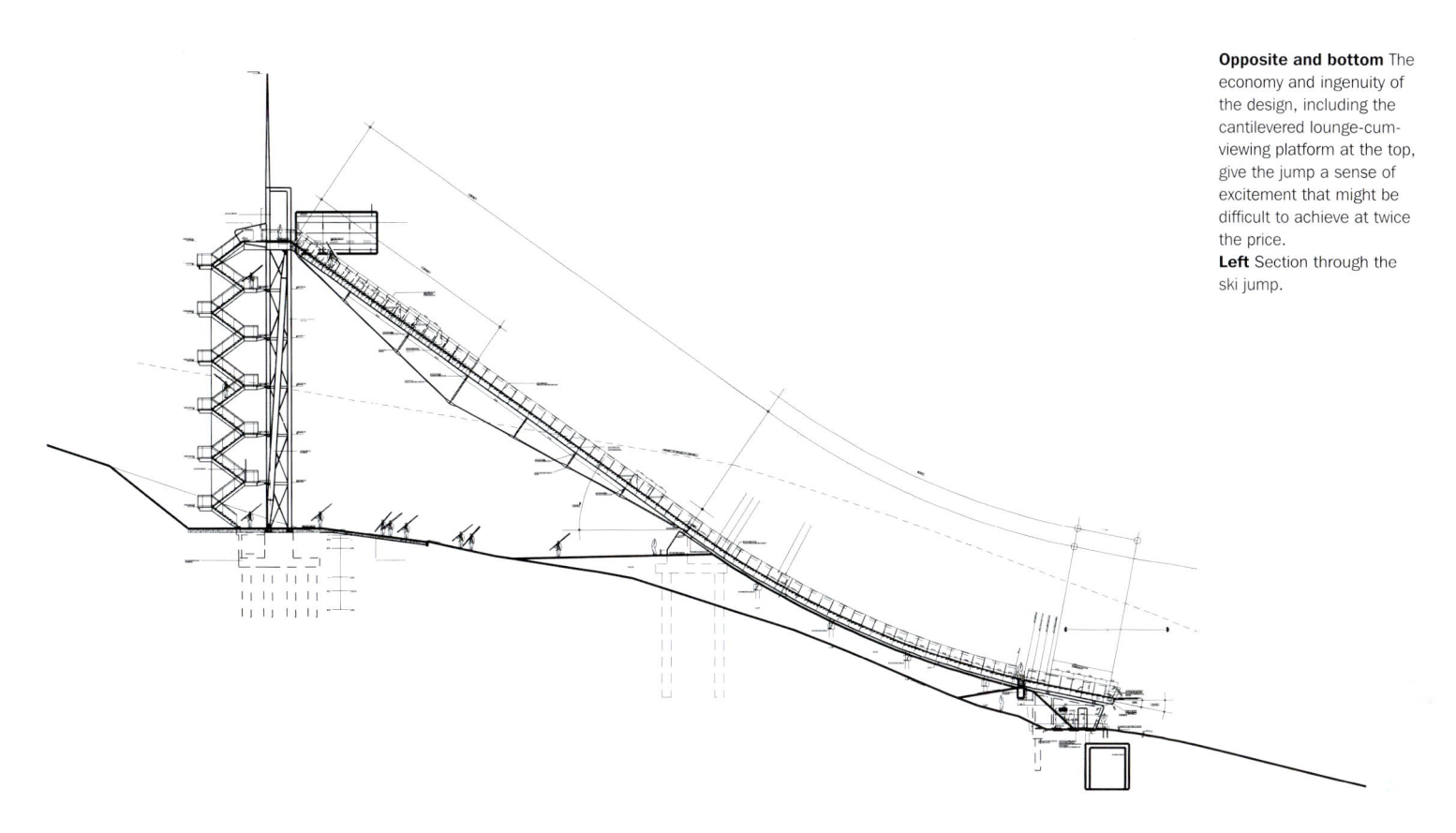

Opposite and bottom The economy and ingenuity of the design, including the cantilevered lounge-cum-viewing platform at the top, give the jump a sense of excitement that might be difficult to achieve at twice the price.
Left Section through the ski jump.

In 2007, when 17-year-old 'teen sensation' Gregor Schlierenzauer won his fifth world cup for ski jumping at Klingenthal in Germany, it was a triumph not only for him but also for UK-based Klingenthal-born architects Axel and Jörg Rostock. Their practice, m2r-architecture, won a competition in 2003 to design a new ski jump for this town near the Czech border. The connection couldn't have been closer – not only are the Rostock brothers and their partner Moritz May keen skiers, but the brothers' grandfather had also been the caretaker for the previous structure.

As part of the former East Germany, the town didn't have a lot of money to spend, so m2r had to come up with a design that would not only support top-level competition but was also economical. The solution, using a great deal of prefabrication, is a jump that works well both in winter and, thanks to the use of artificial surfaces, in summer, and that looks as spare and carefully engineered as the highly trained ski jumpers and their sophisticated skis. It isn't the most elegant of designs and it certainly isn't sculpture. But its economy and ingenuity add to the sense of excitement engendered by ski jumping in a way that a more grounded, considered, extravagant structure would not.

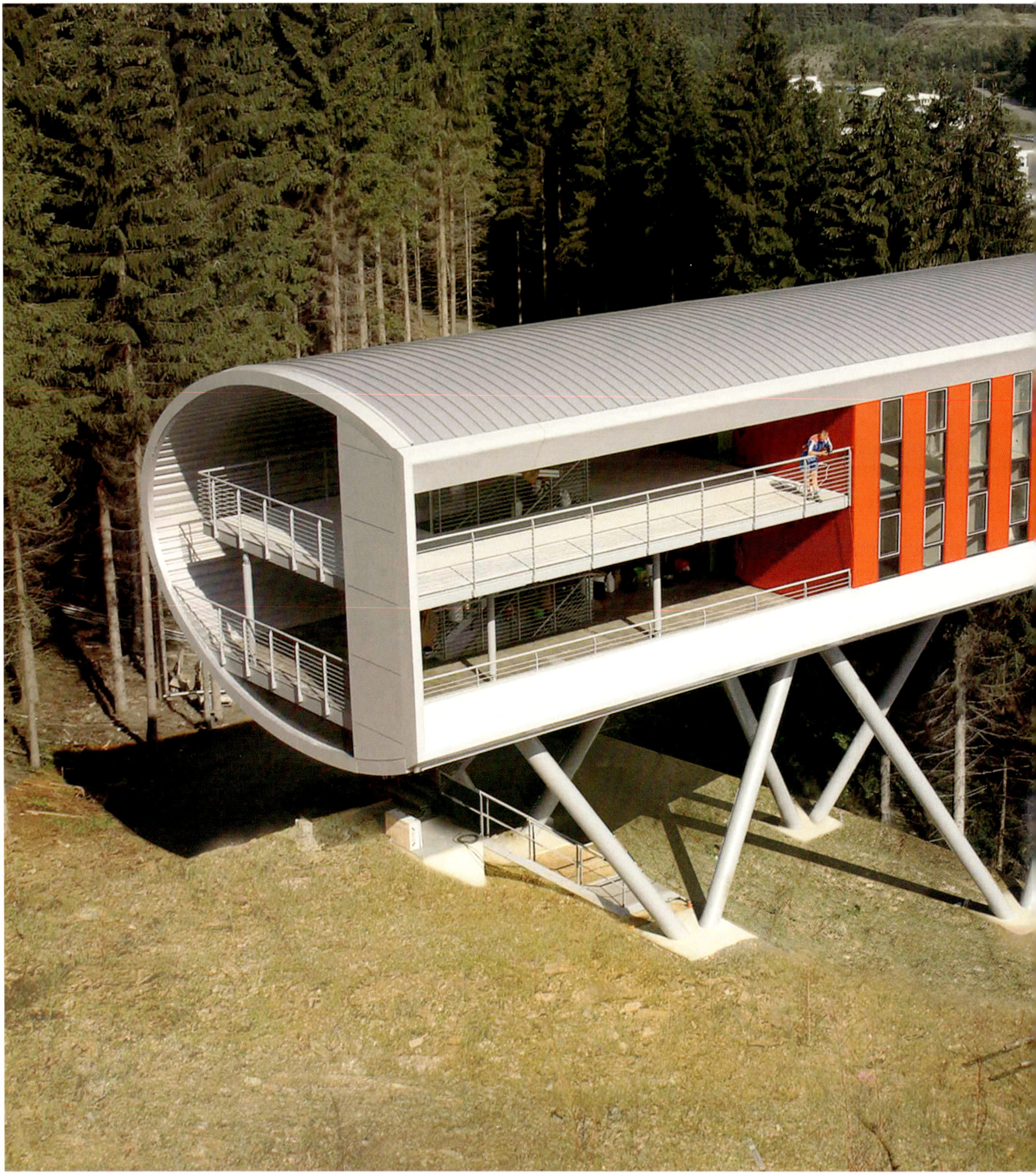

Prefabrication was dictated by the difficulty of access, on top of a steep mountain. And the need for economy meant that every element of the structure was made to work as hard as possible. A main column, designed as a trussed girder, supports all the major elements: the top of the run; a staircase and a panoramic lift to the top; and the lounge in which contestants wait their turn, and which can also act as a viewing platform outside competition periods.

The stairs, which zigzag up beside the tower, are pin-jointed, with hangers descending from the outer edges of each landing supporting the landing below. The lift has been designed to work in temperatures down to −30°C (−22°F), using both heated tracks and ice-breakers to ensure that it keeps going in these extreme conditions.

By supporting the track going down (known in ski-jumping parlance as the 'in-run') with a separate truss below it, the architects have made the structure pre-eminently visible, and added to its drama.

The competitors' lounge-cum-viewing platform is a bravura object. Cantilevering forward 9 metres (30 feet), and tied to the staircase with steel rods, it is an aluminium-clad oval with a flat glazed front face set back behind a rim. This must be a magnificent place from which to look down on the jump, and the naïve might guess that it was the place from which the judging was done.

However, a moment's reflection will show that this is wrong. Judges need to view the trajectory from the side and not from the top. Their tower is situated along the run, well beyond the point at which the competitors fly off the 'in-run' but before they reach the spectators' area. In form it echoes the capsule at the top of the jump, but this time the glazed face is on one side, rather than at the end. Lightness is key again; the capsule sits on a slope, supported on slender, inclined legs slim enough for it to appear to float in certain lights. It has enough space within it to accommodate both the judges and the media – the two sets of people who can ensure the importance of Klingenthal as a top competitive skiing destination, so bringing not only the world's attention but also the employment opportunities and investment that provided much of the motivation for the town to scrape together the money to finance the project. So far, it seems to be money well spent.

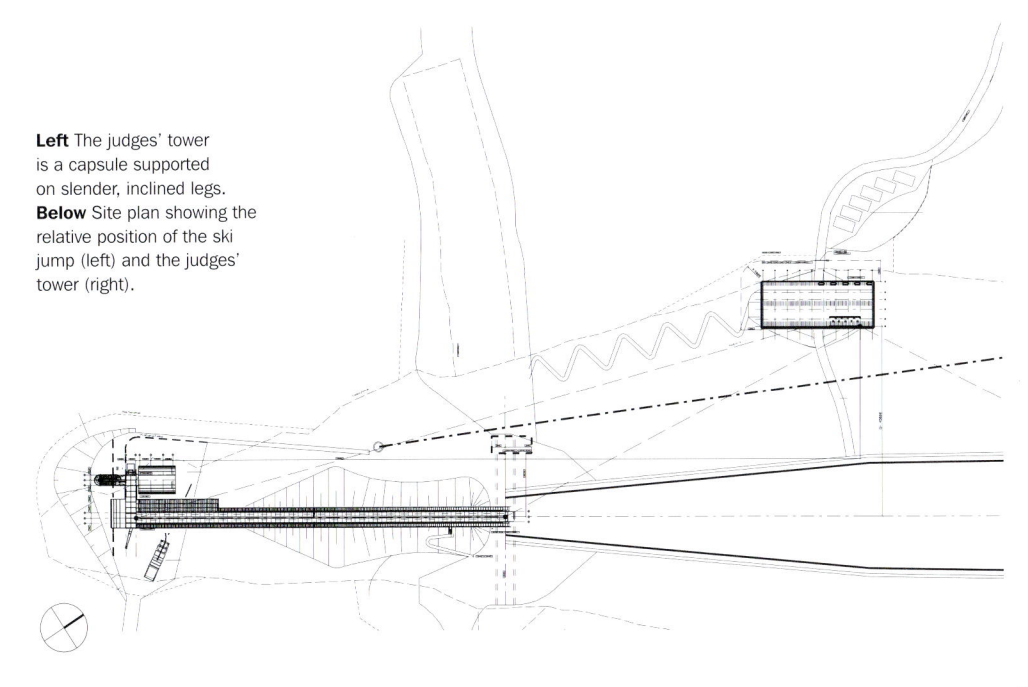

Left The judges' tower is a capsule supported on slender, inclined legs.
Below Site plan showing the relative position of the ski jump (left) and the judges' tower (right).

PORTILLO, CHILE
DRN ARQUITETOS

SKIBOX AND CHALET C7

Height above sea level
2,890m/9,481ft

Average annual snowfall
8m/25ft

Highest temperature in summer 25°C/77°F
Lowest temperature in winter -20°C/-4°F

Opposite The SkiBox includes outdoor space on its podium, preventing visitors from sprawling untidily beyond its bounds.
Right Site plan, showing the new chalets (top left) the hotel (centre) and the SkiBox (right).
Below right The SkiBox is clad in a mixture of local stone and weathering steel.

Portillo, 3,000 metres (9,843 feet) up in the Andes, is an unusual ski resort, and Santiago-based dRN Arquitetos has been working on planned development that could provide new facilities without ruining its unique character.

Dating from the 1880s, Portillo is Chile's oldest ski resort, graced with 8 metres (25 feet) of snow a year and 300 days of sun. Because it is in the southern hemisphere, it attracts keen and professional skiers from North America, looking to ski outside their native season.

Two hours' journey from Santiago, Portillo is unique for the fact that it is not a village – simply a hotel. Although not particularly distinguished architecturally, the hotel is memorable, painted in bright colours, particularly yellow, and offers luxury accommodation and gourmet dining. The rooms have fantastic views of the mountains and Lake Inca.

As the popularity of skiing and summer tourism in Chile has grown, the hotel has expanded, offering cheaper accommodation in a lodge, a hostel and summer chalets. But it is important that as this expansion continues, it doesn't become haphazard. So the hotel called in dRN to devise a masterplan, including the development of a spa.

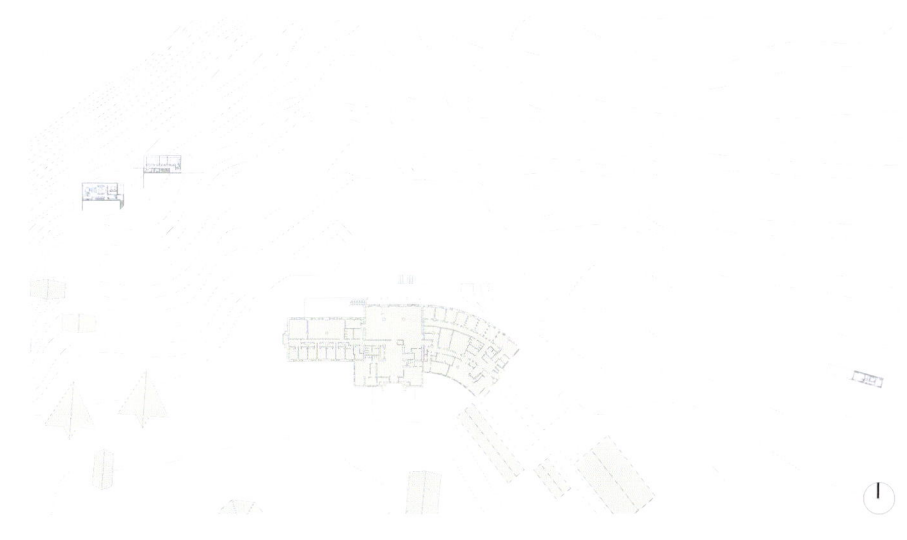

The first part to be completed is what the practice dubs the SkiBox, a 110 square metre (1,184 square foot) building that provides lavatories for skiers, a café and an office for ski patrols. The building is steel-framed and set into a hillside, with the lower, podium level extending beyond the box above, to create a terrace for the café. This lower level, which houses the lavatories, is clad in local reddish-grey stone, very minimally dressed, a choice that makes sense in the summer when the snow melts and the soil and rock are revealed. The upper level, containing the café, the office for ski patrols, and a small warehouse, is largely clad in weathering steel, which folds over from the roof and down the façades. This element appears to float above the podium, as it is separated from it by a strip of glazing.

Also recently completed are two chalets. Set on the edge of Lake Inca, they are an attractive spot for both summer and winter breaks. By setting the upper floor back from the lower floor, the architect has given them an unusual geometry.

Like the SkiBox, the chalets use simple tough materials, and appear as self-contained, carefully placed objects in the landscape. If the client continues to work closely with the architect in this considered manner, the aim of providing more and more varied accommodation without spoiling the magnificence of the setting that made it so attractive in the first place should be achieved.

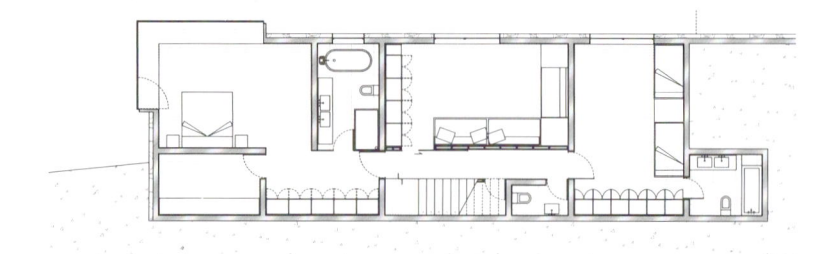

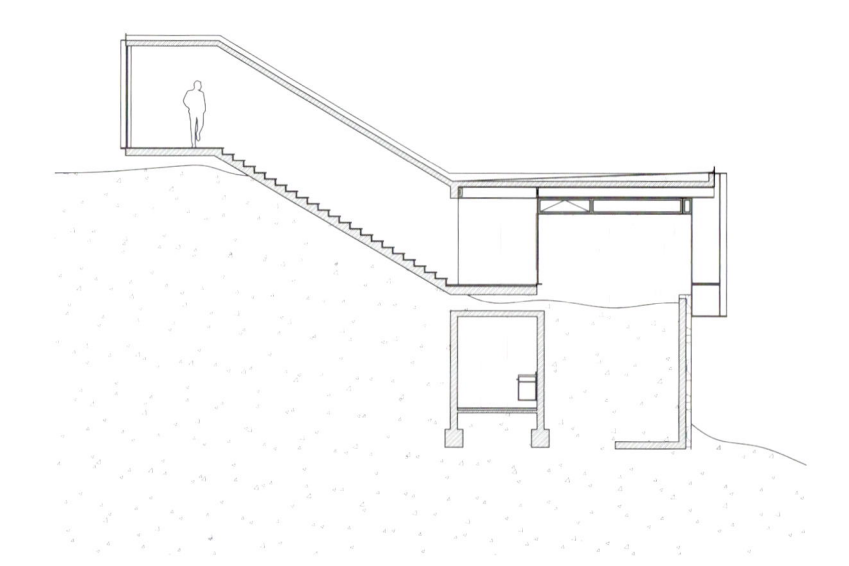

Opposite far left The chalets overlook Lake Inca.
Opposite Upper- and lower-level plans and section of a chalet.
Right The split geometry of the chalets makes them intriguing objects in the landscape.
Below Inside the enigmatic-looking chalets, visitors benefit from large windows and a high degree of comfort.

AROSA, SWITZERLAND
MARIO BOTTA ARCHITETTO

TSCHUGGEN BERGOASE SPA

Height above sea level
1,905m/6,250ft

Average annual rainfall
1,335mm/52½in

Average high and low temperatures
8.7°C/47°F − -12.1c/10°F

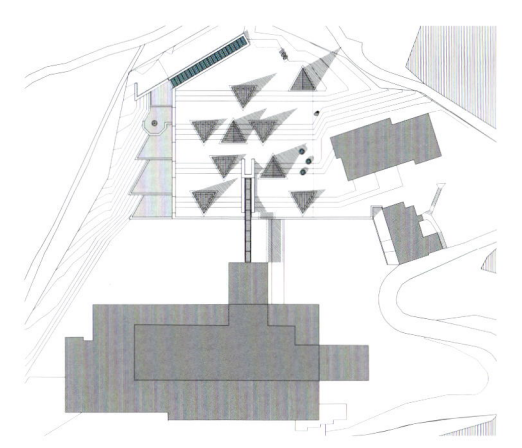

Opposite The giant 'sails', which are the most prominent external elements of the new spa, bring light into all levels of the building.
Above Site plan, showing the connection between the existing hotel and the new spa.
Below Section, showing the pool at the upper level, and the link bridge to the hotel.

What are those things rising above the perfect basin of the town of Arosa in Switzerland? Outlined against the trees in summer, against the snow in winter, could they be giant sails or minor peaks? Whichever metaphor you favour, these visible elements of Mario Botta's spa building are elegant, exciting and enigmatic.

Set into a slope, the building, attached to the Tschuggen Grand Hotel, is otherwise deliberately self-effacing, dug into the mountainside. These great sails, with their curved hoods welcoming in light predominantly from the southwest, contrast with the modest stone-clad wall facing the existing hotel, to which the new building is connected by a glass bridge at second-floor level.

Unusually, the swimming pool is set on the highest, third floor, a decision that seems perverse when you think of the need to support this weight of water. Structurally, this is made a little easier by the fact that the building is set into the hillside, but even more important is the fact that at this level of luxury (this is a five-star hotel), guests expect the best. And the best, in a Swiss mountain resort, is a million miles from the municipal swimming pool that may be buried underground or, at best, at ground level with a few windows looking out onto a car park and a shopping precinct.

Centres such as the Bergoase are known as 'wellness centres' not fitness centres, and the swimming pool is the centrepiece in a collection of sensual treats. What people in the pool want is not simply to plough up and down doing lengths, but to be surrounded by wonderful materials, to have great views of the mountains and to be able to swim outside. In summer, this means being able to get out to a sunbathing terrace. In winter, it means simply following the heated water outside to be enveloped by heat and steam when snow on the terrace is within touching distance, and to relish the contrast.

To increase this pleasure in materials, the swimming pool has one wall in a sinusoidal wave form, tapering away upwards and clad in horizontal stratum of granite. This wall also extends down and spreads under the water, as if one is in a pool that has been carved out of some rock formation or is even, given the temperature, inside a volcano.

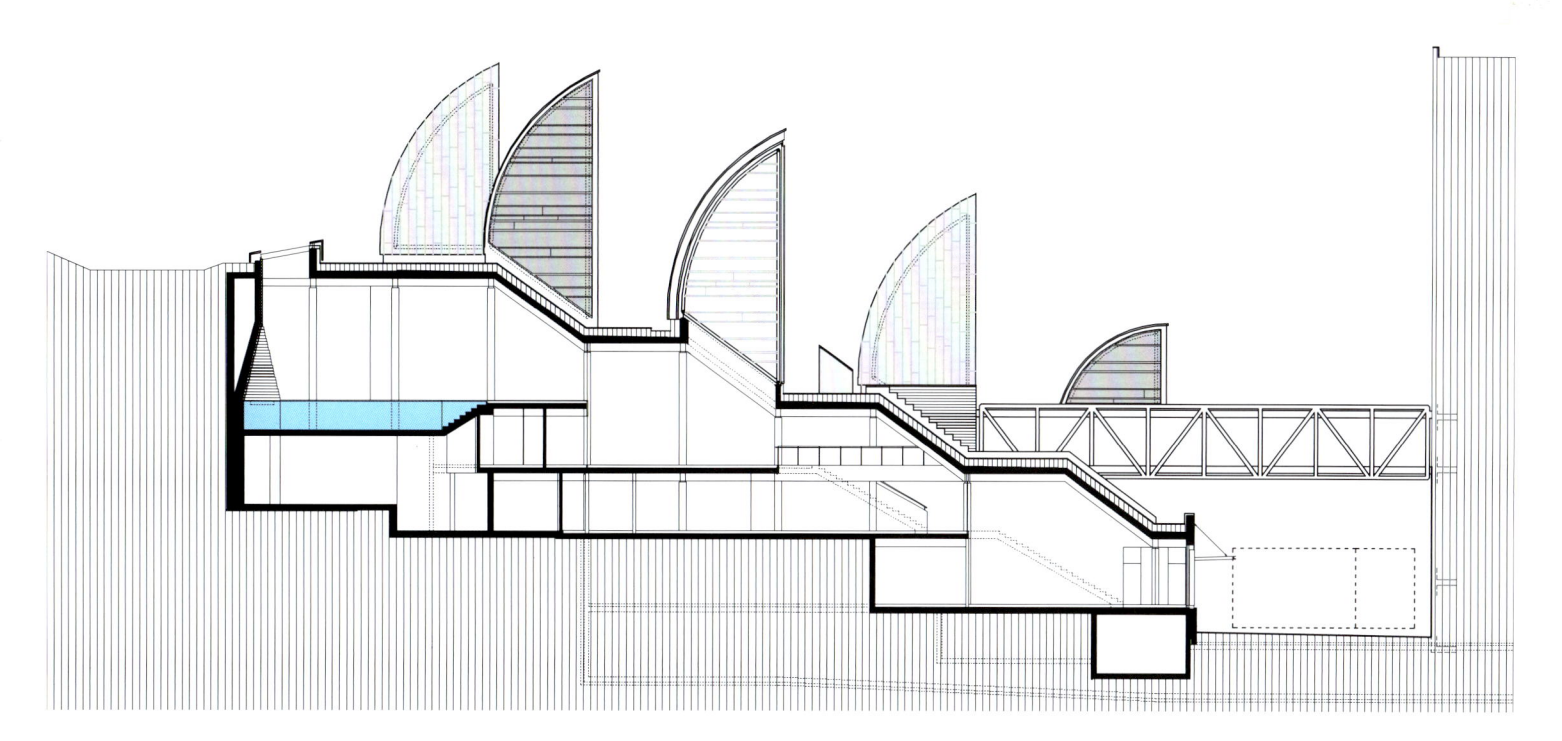

Left From top: third- and second-floor plans.

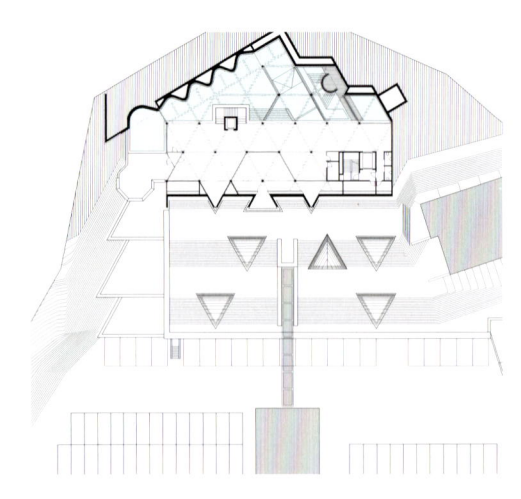

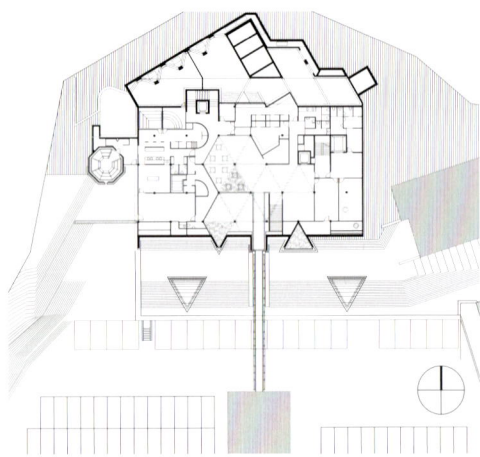

Moving downwards, the second floor contains the main reception, staff areas, the 'sauna world' and the wellness centre. On the first floor are all the treatment areas, and down on the ground floor, where the general public enters, are the fitness suites. And all lit by those great hooded glass windows with glazing bars extending from a central spine, like the ribs of leaves. This is the metaphor that the architect prefers, although the elements look far too tough and permanent to be evanescent and fragile leaves. But whatever they are, as a combination of exciting protrusion into the landscape, a practical means of bringing in light, and advertisements for the comfort and delights within, they couldn't be bettered.

Left High-quality finishes give the feeling of luxury required for a five-star hotel.
Below Striated stone on the sinusoidal wall of the pool gives the impression of being inside a naturally occurring cavern.

GARMISCH-PARTENKIRCHEN, GERMANY
TERRAIN: LOENHART&MAYR BDA ARCHITECTS AND LANDSCAPE ARCHITECTS

OLYMPIC SKI JUMP

Height above sea level
818m/2,683ft

Average annual rainfall
1296mm/51in

Average high and low temperatures
28°C/84°F – -28°C/-18°F

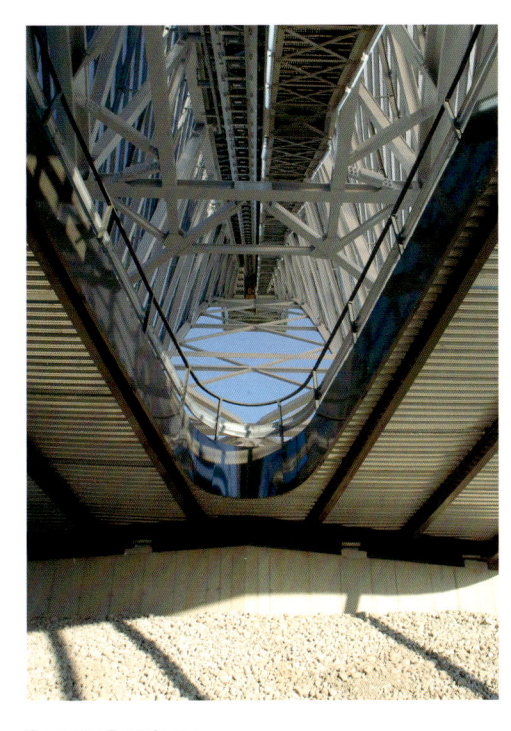

In 2011, when the Alpine World Ski Championships are held in Garmisch-Partenkirchen in Bavaria, southern Germany, fans of the sport will find their eyes drawn to a gleaming white rocket launcher of a structure. The new ski jump for the winter sports resort, designed in part to echo the form of the surrounding hills, is also an audacious cantilevered structure that speaks intensely, even to the uninitiated, of movement and flight and snow.

And it will not have to wait until 2011 to be in the spotlight. Every year, as part of the Four Hills Tournament, a high-profile ski-jumping competition is held at Garmisch-Partenkirchen on New Year's Day. In 2008, this competition inaugurated the new jump.

Skiing seems to be one of the sexy new themes for architectural design, particularly for architects in love with technology. Just as in the 1990s many architects seemed keen to establish their reputations in part on their ability to design bridges (Santiago Calatrava, Future Systems and WilkinsonEyre among others), so the ski jump occupies a similar niche in the opening decade of the twenty-first century. The Garmisch-Partenkirchen jump was therefore the subject of an international competition, which the design team won against such high-profile practices as Zaha Hadid Architects in the UK (already with one such project under its belt), and German practices Auer + Weber and Behnisch Architekten. This ski jump in particular could be considered as the natural progression from a bridge – a demanding engineering structure, but in this case only tethered at one end.

Opposite Seen from a distance, the ski jump, with its 62 metre (203 foot) cantilever, looks like a rocket launcher.
Above View from beneath, showing the escalator.
Below Section comparing the length of the in-run cantilever to that of an Airbus A 380. The curved blue line indicates the jumping trajectory. 1. landing slope; 2. jury building; 3. landing bridge; 4. coaching platform; 5. infrastructure building; 6. in-run cantilever; 7. starting and media platforms

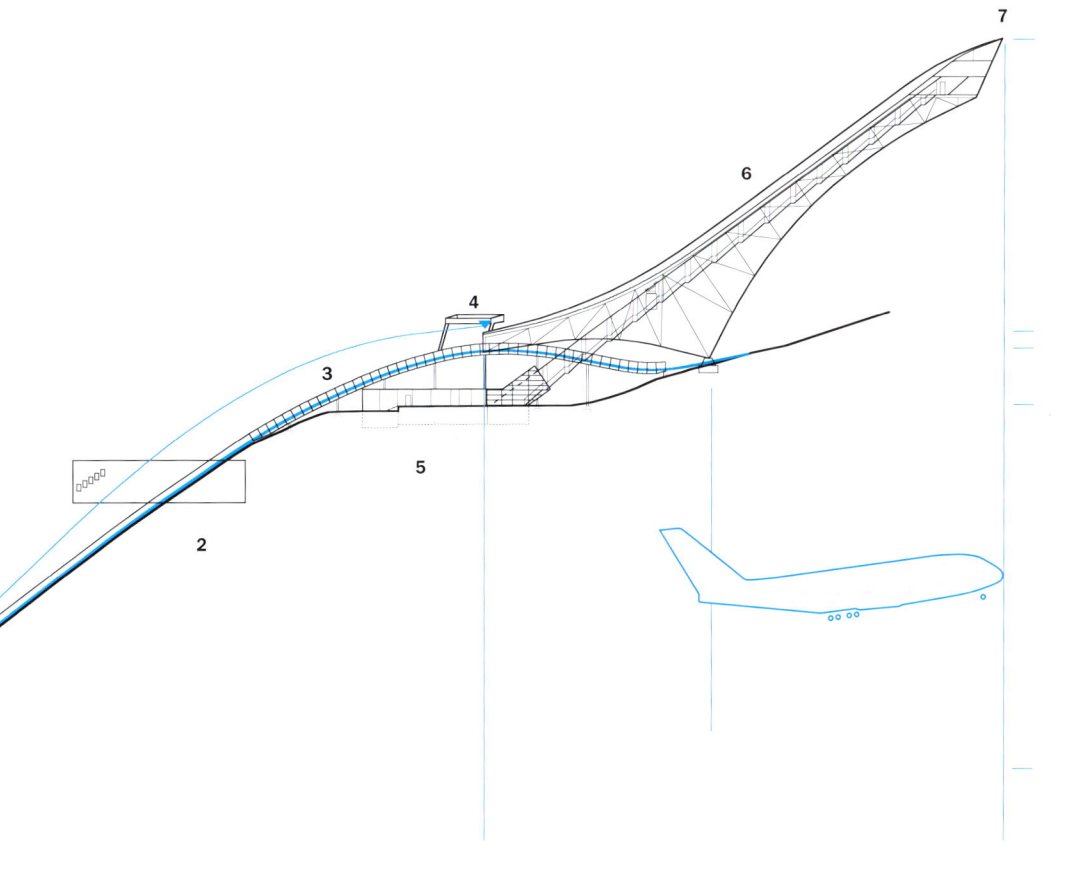

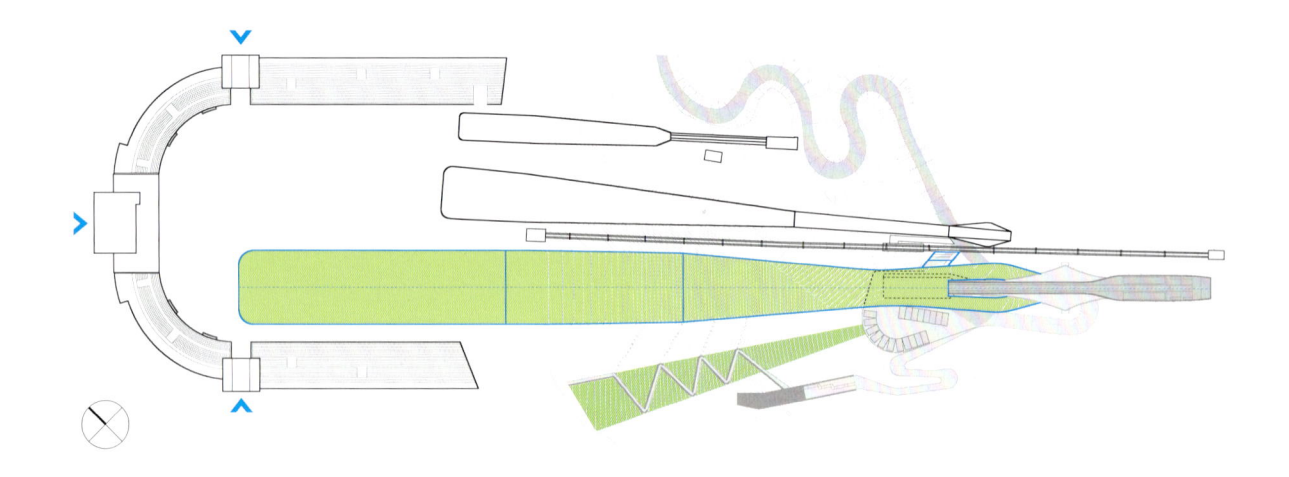

It is the massive cantilever that impresses, and gives the building its sense of excitement. The in-run building, the structure down which the skiers hurtle to take off into space, has a total length of 110 metres (360 feet), of which 62 metres (203 feet) is a cantilever. This length, as the architects point out, is almost equivalent to that of an Airbus – evidently metaphors of flying are not far from their thoughts. The steelwork tracery that makes this possible results in a building that looks a little like an Eiffel Tower tilted at a 45-degree angle. At its base is an infrastructure building, and rising up from the bottom is the 16 metre (52 foot) high table-top structure of the coaching platform, seemingly suspended in space.

Access to the top is via either a staircase of 332 steps or, for those who are lazier or need to conserve their energy for the jump, by an escalator.

If the first dramatic move was the creation of the cantilever, the second was to clad the structure with a translucent polycarbonate, which changes its appearance throughout the day as it reflects the colours of the sky and surroundings. At night, it is lit from within, giving it a ghostly glow.

While the jump is destined to become a television icon for the Alpine World Ski Championships, it is also a great permanent addition to its surroundings – an innovative use of technology that reflects the sport it serves, which progresses every year in terms of technique and slickness.

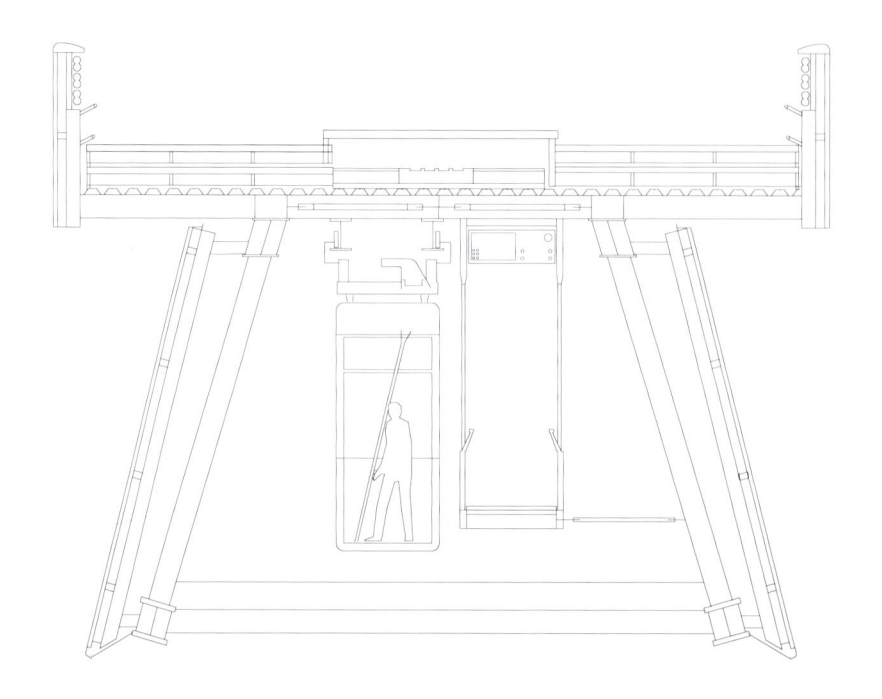

Left Site plan showing the jump and the viewing area.
Below left Section
Below right The in-run track will work with a lower-than-normal volume of snow. In summer a ceramic liner can be added.
Right View looking up to the top of the jump.

JEAN-MARIE MASSAUD, STUDIO MASSAUD

MANNED CLOUD

▲ **Height above sea level**
variable

💧 **Average annual rainfall**
variable

🌡 **Average high and low temperatures**
variable

Even if you like staring at the clouds and imagining shapes in them, you have probably never seen anything as outlandish as the great white whale that will take to the skies if French designer Jean-Marie Massaud has his way. He has come up with the idea of a giant airship that will not only put the elegance back into air travel, but will also put the meaning back into the cliché 'It is better to travel hopefully than to arrive'.

This will certainly not be the way to fly if you are interested solely in speed. Massaud calculates that it will take nearly nine hours to fly from Paris to Rome, or four days to go from Paris to Antananarivo in Madagascar. But this will be a sky cruise, a luxurious journey and a way to see the sights. Massaud, who has designed everything from taps to resort hotels, worked with French aerospace research organization ONERA to look at the feasibility of the design – and initial results were good.

The airship, which will take 40 passengers and have 15 crew, will contain two huge reserves of helium in its bulbous body. Below, in the contemporary version of a basket, will be two decks of accommodation. The first deck, with an area of 500 square metres (5,382 square feet), will include a restaurant, lounge, library and fitness suite, with the second deck containing 20 bedrooms, terraces, a spa and a bar. And right on the top will be the most incredible sunbathing/observation deck.

Maximum speed should be 170 kilometres (105 miles) per hour, with a cruising speed of 130 kilometres (81 miles) per hour, and a range of 5,000 kilometres (3,107 miles) or three days.

Those not averse to a little whimsy may remember the English author A. A. Milne's classic creation, *Winnie the Pooh*, uttering the following ditty:

How sweet to be a Cloud
Floating in the Blue!
Every little cloud
Always sings aloud,
'How sweet to be a Cloud
Floating in the Blue!'
It makes him very proud
To be a little cloud.

Massaud is utterly French, and terribly cool, so this verse is unlikely to be part of his heritage. But his passengers may just find themselves humming it under their breath – you can't get much closer to being a cloud than travelling on this gigantic and oh-so-gorgeous dirigible.

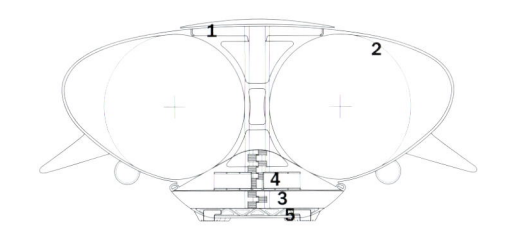

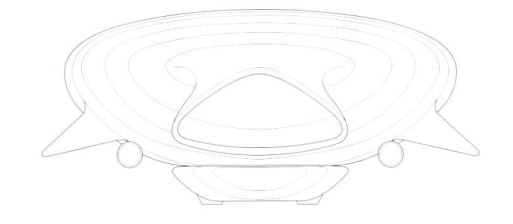

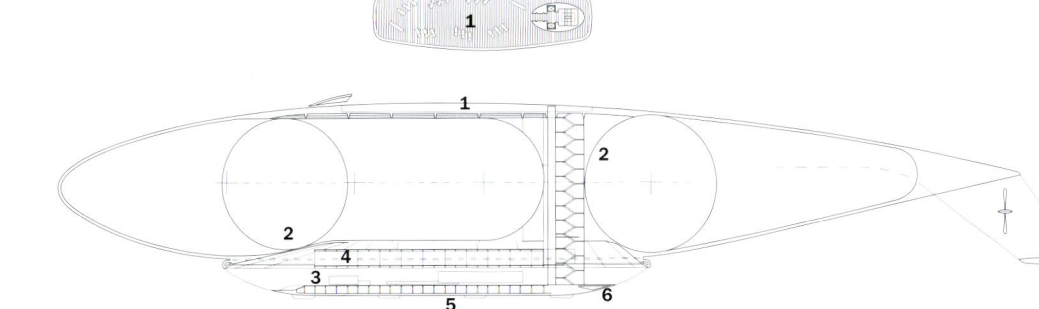

Opposite The giant dirigible will float lazily across the scenery, giving its passengers an experience more akin to a cruise than to the usual urgency and squalor of air travel.
Top Impressions of the interior of the Manned Cloud, where the emphasis will be on comfort and breathtaking views.
Left Cross-section, front elevation and long section.
1. Sundeck terrace;
2. Shape membrane;
3. Public spaces; 4. Rooms;
5. Technical areas;
6. entrance

CHAPTER 4
WET

Left Sweden's floating Utter Hotel has its living space underwater.

As our planet becomes increasingly crowded, the sea is one obvious area where we can expand. This is not new. There have been floating communities for centuries in places like Tonle Sap Lake in Cambodia, and in Kashmir in the north of India and Pakistan.

Land reclamation is not new either. Hong Kong Island has been built outwards progressively, so that buildings that once had coveted waterfront views are now several streets in from the harbour, hidden by their newer, and taller, successors.

But the pressures now are greater than ever before, as growing wealth, opportunity and fear about the future, coupled with sheer technical capability, drive us to seek new places to live, and to enjoy life. At the same time, global warming makes our relationship with water more fraught. The 2007 report of the Intergovernmental Panel on Climate Change predicts that extreme weather events will become more frequent, including storms and flooding. This will be exacerbated for low-lying coastal areas, which will also be affected by rises in sea level. The disastrous floods in Burma's Irawaddy Delta in spring 2008, as the result of a cyclone and subsequent tidal wave, may just be a foretaste.

For the United States, the wake-up call came when Hurricane Katrina devastated the southern city of New Orleans in August 2005. Film star Brad Pitt set up the Make it Right project to provide appropriate housing after the hurricane. He invited 14 internationally known and local architects to come up with solutions that both dealt with the risk of flooding and recognized the local way of life. Many of the architects proposed buildings on stilts to raise them above future floods and one US practice, Morphosis, proposed floating housing.

Flooding is a relatively new problem for the United States to tackle. In contrast, the Netherlands, Europe's most densely populated country, which has 27 per cent of its land below sea level, has been dealing with the need for protection for centuries. Recently its approach has changed. After the devastating floods of 1953, when nearly 2,000 people died, the Delta Act was passed, which aimed to protect habitation behind ever more solid sea defences. However, with rising water levels and population, it became obvious that there would have to be an accommodation with the water if the nation was not to live its life behind walls. As a result, the cabinet drew up proposals in the mid-1990s with titles such as 'room for the river', proposing a new and more symbiotic relationship between dwellings and water. Projects such as the floating housing at Maasbommel (page 166), grew out of these initiatives. They were preceded by projects such as Herman Hertzberger's floating house, functional in every way, but looking rather like a floating concrete silo.

British practice Baca has taken the idea of floating housing further with its 20-million-Euro pilot masterplan for the waterfront at Dordrecht, the third city of the Netherlands, with the explicit intention that the ideas could be developed for use elsewhere. Projects such as Maasbommel are fairly low density, whereas at Dordrecht the ambition is to have 200 people per hectare. 'Much of the challenge,' says Baca's co-founder Richard Coutts, 'comes from questions such as, how will the sewage work?'

The practice has designed a mix of floating homes, amphibious homes (land-based homes that will float at times of severe flooding), flood-resilient homes and 'normal' homes. As important as the houses themselves is the landscaping, with spaces such as play areas that are able to act as water stores. In this manner, the architects calculate, the project should be able to accommodate a one in 1,000-year flood, with no inundation of homes.

In the UK, Baca is working with the Building Research Establishment and a number of other partner organizations to develop similar solutions to protect housing that is to be built on flood plains.

The idea of floating buildings is not confined to housing. Dutch-based Waterstudio.NL, which designed the proposed Floating Cruise Terminal (page 170) started its work with floating housing in the Netherlands but has expanded (literally) overseas. One of its proposals is for a floating rotating hotel in Dubai. The BBC reported in 2007 that Russia is planning a £100 million floating nuclear power station, to provide power in Severodinsk in the country's Arctic north. It will supply electricity to Sevmash, a shipbuilding firm that produces nuclear-powered submarines.

The idea of actually building out into the water rather than floating buildings on it is more demanding but, potentially, more rewarding. Japan's Kansai Airport, for example, is built entirely on reclaimed land. If Hong Kong, Japan and the Netherlands have traditionally been the pioneers of this approach, by examining the driving factors – wealth, growing population and limited usable land – it should not be difficult to guess where the latest boom should be. The tiny but wealthy Emirates have been remaking their coastlines on an unprecedented scale, as they seek to shift their main source of income from oil to tourism. Recession may be slowing some of these projects, but it is unlikely to halt the overall trend. They also have the advantage of shallow seas, decreasing the amount of reclamation needed.

Wet 155

Right The Aquarius underwater laboratory has been used to simulate space travel.
Below Dubai's Palm Jumeirah is an artificial island with immensely dense development.

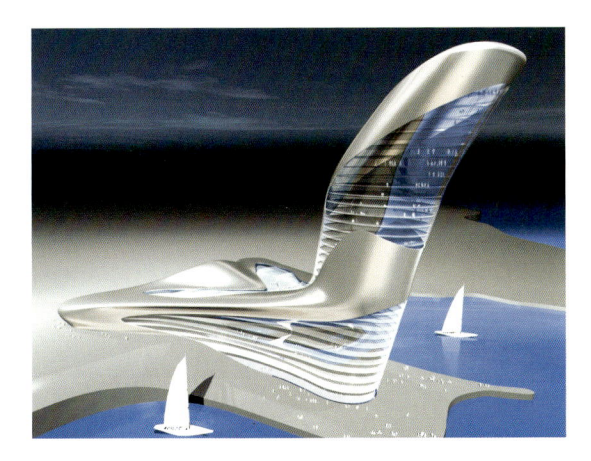

Left Even the land station serving the proposed Hydropolis underwater hotel has been designed to be futuristic.

Dubai has its three palm-shaped groups of islands: the Palm Jebel Ali, Palm Jumeirah and Palm Deira. Launched with great hype, and with homes sold speculatively, most conspicuously to footballers, they are losing some of their glitter. The first residents of the Palm Jumeirah were reported in the *Guardian* newspaper in 2008 to be disillusioned by how closely their homes were jammed together, by the fact that air conditioning was not included as standard in a country where temperatures can reach 46°C (115°F), and by the sheer scale of the project – access is by an eight-lane highway.

Nevertheless, other ambitious projects are planned. Dubai will get The World and The Universe (you can guess the shapes), while Qatar is building The Pearl (actually a string of pearls), which will increase its waterfront by 32 kilometres (20 miles). Bahrain has the Anwaj Islands project.

In Russia, Dutch architect Erick van Egeraat has designed Federation Island, a 330 hectare (815 acre) artificial archipelago, 15 kilometres (9 miles) off the coast of Sochi, in the Russian Black Sea. Built in the shape of the Russian Federation, and apparently reflecting the country's main geographical features, Federation Island will include residences, hotels, and cultural, leisure and recreational facilities.

Thailand has a proposal for Zoran Island, an artificial island off the coast of Phuket, which would allow mega-yachts to moor. The tiny, wealthy Mediterranean principality of Monaco, surrounded by France, is considering an extension on stilts to give the population room to grow.

Again, residential and tourism developments are not the only possibilities. In Denmark, the architectural group Big has come up with a proposal for a 680 hectare (1,680 acre) 'superharbour' centred on the Fehmern Belt Bridge that is proposed between Denmark and Germany. This would, they claim, become a new industrial hub for Denmark, Germany and the Benelux countries, form a gateway to the Baltic, and 'liberate' 20 billion euros worth of prime real estate in Denmark's 12 main cities.

There are many who would consider living on artificial islands. Actually living under water, however, is only likely to appeal as a novelty or in special scientific circumstances. The United States has an underwater laboratory, called Aquarius, 20 metres (65 feet) under the sea near Key Largo, Florida. Like other extreme facilities, this has been used to simulate conditions on the moon. In 2005, six astronauts spent 18 days on a mission out of the Aquarius, using a remotely operated planetary rover, and performing 'moon walks' in pressure suits. They even built a model of a lunar base on the sea floor, an exercise in discovering just how tough such tasks are in a difficult environment.

An earlier underwater laboratory, La Chalupa laboratory originally used to explore the continental shelf off the coast of Puerto Rico, has found a new life, also near Key Largo – as Jules' Undersea Lodge, an underwater hotel. Visitors to the hotel have to be able to dive. The lodge is 21 metres (69 feet) down, and access is from underneath, through a pool in the wet room that forms the central of the three main spaces that make up the lodge. Once inside, however, divers can remove their wetsuits and lead relatively normal lives in two well-appointed bedrooms and a common/dining room – albeit with great diving opportunities, and extraordinary views through the windows.

Less energetic and also more romantic is Sweden's Utter Hotel (*utter* is Swedish for otter). Set in Lake Mälaren, about 1 kilometre (0.6 miles) from the shore, this is like a traditional Swedish red-painted timber hut, floating on a little square raft. As a houseboat it would be nice enough, but there is also a chamber beneath the water. Go 3 metres (10 feet) down a vertical ladder in a tube, and you reach a one-room apartment with windows looking out into the lake. A real 'away from it all' destination, originally developed as an art project by artist and sculptor Mikael Genberg in 2000, it has since become immensely popular.

Both these hotels, however, have an element of roughing it, and now the luxury hotel market has grasped underwater living as the latest novelty. The Poseidon Undersea Resort in Fiji is one such project (page 176), and even more extravagant is the proposed Hydropolis, a jellyfish-shaped extravaganza that would sit on the ocean floor (the first example is proposed for Qingdao, China). Until tourists actually get the opportunity to stay in space (see the next chapter) it is hard to imagine a more exotic destination.

Wet

PARIS, FRANCE
RONAN & ERWAN BOUROULLEC – DESIGNERS

LA MAISON FLOTTANTE

Height above sea level
35m/115ft

Average annual rainfall
641.6mm/25½in

Average high and low temperatures
16°C/60°F – 9.6°C/49°F

Opposite A timber trellis covers the entire interior living and working area and extends over the external spaces.
Left A boat towed the completed house upriver along the Seine.
Below The house was manufactured in a shipyard at Le Havre, at the mouth of the Seine.
Bottom left Section and plan of the principal floor.
1. terrace; 2. living area; 3. kitchen; 4. bathroom/WC; 5. office; 6. bedroom; 7. mezzanine

For many, the mental image of France derives from the paintings of the Impressionists and post-Impressionists, and a number of the key works draw on scenes from in and around Paris, at a time when improved transport links made places newly accessible. The near-Arcadian rusticity celebrated in many of the best-known paintings was already seen to be under threat in some of the works themselves, with factory chimneys appearing on the horizon, and since then many of the sites have changed out of all recognition. The Île de Chatou, however, is one place that has maintained some of its charms, despite being swallowed up by the Paris agglomeration spreading westward.

On the Seine, between Rueil-Malmaison and St-Germain-en-Laye, the island was the setting for Renoir's *Le Déjeuner des Canotiers*, which showed his friends lunching on the shaded balcony of the Maison Fournaise. The Fauvist artists Vlaminck and Derain rented the nearby Maison Levanneur as a studio between 1900 and 1905, and this building has since been renovated as the Centre Nationale de l'Estampe et de l'Art Imprimé (National Centre for Engraving and Printed Art). When the centre wanted to extend to create a residence for visiting artists, it found its heritage both an advantage and a disadvantage. Because of the historic charm of the site, getting permission to build was difficult, but the centre was able to draw on another tradition – that of the *bateaux lavoir*. These were boats, typically moored on the river, where laundresses lived and washed people's laundry in the river. There were two at Chatou between 1860 and 1917.

The Centre Nationale de l'Estampe et de l'Art Imprimé therefore launched a competition for a floating residence, which was won by the increasingly famous product designers, brothers Rowan and Erwan Bouroullec. This was their first architectural commission, and the centre gave it to them partly because it was looking not for a unique piece of architecture but, in a sense, for a 'product', for something that could be reproduced elsewhere. However, the brothers drew on additional expertise by working with architect Denis Daversin and with naval architect Jean-Marie Finot.

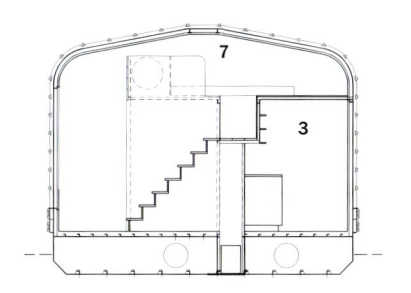

Wet 159

Their solution is a barge that was manufactured at Le Havre, at the mouth of the Seine, and towed upriver for mooring at Chatou. Looking more like an elegant floating railway carriage than a traditional barge, the residence has a constant section, with vertical side walls and a gently arched roof. The steel hull is only 60 centimetres (24 inches) deep, so that the interior sits close to the water level. Windows on the side and at the end are as large as possible, increasing the sense of connection with the water.

A cube in the centre of the boat contains the kitchen, bathroom and lavatory, with a sleeping platform above it. Otherwise, the barge is divided simply into a bedroom, and a large living/working room. At either end of the 23 metre (75 foot) space are external terraces in durable ipe timber. The volume is clad externally in aluminium, with a widely spaced timber trellis, along which ivy could be trained, covering the roof and landward side, and extending over both terraces.

Inside, the space is clad in longitudinally running warm cedar, with dividing walls in plain white. Although the width is only 5.2 metres (17 feet), restrained by navigability, and construction was to a tight budget, the impression is of spaciousness and generosity – a place where anybody would enjoy working, if they could tear their eyes away long enough from the ever-changing riverscape.

Opposite, far left The interior of the barge sits low in the water, so its large windows offer a sense of connectedness with the river.
Opposite left The terrace at the rear of the barge.
Below Moored by the path, the barge harks back to the laundry boats (*bateaux lavoir*) of Impressionist times.

STOCKHOLM, SWEDEN
SCHEIWILLER SVENSSON ARKITEKTKONTOR/ARI LEINONEN

FLOATING SAUNA

Height above sea level
0m/0ft

Average annual rainfall
900mm/35½in

Average high and low temperatures
17°C/63°F – -3°C/27°F

Opposite The sauna is perfectly placed for that essential post-sauna dip – but perhaps not in winter.
Right Section through the floating sauna. The space is divided into areas for (from left to right) the sauna itself, washing and changing.
Below The partially enclosed rear shelters a bench.
Bottom There are all the essential accoutrements for a sauna.

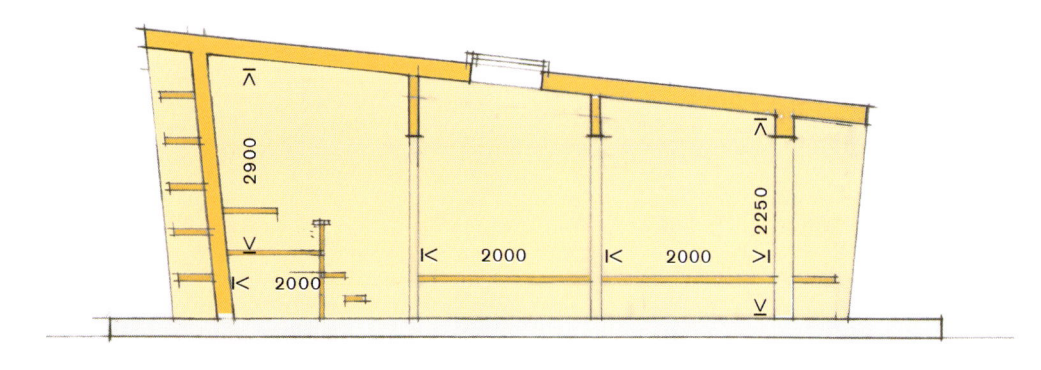

The relationship between saunas and water is an obvious one. Having become as hot as possible in the dry heat of the sauna, enthusiasts want to plunge into cold water. So where better to site the sauna than actually floating on the sea?

This was the conclusion architect Ari Leinonen came to when trying to find a place for the sauna at his parents' summer house in the archipelago outside Stockholm. Leinonen was born in Sweden but his parents are Finnish, so the idea of the sauna was central to their lives. Having come up with the idea of the floating sauna, Leinonen realized that it could appeal to many people, and that Stockholm is an ideal place for it since the archipelago, extending 80 kilometres (50 miles) east of the city, has a staggering 24,000 islands, islets and rocks, many of them containing summer houses.

The one-off design was therefore turned into a prototype, available in three sizes: small (five people), medium (ten people), and large (15 people). All use the same concept – three internal spaces for changing, washing and the sauna itself, set on a timber-decked floating concrete pontoon. The superstructure is of glulam (glued laminated timber), black on the outside and natural wood colour on the inside. It slopes up from the changing area at one end to the more generous sauna space at the other. At the lower end the black box cantilevers beyond the end wall, to shelter a bench that can provide sitting out space in less clement weather, when lolling on the deck would not appeal.

There is a magic to the long Swedish summer nights and, as dusk draws in, this enigmatic black box with its interior lights can transmit sounds of revelry and splashes as those enjoying their sauna slip over the side into the sea. But it looks equally impressive swathed in snow and, since this is a Finnish design and the Finns are notoriously robust about enjoying the natural world in all seasons, it will doubtless find good use in winter as well as summer.

YARAPA RIVER, PERU
TRAVIS PRICE

YACUMAMA LODGE

Height above sea level
126m/413ft

Average annual rainfall
309.8mm/12in

Average high and low temperatures
32.1°C/90°F – 20.8°C/69°F

Holidaymakers who stay at the Yacumama Lodge in Peru enthuse about the quality of the wildlife they see, the warmth of the welcome they receive and the guided tours they go on. Yet few are likely to realize that the centrepiece of the lodge, described as 'a floating boat of thatch', also played a key part in the education of architecture students many miles away, at the Catholic University of America in Washington DC.

Designing and building this floating lodge is just one project that has been carried out over the years as part of a programme called Spirit of Place/Spirit of Design run by architect Travis Price. Price describes this as 'a design-build exploration program primarily for architecture students that has become a major environmental and cultural force in reshaping the built environment. The program also affiliates itself with the fields of anthropology, archaeology, environment, and all the arts.' It has undertaken projects many remote corners of the world – and they don't get much more remote than Yacumama.

On the Yarapa River, a tributary of the Upper Amazon, Yacumama is 120 kilometres (75 miles) west of Iquitos. In just eight days the students built this floating lodge/houseboat, which is appealingly chunky with a symmetric thatched roof looking rather like blond dreadlocks, capped by not one but three jaunty hats. Although it is a project that raises a smile, it is a happy indulgent smile, particularly when one sees the oval-backed chair set on the small deck under the overhang of the roof – an ideal place from which to watch events on the river.

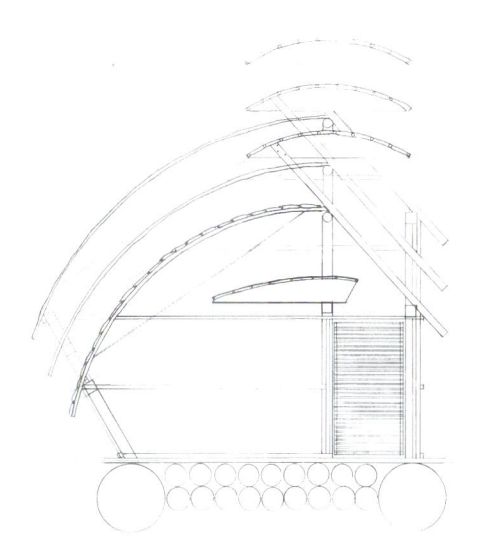

Opposite The floating lodge combines traditional techniques with imported innovations, such as the use of metal on the topmost roof elements.
Top right In this humid and sometimes very wet environment, it is essential to combine shelter with ventilation.
Right Section, showing the raft of balsa on which the lodge floats.

The superstructure is made from a local timber known as ironwood. Commonly used to describe different very hard timbers from around the world, in this case ironwood may be *lignum vitae*, a timber three times as hard as oak, from a tree that grows in a number of places including South America. Whatever its precise nature, the timber is not only very heavy but is also very dense – dense enough to sink. To prevent this, the lodge sits on a raft made from a 1 metre (4 foot) diameter balsa tree felled on the site. With a typical density of only one-third that of other hardwoods (which technically it is), balsa's name derives from the Spanish term for raft. Thor Heyerdahl, for example, used it on his famous raft, the *Kon-Tiki*.

Local Yawari Indians worked with the students on the thatching of the roof, and taught them two different traditional techniques for the two different sides of the roof. However, the upper roof elements, clad in metal, were an innovation to the area, introduced by the students. They provide protection from the torrential rains that fall in violent 20-minute bursts. They also help to reflect light down into the interior, without the heating effect of direct sunlight. And they help with a thermal chimney effect that ventilates the structure and keeps the temperature down.

The lodge even has electric lighting, although not of the conventional variety and not designed or constructed by the students. At night, 2 to 4 metre (6 to 12 foot) long electric eels light up the water, augmented by the occasional shooting star. Such a magical space certainly deserves a special building.

MAASBOMMEL, THE NETHERLANDS
FACTOR ARCHITECTEN BV

FLOATING HOUSING

Height above sea level
4m/13ft

Average annual rainfall
700mm/27½in

Average high and low temperatures
13.4°C/56°F – 5.8°C/42°F

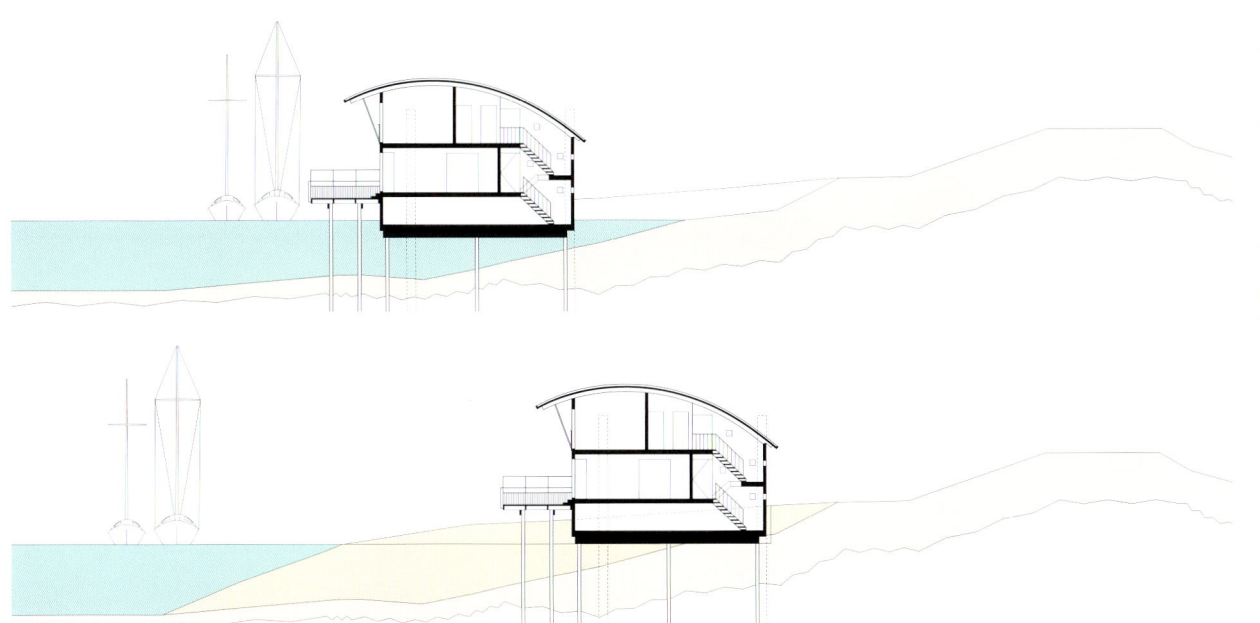

Opposite Houses in the front row, which are floating rather than amphibious, have moorings for boats.
Left Section drawings showing floating housing (above) and amphibious housing (below). Both use the same system of steel piles to raise them above the flood waters.
Below From the front, you can see the reinforced-concrete boxes on which the houses sit.

When floods threatened the new housing at Maasbommel in the Netherlands in September 2005, the residents took swift action. This in itself is not surprising, since the Dutch have a great understanding of the power of water. With 60 per cent of the country below sea level, there is a history of disastrous floods – most recently the North Sea flood of 1953 when 1,835 people in the country died.

Because of this perilous relationship with the sea, the country has pioneered the building of sea defences and the drainage of land, in the process adding words such as dyke, polder and dam to the international vocabulary.

So the fact that the people of Maasbommel reacted to the threat of flooding was not unusual. But instead of running away, they invited their neighbours to visit. This was not out of some masochistic urge, but because the 37 houses at Maasbommel are the first houses in the Netherlands that were designed to be amphibious.

In normal times, these brightly coloured, waterfront houses look like any other. But their attachment is not to the ground. Instead, like boats, they sit on hulls that will enable them to float in the case of floods. Two steel posts 'anchor' them, allowing them to move up and down, but not float away.

Strictly speaking, not all the houses are amphibious. Those set a little back from the waterfront (the River Meuse) are true amphibians, spending most of their time on dry land. The houses right on the water's edge are in fact floating homes, with water beneath them at all times. You can think of them a little like houseboats, but in this case permanently tethered houseboats, with no option of changing location.

In each case the design principles are the same. The steel piles are long enough to allow the houses to rise by up to 4 metres (13 feet) in a flood. The floating reinforced-concrete boxes that form a foundation to the houses were fabricated on a specially designated part of the site and lifted into place. On top of the boxes went the timber frame for the houses themselves, prefabricated in the Czech Republic, and then the houses were finished on site.

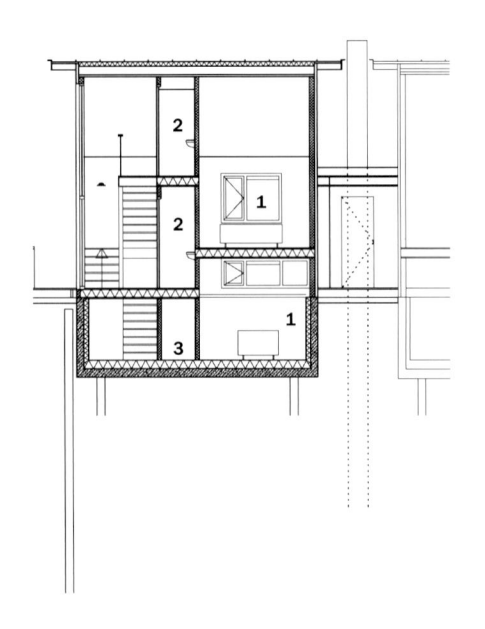

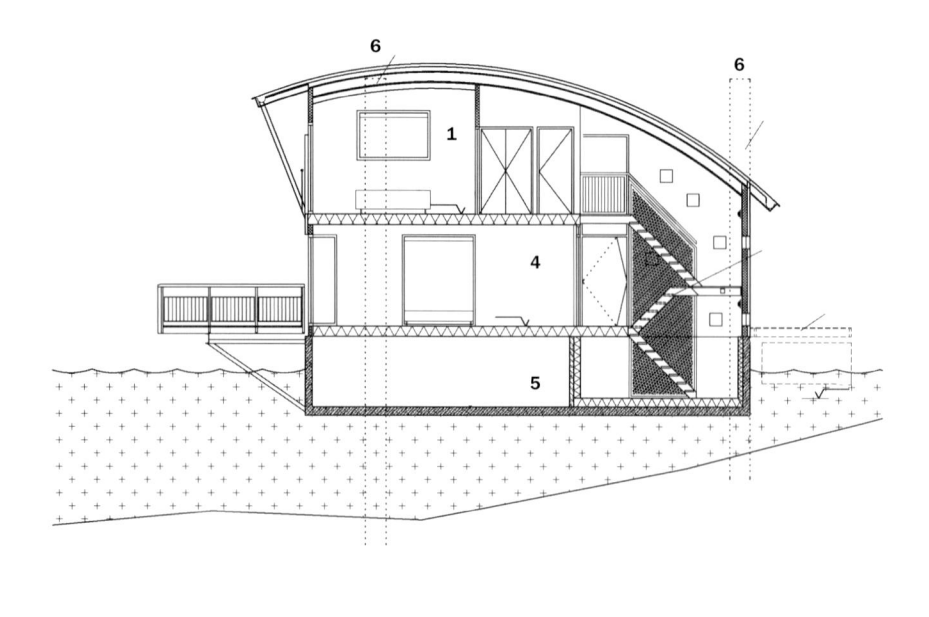

Above Sections through an amphibious house:
1. bedroom; 2. toilet;
3. pump; 4. living room;
5. storage; 6. conducting pole

Opposite Floating technology makes it possible to position houses in this attractive location on the 'wrong' side of the country's sea defences.

With their bright colours and cheerfully curved metal roofs, the houses have a holiday feel to them, accentuated by the balconies and, in the case of the floating homes, boat moorings. What is important about them, though, is that they have been built in a place where previously building could not have taken place – on the 'wrong' side of a dyke, unprotected against flooding. This means that at some stage the houses will be subject to floods. In addition to the ability to rise and fall, they have been designed to be robust enough to cope with the force of surging water and the buffeting it will bring. Equally essentially, all services are in flexible pipework so that they can cope with the change in levels.

Pressure on land in the Netherlands, Europe's most densely populated country, means there is a desire to build almost everywhere. At the same time there is a growing understanding that there have to be areas of land onto which flood waters can escape and where they can be absorbed if the whole country is not to be enclosed by ever-higher walls.

Projects like the Maasbommel houses are not a universal solution, but they are one aspect of the solution. Intended partly to be a pioneering development, the housing has already spawned further ones. In 2005, visitors to the amphibious houses were disappointed as the flood waters receded before they could lift the houses. But at some time in the future, in Maasbommel or elsewhere in the Netherlands, one can expect that such a visit under similar circumstances will reach a satisfactory climax.

Extreme Architecture

Wet 169

DUBAI, UNITED ARAB EMIRATES
WATERSTUDIO.NL

FLOATING CRUISE TERMINAL

Height above sea level
0m/0ft

Average annual rainfall
130mm/5in

Average high and low temperatures
35°C/95°F – 19°C/66°F

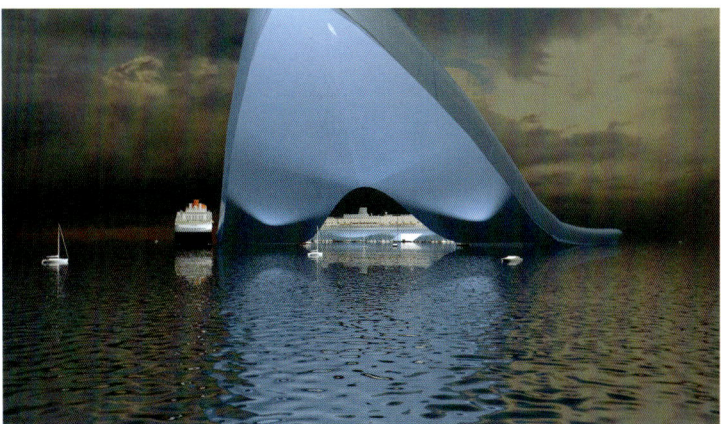

If you have ever been in a small Mediterranean town when a cruise ship arrives, you will understand the logistical barriers to giving passengers the quality of experience they crave. Vast numbers of people pour ashore, swamping a tiny town, and there are long queues for boats to take them back to the mother ship. The alternative is that the ship moors in the docks, often not the most salubrious place. In a city such as Marseilles in the south of France, for example, the immediate environs are likely to appeal only to those with a real love of 'grit' and 'authenticity' – scarcely the stereotypical cruise passenger.

These problems are compounded by the fact that cruise ships are getting bigger. Launched in the spring of 2008, P & O's *Ventura* has a capacity of 3,600 passengers. Even larger and, briefly at least, the biggest in the world, is Royal Caribbean's *Independence of the Seas*, launched at much the same time. Able to carry 4,375 passengers and 1,365 crew, it is 339 metres (1,112 feet) long and 38.6 metres (127 feet) wide. If you can't imagine those figures, go to Venice where you can see the historic buildings and bridges dwarfed by giant cruise ships such as the 3,780-guest *Costa Serena*.

A lot of high-end mass-market tourism has been turned into an increasingly manufactured experience, so it seems appropriate that Dutch-based architectural practice Waterstudio.NL has come up with an idea for a floating cruise terminal – an entirely artificial experience. And the proposed location for that terminal will be the most 'manufactured' of all cities – Dubai.

The design for the terminal is triangular, enabling three of the world's largest cruise ships to moor alongside it. One of the corners is lifted, allowing access to an inner harbour, to be used by smaller ships or water taxis. And in the body of the triangle there will be 165,000 square metres (1,776,045 square feet) of facilities – retail, conference space, cinema, hotels, etc. So passengers on cruise ships will be able to disembark, shop to their hearts' content or use some of the other facilities. If they want to travel ashore, the floating terminal will make the whole process of transfer painless.

Waterstudio is an ingenious practice, which has dedicated itself to the development of projects in the water. If this terminal is successful, it could be replicated elsewhere in the world. And then one could imagine a new generation of cruises, traveling from floating terminal to floating terminal, buying souvenirs and sampling 'local' cuisine and entertainment – and never having to interact with the real world at all. Genius.

Opposite A giant cruise ship moored at the terminal. The view here is from the inner edge, where small boats can moor, looking across the body of the terminal which houses shops and hotels.
Above left One giant cruise ship can moor on each of the three sides of the terminal.
Above One end of the terminal tips up like the maw of a giant whale, to allow smaller boats to enter the inner harbour.

ZARAGOZA, SPAIN
CARLORATTIASSOCIATI

DIGITAL WATER PAVILION

Height above sea level
195m/639ft

Average annual rainfall
350mm/13¾in

Average high and low temperatures
40°C/104°F – 0°C/32°F

Opposite The pavilion with its curtain of water.
Above The roof partly down.
Above right The roof in the fully lowered position, with the pavilion sitting in a pool.

As a child, staying with my grandmother at the English seaside, I loved visiting a swimming pool that had an enormous umbrella-shaped fountain. It was possible to rush through the cold falling water and sit 'inside' the fountain, enclosed by the wall of water.

This concept of water as an enclosure has been exploited by Carlo Ratti, of carlorattiassociati and the head of MIT's SENSEAble City Laboratory, in the design for a pavilion in Zaragoza. Cleverly, the pavilion is retractable, so that when it is not in use or when the wind is too strong it can 'disappear' into the ground. The pavilion is part of not one but two initiatives in this inland Spanish city. It was built for the 2008 Expo, which had as its theme Water and Sustainable Development. And it also forms part of La Milla Digital, a project to focus on the digital potential of the city. So it is appropriate that the pavilion, which sits on the specially created Paseo del Agua (water street) that runs from Zaragoza's Delicias station to the Expo, uses 'digital water' – projecting images onto the wall of water.

The pavilion consists of four main components. Two boxes contain the tourist information centre and the café with a terrace on top. These elements also serve a structural purpose, helping to stabilize the roof, which they penetrate when it is lowered. The other elements are the 'wet' roof itself, and a series of tables and benches.

Hydraulic rams buried in the ground lift and lower the roof as required. Digital messages are projected not only onto the water walls but also onto internal walls. Nozzles on the edge of the roof slab project water onto it, so that not only is the slender roof covered with water, and seemingly made from it, but the curtains of water that form the 'walls' also drop down from here.

There were technical challenges to overcome, such as creating a flooring material that can allow water to pass through – the architect selected a foamed aluminium. But through the choice of materials and approach the architect has created a water pavilion that is eye-catching in one of Europe's driest countries, that will have a continued life through the presence of the café and, by its use of digital projection, can change its message over time.

Left Carefully considered lighting makes this an attractive space at night as well as during the day.
Below Inside the pavilion, visitors are surrounded by a wall of water.
Opposite Section and plan of the pavilion.
Opposite below The opportunity to play in water is welcome in hot, dry inland Zaragoza.

Wet 175

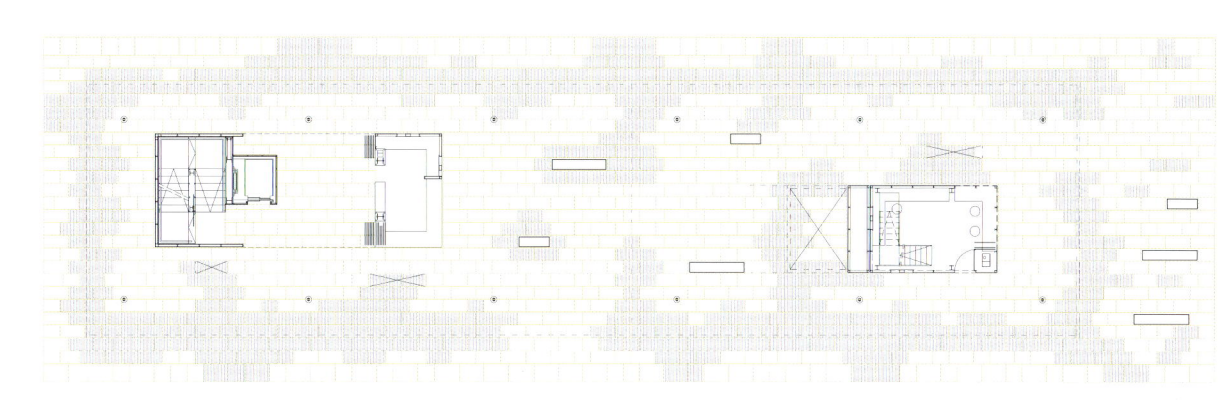

FIJI
POSEIDON UNDERSEA RESORTS

POSEIDON UNDERWATER HOTEL

Depth below sea level
12m/40ft

Average annual rainfall
252mm/9¾in

Average surrounding water temperature
28°C/82°F

The phrase 'sleep with the fishes' will become a whole lot less sinister once the Poseidon Underwater Hotel opens alongside a 'mystery' Fijian island. Using technology developed by US Submarines Inc, a company that has been working with sub-sea vehicles for 13 years, the promoters are prefabricating all the key elements, mainly in the United States, and reckon they will be able to install the whole affair in a mere 48 hours.

The offer is that visitors will, as part of a week-long holiday on the island, spend two nights living 12 metres (40 feet) under water, in a luxury pod that is 70 per cent transparent and where visibility is up to 200 metres (656 feet). In rooms that have all the usual accoutrements of a high-end hotel, they will be able to look out on the marine life of the coral reef, switching on exterior lights when they want to attract the wildlife. There will be 24 of these 10 metre (33 foot) by 5.1 metre (16.7 foot) pods (plus one 93 square metre/1,000 square foot Nautilus suite, a recreation of Jules Verne's fictional submarine in *Twenty Thousand Leagues Under the Sea*). Curved, and steel-framed, the pods will be clad with 100 millimetre (4 inch) thick Plexiglas, which is both very strong and highly transparent. There will be a 'privacy film' instead of curtains to protect the people staying in the pods when their neighbours go out exploring too early in the morning.

The 24 pods will line up along a corridor, with communal spaces (including a chapel for underwater weddings) at either end. Access will be by a lift coming down from a water-level reception.

Each of the rooms will have a carbon-fibre watertight door that is outward opening, and can seal it completely. A similar door will lead from the corridor to the module. If it is necessary to remove a module, these two doors will be closed, and the space between will be flooded.

This process will be used in reverse for installation. A semi-submersible ship will tow the main structure, which has only slight positive buoyancy, into place, and then ballast it. Next the umbilicals will be attached (power, water, sewage, etc.) and then each unit will be taken down in turn, and fixed by divers.

The units will be at atmospheric pressure, so there will be no need for any adjustment, and with a lagoon water temperature of 28°C (82°F), the units are likely to need cooling rather than heating. In case of emergency, each unit has a removable dome and trained divers will be able to lead people to safety. But this is not the kind of adventure that the promoters are promising; instead they offer a mixture of diving, outings in deep submersibles, spas and sports.

They believe that their technology makes construction more efficient and less expensive than, for example, the proposed Hydropolis Underwater Hotel in Dubai – which is evidently what permits them to come up with an introductory offer of just $15,000 per head for a week's stay!

Opposite The 24 units will lead off a corridor, with communal facilities at either end. Entrance will be at water level.
Left Prefabricated bedroom pods will be ballasted into position and attached to a central corridor.
Below From the well-appointed bedrooms, guests will have up to 200 metres (656 feet) of visibility through Plexiglas of the clear waters around Fiji.

JACQUES ROUGERIE ARCHITECTE

SEAORBITER

Height above sea level
0m/0ft

Average annual rainfall
variable

Average high and low temperatures
variable

In 2011, if all goes well, holidaymakers on cruises in the Mediterranean may spot a vessel unlike any other. Drifting through the sea like an upended plane wing will be the upper part of the SeaOrbiter, designed by French architect Jacques Rougerie, at the start of its year-long circumnavigation of the globe.

Extraordinary though the above-surface part of this craft will be, looking like a water-borne version of one of Calatrava's more fantastical buildings in Valencia, it is what goes on under the water that will be the more remarkable – and which will keep afloat a form that looks inherently unstable.

Part research station, part PR mission, and part training ground, the SeaOrbiter is a carefully researched project that has been born from the fertile imagination of an architect whose career has resulted in many successful and avant-garde land-based buildings, but who has never lost a utopian enthusiasm for the marine environment.

The wonder of those Mediterranean voyagers when they spot the SeaOrbiter will not equal that of the people in Jules Verne's *Twenty Thousand Leagues Under the Sea* when they are first nudged by Captain Nemo's craft. Unlike Nemo's vessel, the SeaOrbiter will never be entirely submerged and Rougerie, unlike Nemo again, is keen to publicize rather than conceal his exploits.

But the parallels are obvious. The fictional Nemo was exploring a world that was little known and making 'discoveries' (some good guesses by the author, others later disproved), and discovery is also the major aim of the SeaOrbiter. Furthermore, as with Nemo and his colleagues, the inhabitants of the SeaOrbiter will be spending considerable amounts of time on, in and under the water.

The project has another precursor in the work of Ant Farm, a group of experimental architects and artists formed in San Francisco in 1969. One of their never realized proposals was for the Dolphin Embassy, a sea station in Australia that would allow interspecies communication by using then new video technologies. The structure would sail with the help of a solar mechanism.

The SeaOrbiter is different because there has been serious work on the technology and on viability. A scale model was tested rigorously in Norway, and showed the craft's ability to withstand the roughest weather, allowing plans to progress for construction to start in 2009. The finished vessel will be 51 metres (167 feet) high, of which 31 metres (102 feet) will be under water. This underwater section will be divided into two zones. The first will be kept under atmospheric pressure, and will communicate with the above-water zone, but will allow the crew of ten to observe the sea through portholes and panoramic windows. Noise emission will apparently be very low, so sea creatures should not be scared away.

The other underwater zone of the vessel will be pressurized to the pressure of the sea, and will communicate directly with it. This part will be occupied by eight 'aquanauts' who will spend their time in and out of the water making direct observations. In addition, cable-operated robotic video cameras will be able to travel as deep as 600 metres (1,969 feet).

Through this variety of approaches the aim is to have three broad areas of study: monitoring pollution, learning more about marine diversity, and climate studies. A fourth area of study will be not of the ocean itself but of humankind. Both NASA and the European Space Agency are interested in using the SeaOrbiter to learn more both about human physiology and the difficulties its occupants have in carrying out mechanical and other tasks in such circumstances. This will be a great analogue for life in space, and will build on work that has already been done with the underwater laboratory in Florida. To this end, one of the collaborators is Bill Todd, the director of NASA's delightfully named NEEMO (NASA Extreme Environment Mission Operations) undersea training programme.

In addition, the SeaOrbiter will attract a great deal of attention and can be used for educational purposes, both for information about itself and through films, the Internet and other media. Expect books, exhibitions and other extensive coverage.

Jules Verne's Captain Nemo discovered a sea tunnel linking the Red Sea and the Mediterranean. Given our much more sophisticated knowledge of geology, surprises on that scale are unlikely, but Jacques Rougerie's initiative is likely to build considerably on the knowledge acquired by his fellow countryman with whom he shares a forename: Jacques Cousteau.

Opposite left The above-water element of the Sea Orbiter looks inherently unstable.
Opposite right Like an iceberg, the larger element is under water. The lower part will be pressurized to the pressure of the sea, allowing divers to come and go as they study the oceans.

CHAPTER 5
SPACE

Far left The Phoenix lander touchdown on Mars in summer 2008 brought manned space flight to that planet a little nearer.
Left The first moon landing in 1969 was by astronauts who travelled in cramped conditions that would not be suitable for longer missions.

I first realized how close we have come to 'ordinary' people going into space at a dinner in London in April 2008. It was held in a magnificent livery hall in the City, the acme of tradition, and one of my neighbours was a youngish man who had signed up to travel in the first year of operation of the Virgin Galactic spaceship. 'I've always been a space nut,' he said, 'and I can afford it. It's a no-brainer.' The cost of two hours in sub-orbital space? A cool $200,000.

Only a few weeks later, on 25 May, the Mars Phoenix lander touched down on the Arctic plain in the north of the planet and started taking samples of rock and looking for ice. For many of us the moon landings may have just seemed like a blip in history, but a serious programme, being organized in the United States and by the European Space Agency (ESA) aims to take more human beings to the moon, and on to Mars and even beyond.

It is all a little later than some would have expected. *Weekend* magazine, on 22 July 1961, predicted that 'by the year 2020, five per cent of the world's population will have emigrated into space'.

In 1967 Barron Hilton, then chairman of the American hotel chain, spoke at a space conference about the possibility of having Hilton hotels in space. He said: 'A basic rule of the hotel industry is that a hotel, whether on earth, in space or on the moon, should not be built unless there is a proven need for it. If you ladies and gentlemen can get space travellers into circulation, we will have Hiltons for them to stay in. Possibly other hotel companies would join with us in a cooperative venture. We really don't feel that we have to beat our competition to the moon, but just between us, we might try.'

Since then there have been many proposals, from Hilton again, from giant American architectural practice WATG and from sheer fantasists, about the possibility of space tourism, either orbital or on the moon. Now it is difficult to tell fantasy from possibility. Patrick Collins, a space-tourism expert and professor of economics at Azabu University, Japan, has said that just ten per cent of existing governmental space budgets would be needed to make space tourism a $100-billion-a-year business. In a speech he gave in 2004 at the Space Technology and Applications International Forum he said: 'The growth of sub-orbital tourism could lead on to orbital tourism services, for which there is known to be very large potential demand.'

Virgin Galactic, we know, is serious enough to be commissioning spaceships and has already had its spaceport designed by Foster + Partners (page 186). Equip.Xavier Claramunt (page 190) seems to be utterly serious about its Galactic Suite. Hans-Jurgen Rombaut's concept of a Lunar Hotel (page 196) appears much more fanciful, but he is talking about 2050, and who knows? By then, if everything goes to plan, NASA will have had a base on the moon for over 25 years.

Amidst all the uncertainty, there are two things we can be sure of. Creating bases in space will be very expensive (currently putting just 1 kilogram/2.2 pounds into space costs about $10,000), and there will be a need for architects. David Nixon, a British architect who has worked for most of his career on designs for space, told me: 'This field is heavily controlled by the engineering community. When architects and designers are brought in they make a difference, at broad conceptual level and at a highly detailed level.' Their input will be increasingly important because of the length of time people will be spending in space, and the changing demographic of the visitors. Just as the earliest Antarctic pioneers suffered conditions that would no longer be considered acceptable, so did the pioneers of manned space flight. The Gemini spacecraft that flew ten manned flights lasting up to ten days in 1965 and 1966, had a volume of 2.55 cubic metres (90 cubic feet) and travelling in them was described at the time as like being locked in the front seat of a VW Beetle.

Nixon worked on designs for the habitation modules of the International Space Station. His proposals were abandoned in a round of cuts and the result, he says, is a cramped design with astronauts having to 'tiptoe in weightlessness' through protruding equipment within a space that has a maximum diameter of 2.4 metres (8 feet). He equates the level of comfort experienced by the highly trained astronauts with being in 'a five-star hotel without any private bathrooms'.

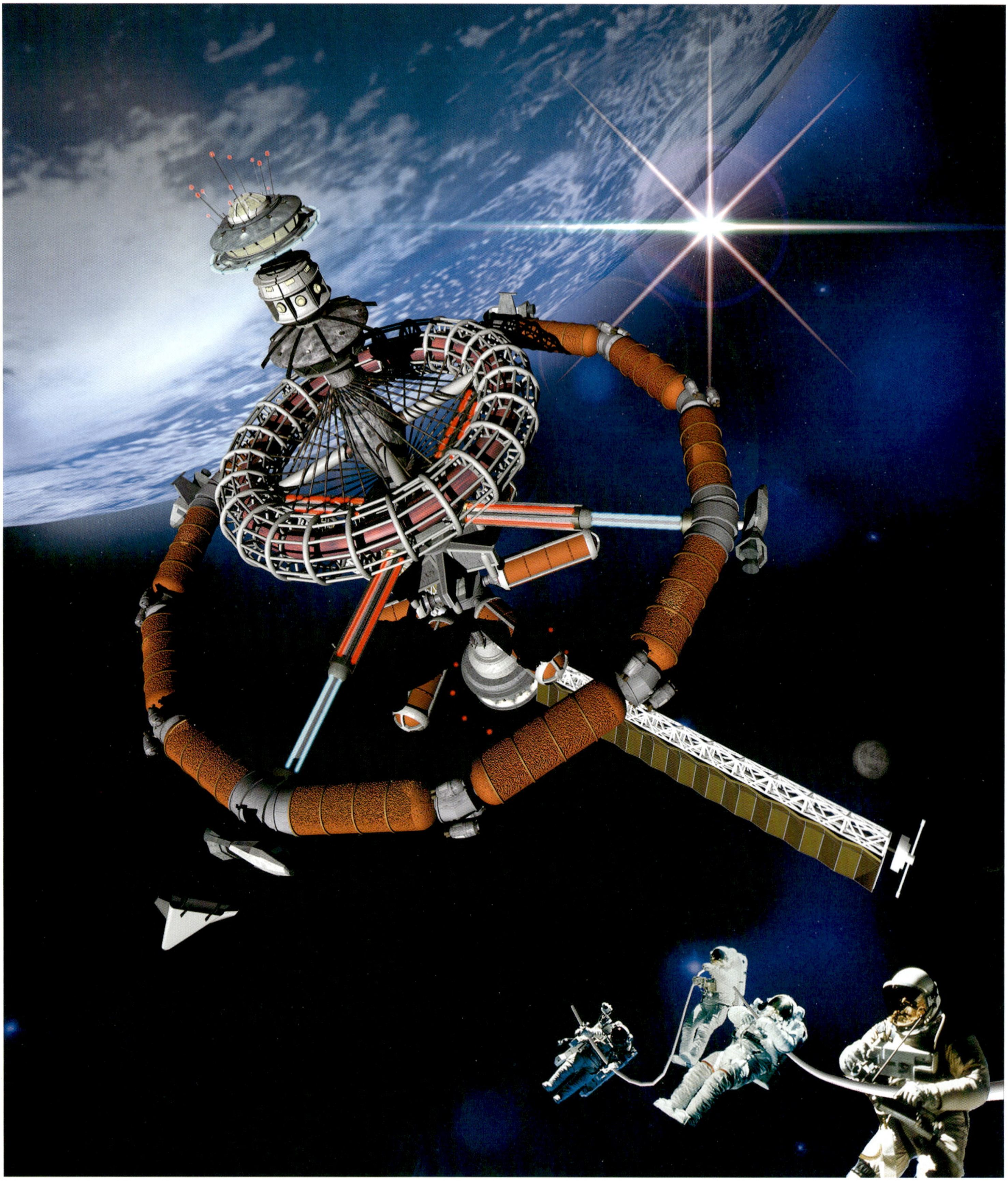

Opposite Visualization of a space resort by American architectural practice WATG.
Right Cost-cutting resulted in far from ideal conditions at the International Space Station.
Far right The Biosphere 2 project in the 1990s demonstrated just how badly enclosed communities can go wrong.

With a mission to Mars expected to last at least two years, including a year on the surface, this level of discomfort will not be tolerable. As well as satisfying the astronauts' physical needs, architects' skills will be needed to ensure their mental well-being in such an alien environment. In order to learn as much as possible on earth that could be applicable in space, NASA has carried out underwater missions (see Wet, pages 154–6) and has annual Desert RATS expeditions (RATS is short for Research and Technology Studies) to remote locations in Arizona or California, which simulate conditions in space. The European Space Agency is testing both technology and psychology at the Concordia Station in the Antarctic (page 184).

Even more directly, Olga Bannova of the Sasakawa International Center for Space Architecture (SICSA) has worked with Ian Smith of the Applied Computing and Mechanics Laboratory at the Ecole Polytechnique Fédérale de Lausanne (EPFL) on a joint US–Swiss research project for a new research station on the Greenland ice cap. As well as improving the environmental performance of the existing station, the construction of the new station would provide a test bed for building techniques in space and an environment with a lot of similarities to space. She lists these as follows:

- The summit, which is 3,200 metres (10,500 feet) above sea level, is one of the earth's highest and driest environments, and has a relatively low atmospheric pressure most like Mars.
- Temperatures are as low as -50°C (-58°F) during winter, which is similar to those on the moon and Mars.
- Wind range can reach 21 metres (69 feet) per second. Snowstorms in these locations have similarities to dust storms on Mars, which may create difficulties similar to snow drifting.
- Arctic environments and the moon both experience long days and nights, thereby affecting surface operations. The Arctic has almost five months of darkness and extreme cold while a lunar night is the equivalent of 14 earth days.
- Greenland terrain contains sterile areas that are devoid of life in any form, which is similar to conditions found on the moon and Mars.
- The permafrost environment in Greenland is similar to surface conditions on Mars.

Earlier ambitious simulation projects indicate just how essential it is to get both physical and psychological factors right. One of the most important of these projects ended in a worrying degree of disarray. This was Biosphere 2, a 1.27 hectare (3.14 acre) structure originally built as an artificial closed ecological system in Oracle, Arizona, by Space Biosphere Ventures. Completed in 1991, it was used for two missions, during which people were enclosed in the biosphere and were required to be entirely self-supporting.

The first mission lasted for two years, but oxygen levels became so low that two injections of oxygen were needed. The reasons for this were never entirely understood. Even more disturbing was the second mission, which was intended to run for ten months from 6 March 1994. However, there were arguments both with the management team and within the 'crew' of the biosphere, which resulted in deliberate vandalism and several people leaving, so the mission was aborted after six months. What was upsetting in Arizona would be disastrous and life-threatening if it happened in space.

Still, NASA and ESA are determined to go ahead with their programmes, and both Russia and India are developing plans for manned space flights. These missions will demand an architecture of extremes that will make all the other projects in this book seem straightforward and almost cosy. Love or hate the whole concept of the colonization of space, it offers architects an opportunity to create environments that will be more important to their users than ever before.

Space 183

ANTARCTICA
SERVEX

CONCORDIA STATION

Height above sea level
3,233m/10,607ft

Average annual rainfall
20–100mm/ ¾–4in

Average high and low temperatures
-50.8ºC/-59ºF – -84.4ºC/-120ºF

Imagine being on a mission to the moon or to Mars. It will be cold, you will be cut off from almost all communication and certainly from the ability to escape. You will need to be self-sufficient, and able to deal with your problems as they arise. The challenges will be both physical and physiological. How will you cope?

For most individuals, this is a fairly theoretical set of questions. For the agencies planning to send people into space, however, it is essential to have at least some of the answers before a vastly expensive mission takes place. And one place where the European Space Agency (ESA) is looking for answers is at the Franco-Italian Concordia Station in the Antarctic.

Even by the standards of the Antarctic, Concordia is inhospitable. Sited on what is known as Dome C, a high point on the Antarctic ice, it is 3,233 metres (10,607 feet) above sea level – equivalent to an elevation of almost 4,000 metres (13,123 feet) on the equator. With air pressure of only 645 hPa, residents suffer from chronic hypobaric hypoxia, a shortage of atmospheric oxygen that can produce both long-term and short-term health problems.

And it is really cold. On 3 September 2007 all records were broken, with a minimum temperature in the area of –84.4ºC (–120ºF). And it is remote. Concordia is 1,100 kilometres (684 miles) inland from the French research station at Dumont D'Urville, 1,100 kilometres (684 miles) inland from Australia's Casey Station and 1,200 kilometres (746 miles) inland from the Italian Zucchelli Station at Terra Nova Bay. Russia's Vostok Station is 560 kilometres (348 miles) away, and the geographic South Pole is 1,670 kilometres (1,038 miles) away.

In the long polar winter, which runs from February to November, Concordia is inaccessible, with the 16 people who are overwintering there unable to leave.

When the clients for the station, the Institut Polaire Français – Paul Emile Victor (IPEV) and the Programma Nazionale di Ricerche in Antartide (PNRA), chose this location they didn't do it out of some sadistic impulse towards the scientists who would be working there, but because its position makes it excellent for certain studies – for astronomy and glaciology, and for studying the ozone layer. But, with the survival challenges it poses, it is also good for studying how people in space would react to isolation and extreme physical conditions.

The station consists of three linked buildings. Two are cylindrical, three storeys high and designated respectively as 'quiet' and 'noisy'. The quiet building contains the sleeping quarters, the communications room, laboratories and hospital. The noisy building houses the workshop, the kitchen and the restaurant. The third building consists of 11 container-size modules, and accommodates the wastewater treatment plant, electric power plant, the boiler room and a second workshop.

Waste-water treatment is one area where there has already been a synergy with the ESA. In both the Antarctic and in space it is vital to leave no trace of pollution, and the ESA has developed a method of grey-water and black-water recycling that has been applied at the Concordia Station.

The two 'cylindrical' buildings, designed to minimize the external area and hence heat loss, in fact have 18 sides each. Their diameter is 18.5 metres (61 feet) and they are 12 metres (39 feet) high. Six columns support the 200 ton weight of each building, which sits on a 3.5 metre (11.5 foot) high snow berm. A hydraulic system allows the columns to be lifted by 40 centimetres (16 inches) to compensate for any sinking into the ice. Snowfall at the Concordia Station is very low, with only 2 to 10 centimetres (0.8 to 4 inches) per year, so unlike stations nearer the coast there is not a problem with burial by drifting snow.

The steel structure, of high-grade steel intended to resist the cold, is clad with sandwich panels of expanded polyurethane covered with glass fibre, with a total thickness of 16 centimetres (6 inches). The system provides good insulation and is also fire resistant. Panels are jointed with a combination of silicone fixative and timber wedges to avoid any cold bridging to the metal structure.

Construction at Dome C started in 1999, and was completed in 2004. In the first winter season, ESA sponsored a number of tests on the resident team, looking at both physiological adaptation and group identity. Further research was planned.

To most of us, this environment may seem extraordinarily hostile and devoid of familiar comfort. However, compared to space, it is positively homely. Lessons learnt in the Antarctic should at least make the ordeal of living in space a little more bearable.

Opposite One of the cylindrical buildings at Concordia is designated as noisy and the other as quiet. Both have been designed to resist extraordinarily inhospitable conditions that have valuable parallels with conditions in space.
Above The station is a long way from anywhere, in the middle of nothing.

UPHAM, NEW MEXICO, USA
FOSTER + PARTNERS

SPACEPORT AMERICA

Height above sea level approx 1,220m/4,000ft

Average annual rainfall 20mm/¾in

Average high and low temperatures 25°C/77°F – 5.6°C/42°F

You just know that Norman Foster would love to go into space. Adventurous and fit (he is a highly competitive skier), he always gives the impression that the world is just slightly too small for his ambitions. You can imagine how we would like to extend his influence to elsewhere in the universe.

As a man in his seventies, however, the closest he is likely to get is as the designer of Spaceport America, the equally entrepreneurial Richard Branson's project to build the world's first privately funded spaceport, at Upham in the New Mexico desert in the United States.

Offering two-and-a-half hour flights for $200,000, and claiming that it hopes to start operating as early as 2009, Virgin Galactic is allowing people to register now on a website that is almost as matter of fact as Virgin Atlantic's when it offers to convey people across the Atlantic. Astronauts (Branson assures potential passengers they will be entitled to this title), will enjoy a two-stage flight in vehicles that look faintly inspired by 1960s science fiction, and will be allowed to wander about to experience weightlessness.

Evidently the spaceport will be a key part of their experience – and the total experience for the many non-flying visitors who will be expected. So the design needs to be both attractive and functional.

First flights will be from an existing space station in the Mojave Desert, but the permanent building that Foster is designing will be in the desert of southern New Mexico, near the abandoned town of Upham. The nearest accessible town by road is Las Cruces, 66 kilometres (41 miles) away, although the wonderfully named Truth or Consequences is only 35 kilometres (22 miles) away cross-country.

So this will be very much a destination building, and Foster's design pays great attention to the process of arrival. The low-lying structure, only 15 metres (50 feet) at its highest point, is almost entirely earth-sheltered, and visitors will approach it along a narrowing slot between two walls that will be used to display exhibitions on the history and culture of the region, and the history of space travel. Despite the plan being almost circular, not a shape that is the most conducive to segregation, there will be careful division to ensure that areas such as the control room are visible but out of reach.

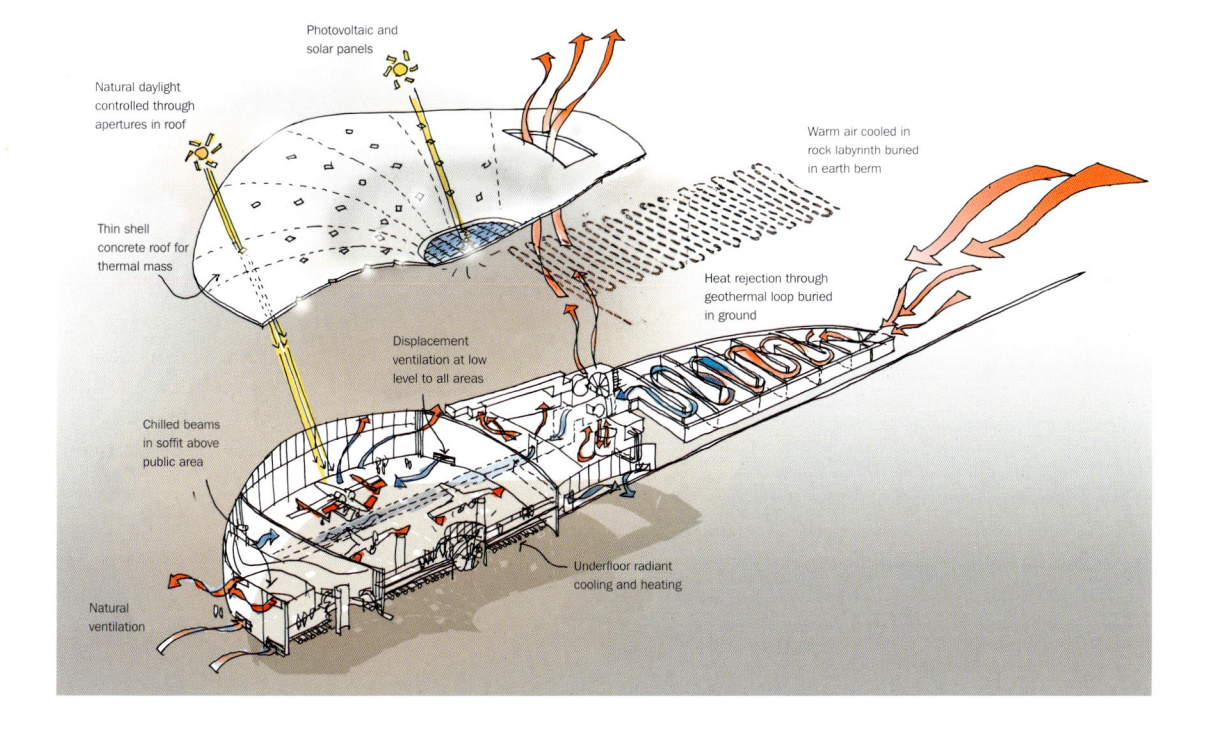

Opposite Partially buried in the desert of southern New Mexico, the spaceport will be buffered as much as possible from the extreme environment – and will save its surprises until visitors actually arrive.
Top Cut-away visualization of the interior, in which functions are carefully segregated.
Left The environmental strategy will be as sustainable as possible, making the most of ventilation and using a thermal labyrinth in the underlying ground.

Space 187

By partially burying the building, the architect will buffer it from the extremes of heat and cold experienced in the desert. The orientation will allow it to take advantage of westerly winds for ventilation in the mid season. The intention is that the building will achieve Leadership in Energy and Environmental Design (LEED) Platinum accreditation, the highest environmental standard in the United States. A thermal labyrinth in the rocks under the berm that encloses the building will cool air for use indoors, and there will be underfloor radiant heating or cooling according to the season.

A large central skylight will bring in daylight, and glazing set against the shallow arched forms at the sides will allow views of the vehicles on the ground and as they take off.

If the brand-new astronauts cast an eye back to the desert, they will see a building that deliberately blends into its landscape, a teardrop-shaped form diminished by the runways surrounding it. They are unlikely to reflect on the irony of a building designed to be environmentally friendly that can only be reached by car and is used to promote energy-intensive flight. But when they return to earth, exhilarated but perhaps a little disappointed that the big adventure is over, they will at least be able to benefit from spending time in a building carefully designed for their enjoyment.

Opposite Entrance will be through a narrow slot in the earth-sheltered structure, with the walls doubling as exhibition space.
Below Once inside, visitors will have views of the spacecraft on the tarmac and taking off.

CARIBBEAN/SPACE
EQUIP.XAVIER CLARAMUNT

GALACTIC SUITE

Distance from earth
450km/280m

Below The first operations will be conducted with Soyuz rockets and capsules, but farther in the future reusable private vehicles will access the Galactic Suite space resort.

Right Training and recovery will take place in high-class conditions at an undisclosed Caribbean location with accommodation, recreational and technical segments.

If the idea of a trip with Virgin Galactic (page 186) feels a bit tame to you, one organized by Galactic Suite might be more to your taste. Describing itself as 'one of the leading companies in the emerging space tourism industry', and, founded in Barcelona in 2007, it 'creates and develops cutting-edge concepts to improve the orbital tourism experience'.

Its founder is Xavier Claramunt, an architect with a practice called Equip.Xavier Claramunt in Barcelona, which blends architecture, interior design and jewellery. His interest in outer space led him to set up the space tourism company Galactic Suite.

With impressive-sounding backers and collaborators, the company claims that it will be putting its first tourists into orbit for stays of around four to six days in 2012.

The ticket price is an eye-watering 3 million euros, but this does include 16 weeks of pre-flight training on an undisclosed Caribbean island and two weeks of post-flight recovery. Some holiday. But, apparently, by the end of 2007 the company had already received 38 pre-reservations.

The idea is that tourists will do their training in luxurious surroundings at the spaceport on the island, then fly into space and be taken to a hotel in orbit 450 kilometres (280 miles) above the earth. The four tourists and two crew will bring all their supplies to the hotel, which will be empty between visits – the designer likens it to a mountain refuge, which is also not occupied on a permanent basis.

As befits a tourist experience, visiting the hotel should be much more luxurious than going into space on a working basis. Claramunt envisages conditions a world away from those on the International Space Station, where the astronauts squeeze into the pockets of space left over from the space taken up by the station's vital functions.

The Galactic Suite hotel will have five modules: three for accommodation, one recreational module and one service module. Every module will have a large window for earth- and star-gazing. The living modules will be individual private spaces for rest and relaxation, with a minimum of life-support equipment so that the amount of room can be maximized.

Space **191**

Above The first view of the hotel will be from the arriving spacecraft before docking manoeuvres.

The recreational module will allow the residents to enjoy sports under micro gravity conditions. Facilities will include space cycling, treadmills and resistance equipment. More prosaically, the toilets and sickbay will also be in this module, as well as the 'space spa', which the designers describe enticingly as 'a recreational water activity inside a bubble 2 metres (6.5 feet) in diameter'. The service module, as well as housing the bulk of the life-support equipment and the docking ports, will be where group activities take place, including meals and sending transmissions to earth.

In all the modules, the technical equipment will be concealed behind undulating walls, which the designers describe as like 'a hilly Tuscan landscape covered in the most glamorous, sensual materials suitable for use in space'.

The developers have not yet decided on their final choice of vehicle to transport the tourists, as they say that there are several projects under way to develop private space-flight vehicles. Initial access will be by Soyuz launches from Baikonour in Russia, but eventually there will be dedicated vehicles travelling from the Caribbean resort. These will be more luxurious than current spacecraft and Galactic Suite are looking at the use of Maglev (magnetic levitation launch technology) as a possible option in the future.

Ironically, however, the longest part of the experience will be on earth, so the design of the spaceport will be key – and, of course, a little less speculative since we can all understand how key elements, such as the plumbing, will work.

One part of the spaceport will be a luxury hotel, a field that Claramunt understands since his practice has considerable experience in hotel design. This, however, will be more ambitious than the standard urban hotel, with some floating suites and others hanging from cliffs. There will be a total of 200 rooms to accommodate not only the space tourists and their families but also more casual visitors who want to witness the whole procedure without actually going into space themselves.

The technical area will have all the facilities for take-off and landing, plus a landing area for private jets, maintenance facilities, and a harbour for deliveries of technical equipment and fuel. The training area will include a human centrifuge. The recreational area will partly be geared towards day visitors and partly to the space tourists' families, and will have a platform overlooking the launch and landing area.

In order to make space tourism a reality there are enormous technical challenges to overcome, as well as the challenge of providing the type of experience that is way beyond the comfort level of current stays in space. Would the very well-heeled put up for six days with sanitary conditions and food that would make a backpacker's hostel sound like luxury? Can these issues be resolved? The reports from the first visitors may make entertaining reading.

Right Undulating walls of sensual materials will conceal vital equipment while providing maximum empty space to enjoy weightlessness.
Below View of the space resort with its final configuration of five modules – three for accommodation, one for recreation and one service module.

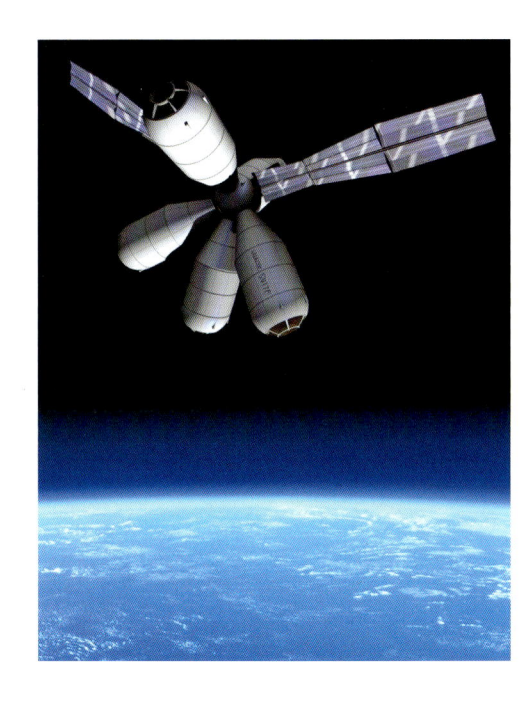

Space

ARCHITECTURE AND VISION

MOONBASETWO

Distance from earth
384,000km/238,400m

Average high and low temperatures
107°C/225°F – -153°C/-243°F

Solar energetic particles that could eventually trigger cancer are just one of the hazards that astronauts spending a considerable time on the moon could encounter – and that have to be designed against in any kind of habitation. Although recent reports by the University of Washington show that certain areas of the moon are protected for seven days out of 28 by the earth's magnetosphere, this is obviously not very helpful for anybody setting up a semi-permanent base.

Instead, Architecture and Vision, which has been working on MoonBaseTwo, has come up with a solution for the astronauts while they are within the base: shielding with regolith. Not heard of it? Well, although it was first defined in 1897 by George P. Merrill, who called it the 'entire mantle of unconsolidated material, whatever its nature or origin', it isn't really an important term on earth, where instead we use words like 'soil' and 'alluvium'. On the moon, however, regolith is really important as it is the dusty covering that occurs over the bedrock almost everywhere. If you have ever wondered why you could see that astronaut's footprint taken on the Apollo 11 moon mission, it was because he was standing on regolith rather than on bedrock.

Since rock provides great protection against radiation, the idea is that the walls of the igloo-like MoonBaseTwo will be filled with regolith. Since the base will also be pressurized to the earth's atmospheric pressure, astronauts will be able to relax in it without wearing protective clothing – an important factor for their psychological as well as physical well-being.

The base will be on the edge of the Shackleton crater, at the lunar south pole. An advantage of this location is that it minimizes the length of the lunar night (equivalent to 14 earth days) and hence maximizes the amount of solar energy that can be collected for power generation.

The MoonBaseTwo will be transported by the new Ares V cargo rocket, and will, in its transportation mode, be only 6 metres (20 feet) long and 7.5 metres (25 feet) in diameter. It will open up to a diameter of 20 metres (66 feet) and a height of 10 metres (33 feet). The architects calculate that the amount of space individual people need is greater on the moon than on earth, because the reduced gravity means they will have a larger vertical range of movement – i.e. they will bounce about more. The base will provide room for four (though it can fit up to six) astronauts to live there and also to carry out research.

Getting the astronauts out of their suits is the first step in improving their well-being. In addition, the softness of the spaces will make existence more 'normal'. And neither has the architect neglected the need for privacy – living accommodation will be in individual 'pods' suspended from the ceiling of the space.

The ends of the 'igloo' will house airlocks and also a docking station for a moon rover, the vehicle that will transport the astronauts around the moon. The architect has addressed a whole range of issues including housekeeping – dust collection will be either by hand or by robot. The idea is that astronauts will live in the building for up to 6 months, and it will be the only place where they can experience even a fraction of terrestrial 'normality'. If you think of the mission as a 6-month camping trip for which you have to take all your supplies – and never come home for a hot bath – its enormity becomes a little clearer.

As does the role of architects, in designing a structure that is not only functionally effective, but one in which it is also possible to live and not go mad. The challenge is an extraordinary one, and the project should teach us as much about human behaviour as about interplanetary science.

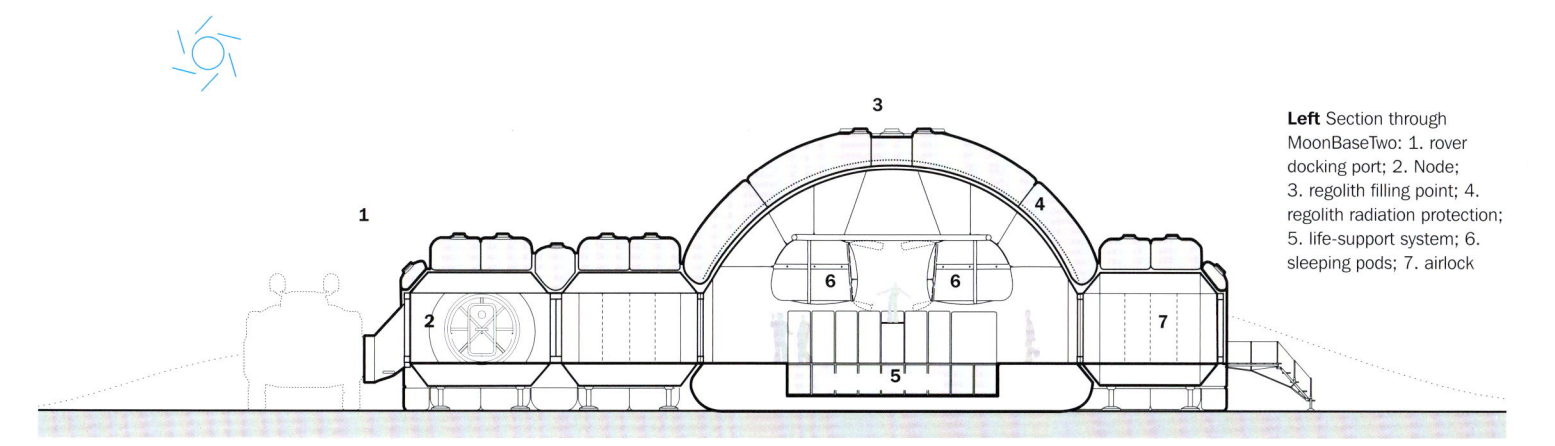

Opposite MoonBaseTwo should provide some semblance of home comforts for astronauts spending up to 6 months on the moon.
Left Transport and configuration sequence: 1. rocket launch; 2. landing on moon; 3. pick-up; 4. self-deployment; 5. membrane inflation; 6. regolith filling

Left Section through MoonBaseTwo: 1. rover docking port; 2. Node; 3. regolith filling point; 4. regolith radiation protection; 5. life-support system; 6. sleeping pods; 7. airlock

HANS-JURGEN ROMBAUT–LUNAR ARCHITECTURE/WONKA

LUNAR HOTEL

Distance from earth
384,000km/238,400m

Average high and low temperatures
107ºC/225ºF – -153ºC/-243ºF

Opposite The diminished gravitational pull of the moon makes it possible to build very slender towers.
Below left The hotel will be built as much as possible from locally available materials.
Below right Flying around in 'bat' costumes will be one of the attractions on offer. Notice the suspended sleeping pods, which visitors can move up and down as they wish.

There is something immensely appealing about a mix of fantasy and hard-headed thinking. So when Dutch architect Hans-Jurgen Rombaut designed a hotel on the moon, which he believes could open in 2050, he came up with lots of exotic visualizations that would sit happily in space comics, but also tackled practical applications – radiation, redundancy and resources.

His vision for the earth is relatively apocalyptic. He predicts that in 2054, when his hotel should have been open for four years, the population of the world will have reached 9,309,051,539 (I love that last '9'), and the effects of global warming will be in full flow, so that 'El Niño will look like a cool breeze'. With resources under pressure, and the average lifespan exceeding 100 years, people will be working until they are 70. They will certainly want a holiday somewhere relaxing – what could be better than the moon?

Already, with increasing affluence, the idea of resort hotels where one basks in luxury and spends a large proportion of one's time within the hotel's confines is growing in popularity. The Lunar Hotel just takes this idea a stage further.

Looking as if it is going to take off at any moment, the hotel consists of two slender 160 metre (525 foot) high towers linked by bridges. The envy of architects of earthbound tall buildings, who want their constructions to be ever taller and slimmer, these towers can be far more delicate-looking than their terrestrial equivalents, since the gravitational pull is only one-sixth of that on earth, and maximum wind speeds are much lower.

This does not mean, however, that architecture is easy, since there is a whole load of other issues to contend with. The external temperature range is enormous, from −153ºC (−243ºF) to 107ºC (225ºF), the building needs to provide an artificial atmosphere, and it needs to protect residents from damaging lunar radiation. The building would be clad in moon rock, with a 35 centimetre (14 inch) deep layer of water behind it, which would serve a double function by helping to modulate the temperature while also absorbing radiation. Windows would be created by simply cutting away the moon rock.

The rock would be quarried when the underground portion of the building was constructed – this would mainly be used to house the staff, as it would have the highest degree of protection against damaging radiation; since they would be on the moon on a semi-permanent basis, their exposure would be higher than that of transient visitors. Glass and tiles made from moon dust could also be made on site, so minimizing the use of materials that have to be transported expensively from earth.

Having two towers is part of the concept of compartmentation in the design, which allows part of the building to remain in use even if other parts are damaged, for instance in a fire or by being hit by a piece of space debris. But it does not mean the towers will be identical in function. Rombaut intends one to be 'physical' and the other 'spiritual'. In the physical tower, people will be able to enjoy activities made special by the low gravity – swimming, and leaping out of the water; abseiling and 'flying' in bat-like suits.

In the spiritual tower there will be meditation and spa facilities plus opportunities to look out at the lunar landscape and the stars, and observe the earth through telescopes.

Sleeping accommodation will be in 'pods' hanging from slender steel cables, which the residents can raise and lower themselves to enjoy different views. Although there will be lifts, visitors will be encouraged to use the steep ramps to navigate the hotel, in order to minimize the muscle wasting caused by low gravity.

Rombaut envisages the average trip lasting one to two weeks so that visitors can enjoy at least one sunrise or sunset in the lunar day, which is equivalent to 14 earth days. Travel from earth to the moon would take about two days, and the landing place would be a relative distance from the hotel, as landing produces severe dust clouds. A surface vehicle will take guests to the hotel, which will be set on the rim of a 5 kilometre (3 mile) deep canyon.

Excursions may include moonwalks or trips out in a space vehicle, but both will be fairly arduous. Like so many resort hotels, this will be its own self-contained little world – at least in this case there will be no residual guilt about not injecting money into the native economy or getting to know the locals. And if all this is beginning to seem a little prosaic, not to say practical, don't forget the name Rombaut has given to his hotel: 'Lunatic'.

ARCHITECTURE AND VISION

MARSCRUISERONE

Distance from earth
100million km/62million m –
380million km/235million m

Average high and low temperatures
20 °C /68 °F – -140 °C/-220 °F

Opposite MarsCruiserOne will play a key role in exploring the planet and taking scientific samples. **Left** The large wheels, which have no hubs, increase the amount of usable space.

It looks like the ultimate boy's toy – a futuristic vehicle, with huge wheels more than twice the height of a man, that can travel forward, backwards and sideways, allowing astronauts to yomp across the undiscovered surface of Mars.

In fact, yomping is the last thing this vehicle will be doing. It will travel at a stately 5 to 10 kilometres (3 to 6 miles) per hour, containing its crew for up to two weeks and allowing them to carry out their work without, in any way, polluting the environment. That includes taking all – yes, all – their waste back to base with them. And, of course, the people inside the vehicle have to live, eat, sleep and explore within, and occasionally outside, it for two weeks without going crazy.

So the MarsCruiserOne, which is designed following NASA and European Space Agency (ESA) predictions that man will go to the planet in 2032, is not just a problem in propulsion and environmental protection. It is also about creating a liveable and workable space under extreme conditions – in short, it is a piece of architecture.

The large wheels have a key role to play in this. Driven from the rim by linear electric motors, they have no hub and so maximize the internal space. By placing the living and working space within the wheels rather than above them, the design team has both increased this space and allowed the occupants to stand upright within it.

The reason that maximizing space is so important is that there is an absolute limit on the exterior dimensions of the cruiser. It will travel from earth in a container fitted to the launch vehicle's upper stage, and will have a maximum diameter of 5 metres (16 feet) and a maximum length of 10 metres (33 feet). The wheels have other advantages. Because the vehicle will be able to travel sideways, docking with the main vehicle or even with another rover will be simplified. And it can also safely approach the edges of craters and other geological features.

This certainly needs to be an all-terrain vehicle – there are no roads on Mars. The cruiser will be able to roll over obstacles between the wheels that are up to 500 millimetres (20 inches) high. And each wheel can go over an obstacle up to 300 millimetres (12 inches) high. The cruiser will use a similar suspension and dampening system similar to that adopted in Formula One racing cars.

Interior layout will be key to the success of the vehicle. At the front will be the cockpit, with the drivers' seats and storage. The seats will be used not only for driving, but also for eating and sleeping. The main window will be in front of the seats and will offer good views not only if the occupants are sitting but also if they are standing in front of it.

About half the space will be needed for storage and food, and waste – predominantly the last. In addition, there will have to be 'toilet and hygiene facilities', the latter consisting of wet towels that will be taken back to the main base for cleaning.

Also essential will be a 'glove box' for the collection of samples. From the inside, access to this will be with gloves or by robot manipulation; from the outside a robot arm will deliver samples to the box. This is one of the complex processes required to ensure that there is no contamination, either from Mars to Earth or in the other direction.

This will make the process of exploring the red planet a matter of being punctilious rather than foolhardy. Exploration will be a relatively slow, constricting and at times even boring experience, with everyday activities that we take for granted on Earth occupying an inordinate amount of time. But though it will be far removed from the uninhibited yomping that a first view of the cruiser might suggest, it will be one of the most exciting and extraordinary adventures ever.

ENDMATTER

PROJECT CREDITS

Amundsen-Scott South Pole Station
Architect Ferraro Choi and Associates Ltd. www.ferrarochoi.com
Client National Science Foundation
General Contractors Antarctic Support Associates; Raytheon Polar Services
Structural Engineers BBFM Engineers, Inc.
Mech/Elec. Engineers, Fire Protection PDC Consulting Engineers
Communications Allied Signal Technical Services Corp.
Food Service George Matsumoto & Associates
Snowdrifting Analysis, Acoustics, Air Quality Analysis Rowen Williams Davies & Irwin
Materials Handling Semco, Sweet & Mayers, Inc. (SS&M)

Aurland Lookout
Architect, Interiors and Landscape Todd Saunders and Tommie Wilhelmsen
www.saunders.no
www.tommie-wilhelmsen.no
Client Norwegian Transport Department
Contractor Veidekke AS
Structural/Mechanical and Electrical Engineers Node AS
Road Engineers Asplan Viak

Cape Schanck House
Architect Paul Morgan Architects
www.paulmorganarchitects.com
Project Team Paul Morgan, Sophie Dyring, Karla Martinez, Yau Ka Man, Timo Carl, Jo Scicluna, Tek Chee Chow
Owner/Builder Paul Morgan
Landscape Architect Sally Prideaux
Structural Engineer Doug Turnball (TD&C)
Civil Engineer Wirrawonga
Quantity Surveyor Prowse Quantity Surveyors P/L
Building Surveyor BSGM
Builder Drew Head
Carpenters Shane McGree, John Kunert
Structural Steel Jack Engineering
Plasterer Risebud Plaster
Painter Chiaroscuro
Plumber MAS Plumbing & Gasfitting
Electrician Scott Gibbins Electrics
Cement Pavers Dromana Concrete Products

Carmenna Chairlift Stations
Architect Bearth & Deplazes Architekten
www.bearth-deplazes.ch
Project Team Valentin Bearth, Andrea Deplazes, Daniel Ladner with Patrick Seiler
Client Arosa Bergbahnen AG
Structural Engineer Ribi & Mazzetta, Bauingenieure & Planer AG
Test Engineer Fredy Unger, dipl, Ing.
Cable Car Builder Garaventa
Cable Car Controller Frey AG
Structural Physicist Edy Toscano AG

Casa Segura
Architect Robert Ransick
www.casasegura.us
Collaborators Blake Goble, B Space Architecture + Design, New York; Alberto Morackis and Guadalupe Serrano, Yonke Arte Público, Nogales, Mexico; Paola Sanguinetti; Ryan Moran; Çarlo Montagnino

Central Market, Koudougou
Architects Laurent Séchaud, architect EAUG and Pierre Jéquier, architect EPFZ (Swiss Agency for Development and Cooperation www.ddc-burkina.org)
Client Koudougou Municipality
Project Management Engineer Joseph P. Nikiema , Establissement Public Communal pour le Développement
Sponsor Swiss Agency for Development and Cooperation

Concordia Station
Architect SERVEX
Project Team Gianluca Pompili, Jean-Paul Fave
Client/Contractor IPEV Institut Polaire Francais Paul Emile Victor (French Polar Institute); PNRA Programma Nazionale di Ricerche in Antartide (Italian Polar Institute) www.institut-polaire.fr
Steel Structure JOUFFRIAU (Fr)
Outside Panels TANCARA (It)
Inside Panels CLESTRA Hauserman (Fr)
Ceiling METECNO (It)
Pills FLAGERBA (It); AUTOMATEX (Fr) Ground Overlay MONDO (It)
Power Station CRCT (Fr)
Water Treatment Systems European Space Agency

Delta Shelter
Architect Olson Sundberg Kundig Allen Architects
www.askaarchitects.com
Project Team Tim Kundig FAIA, Ellen Cecil, Debbie Kennedy
Client Michal Friedrich
General Contractor Tim Tanner
Engineers Monte Clark Engineeering (structural); Turner Exhibits (shutter engineer)
Metal Roofing AEP Span
Steel Framing Farwest Ironwork
Aluminium Windows Milgard
Doors CECO (steel entrance door) Fleetwood (sliding class) Interior Plywood (Weyerhauser)
Furnishings Cassina (Leaf Chair); Knoll; Chista; Poltrona

Digital Water Pavilion
Architect carlorattiassociati
www.carloratti.com
Preliminary Design Project Team Walter Nicolino and Carlo Ratti with Claudio Bonicco
Executive Design Walter Nicolino and Carlo Ratti with Matteo Lai.
General Project Team Matteo Lai, Claudio Nonicco, Andrea Milano, Gricelys Rosario, Dario Parigi, Eva Stiperski, Paolo Porporato, Riccardo Sirtori, Claudio Gerenzani, Justin Lee, Andrea Lo Papa, Petro Leoni, Julia Schlotter, Anna Chiara Frisa, Walter Nicolino, Carlo Ratti
Client City of Zaragoza and Expoagua Zaragoza 2008
Interactive Water Wall Concept MIT Media Laboratory, Smart Cities Group (William J. Mitchell, Director)
Team Guy Hoffman, William J. Mitchell, Carlo Ratti, Andres Sevtsuk, Andrea Vaccari
Main Contractor Siemens
Structural and Mechanical Engineering Ove Arup & Partners, Madrid and London
Landscape Design agence ter
Graphic Design Studio FM Milano
Site Supervision: Typsa, Madrid
Masterplan Milla Digital: MIT Department of Urban Studies and Planning, CDD Group
Expo Gateway Preliminary Design MIT senseable city lab (Carlo Ratti Director)
Water Engineering Lumiartecnia Internacional

Echigo-Matsunoyma Museum
Architect Takaharu + Yui Tezuka
www.tezuka-arch.com
Project Team Masahiro Ikeda, Makoto Takei, Hiroshi Tomikawa, Ryuya Maio, Masafumi Harada, Miyoko Fujita, Mayumi Miura, Taro Suwa, Takahiro Nakano, Toshio Nishi, Tomohiro Sato
Client Matsunoyama-machi/Secretariat of Tokamachi Regionwide Areas Municipal (Munical) Cooperation
Architectural and Structural Design Tezuka Architects, Tezuka Lab at Musashi Institute of Technology, Masahiro Ikeda Co. Ltd.
Facility Design ES Associates, Environmental Total Systems
Lighting Design Masahide Kakudate (Masahide Kakudate Lighting Architect & Associates, Inc.)
Acoustical Design Nagata Acoustics Inc.
Landscape Design Shunsuke Hirose
Art Fuamu Kitagawa + Art Front Gallery
Artists Toshikatsu Endo, Takuro Ousaka, Yukiko Kasahara+Haruna Miyamori, Tadashi Kawamata, Taiko Shono

Engbarth Residence
Architect Jeffrey H. Page RA
www.diarconsult.com
Project Team Jeff Page, Mahsa Page
Client Jeff & Kelly Engbarth
Main Contractor Moretti Builders
Engineer Chuck Doell
Interiors Level 9

Floating Cruise Terminal
Architect Waterstudio.NL
www.waterstudio.nl
Project Team Waterstudio.NL, Dutch Docklands, Royal Haskoning
Client Private

Floating Housing, Maasbommel
Architect Factor Architecten bv
www.factorarchitecten.nl
Client Dura Vermeer bv & A. van Ooijen
Constructor Advin West bv
Consultant Boiten Raadgevende Ingenieurs Ammersfoort bv

Floating Sauna
Architect Scheiwiller Svensson Arkitektkontor/Ari Leinonen
www.ssark.se
Client Modern Living
Main Contractor X-House
Sauna Tylö
Pontoon Pontona

Galactic Suite
Designer Equip.Xavier Claramunt
www.galacticsuite.com
Project Team Xavier Claramunt, Joan Cuevas Pareras, Miquel de Mas, Marc Zaballa
Client Galactic Suite

Galzigbahn
Architect driendl*architects
www.driendl.at
Project Team Georg Driendl, Martin Barnreiter, Franz Driendl, Daniel Erdeljan, Zuzana Talasova, Judith Sagl
Client Arlberger Bergbahnen AG
Main Contractor Ingenieurbüro Brandner
Structural Engineer Ingenieurbüro Brandner (structural engineering reinforced concrete construction); Bernard Ingenieure ZT GmbH (structural engineering, steel-glass construction)
Construction Companies Unger (steel construction), Strabag (concrete), Foidl (glazing)

Halley VI Antarctic Research Station
Architect Hugh Broughton Architects
www.hbarchitects.co.uk
Client British Antarctic Survey
Main Contractor Morrison Construction
Structural Engineer Faber Maunsell
Services Engineer Faber Maunsell
External Cladding Consultant Billings Design Associates
Colours Psychologist Colour Affects
External Envelope The Antarctic Marine & Climate Centre (PTY) Ltd. (South African consortium formed by: MMS Technology (PTY) Ltd., Petrel Engineering (PTY) Ltd., Outside)
Hydraulic Legs Bennett Associates
Main M&E Sub-Contractor Merit Merrell

House RR
Architect Andrade Morettin Arquitetos
www.andrademorettin.com.br
Project Team Vinicius Morettin, Marcelo Morettin, Merten Nefs (coordinator), Marcio Tanaka, Marcelo Maia Rosa, Marina Mermelstein, Renata Andrulis
Client Private
Construction Vicente Ganzelevitch
Structure Ita Construtora
Foundations Eng. Pedro Negri
Electrics Eng. Nilton José Maziero
Suppliers Masisa Brasil (OSB); Udinese-Papaiz (mosquito screen); Reka, Luminárias Projeto (lighting), Sicmol (glass tablets); Estrumec (cladding and metal frames)

Ice hotels and bars
Icehotel Jukkasjärvi
Artistic Director and Architect Arne Bergh
Sculptor Åke Larsson
www.icehotel.com

Icehotel Quebec
Artistic Director, Quebec Serge Péloquin
Architects Brière Gilbert + Associés
Head of Production Gilles Roy
www.icehotel-canada.com

Absolut IceBar London 2008
Designers David & Martin

Absolut IceBar Stockholm 2008
Designers Daniel "Ikaroz" Diaz and Pierre "Slak" Johansson
Collaborators Mark Armstrong and Mikael Nilsson

Absolut IceBar Copenhagen 2008
Designers Anders Eriksson and Anders Ronnlünd

Lunar Hotel
Architect Lunar Architecture/Wonka
www.lunararchitecture.com
Project Team Hans-Jurgen Rombaut

Magma Arts and Congress Centre
Architect Artengo Menis Pastrana
www.menisarquitectos.com
Project Team Fernando Martin Menis (Principal in Charge), Felipe Artengo Rufino, José Maria Rodriguez Pastrana (Partners), Esther Ceballos, Andreas Weighnacht, Ana Salinas (Assistant Architects), Esther Ceballos, Fernando Menis, Carlos Lapresta (interior design)
Client Canary Islands Government
Technical Architects Rafael Hernandex, Andrés Pedreño
Construction Company UTE CONGRESS (ACCIONA+PPL)
Consultants Victor Martinez Segovia (Structural Engineer); Juan José Gallardo (urban environment); Milian Associats SL (Electrical Engineer); Audioscan SL (acoustic); Carlos Belda (lighting)
Lamp Design Juan Gopar
Signage Miriam Durango

Maison Flottante
Designer Ronan & Erwan Bouroullec
www.bouroullec.com
Client CNEAI (Centre National de L'Estampe et de L'Art Imprimé)
Collaborators Architects Jean-Marie Finot and Denis Daversin

Manned Cloud
Architect Jean-Marie Massaud, Studio Massaud
www.massaud.com
Scientific Partnership and Project Development ONERA (Office National d'Etudes et de Recherche Aérospatiale)

MarsCruiserOne
Designer Architecture and Vision
www.architectureandvision.com
Project Team Arturo Vittori, Andreas Vogler
Client Centre Pompidou, Paris
Engineers SR Consultancy/Stephen Ransom, G-Engineering, Explora
Illustrations Alessandro Natalini
Partnerships and Collaborations EOS, McNeel Europe (Rhino 3D), Maxon (Cinema 4D), Self Group
The project is based on the Mobile Pressurized Laboratory (MPL) concept of EADS Space Transportation

MoonBaseTwo
Designer Architecture and Vision
www.architectureandvision.com
Project Team Arturo Vittori, Andreas Vogler
Client Museum of Science and Industry, Chicago
Consultant Thales Alenia Space (Maria-Antonietta Perino, Massimiliano Bottacini)
Model Self Group

Mountain Lodge
Architect, Interiors and Landscape div.A arkitekter as
www.diva.no
Project Team Christopher Adams, Kirstin Bartels, Henriette Salvesen
Client Private
Contractor Bøygard bygg AS
Quantity Surveyor AS Bygganalyse
Structural and M+E Engineer Stormorken & Hamre AS

Nk'Mip Desert Cultural Centre
Architect Hotson Bakker Boniface Haden architects + Urbanistes
www.hotsonbakker.com
Project Team Bruce Haden (Principal-in-Charge), Brady Dunlop (Project Architect), Norm Hotson, Stephanie Forsythe, Tina Hubert, Julie Bogdanowicz
Client Osoyoos Indian Board
Landscape Architect Phillips Farevaag Smallenberg
General Contractor Greyback Construction
Structural Engineering Equilibrium Consulting Inc.
Mechanical Engineering Cobalt Engineering
Electrical Engineering MCL Engineering
Code LMDG Code Consultants
Exhibit Design Aldrich Pears Associates
Acoustic BKL Consulting
Theatre Design Douglas Welch Design
Theatre Electrical Acumen Consulting Engineers
Live Displays Bufo Incorporated
Retail Retail Excellence

Nordpark Cable Railway
Architect Zaha Hadid Architects
www.zaha-hadid.com
Project Team Zaha Hadid with Patrik Schumacher (design), Thomas Vietzke (Project Architect), Jens Borstelmann, Markus Planteu (Design Team) with Caroline Andersen, Makakrai Suthadarat, Marcela Spadaro, Anneka Wagener, Adriano di Gionnis, Peter Pichler, Susann Berggren
Client INKB (Innsbrucker Nordkettenbahnen GmbH)
Building Management Malojer Baumanagement GmbH & Co.
Façade Planning Pagitz Metalltechnik GmbH
Main Contractor Strabag AG
Engines and Cables Contractor Leitner GmbH
Planning Adviser ILF Beratende Ingenieure ZT
Structural Engineers Bollinger Grohmann Schneider (roof); Baumann&Obholzer ZT_GmbH (concrete base)
Bridge Engineers ILF Beratende Ingenieure ZT Gesellschaft GmbH
Lighting Zumtobel Lighting GmbH

Olympic Ski-Jump
Architect terrain: loenhart&mayr BDA architects and landscape architects
www.terrain.de
Client City of Garmisch-Partenkirchen
Contractor Birsschnau GmbH & Teerag AG
Structural Design and Structural Planning Mayr+Ludescher Partners
Design and Planning of the Jurybuilding, Technical Equipment Architects Sieber+Renn

Poseidon Underwater Hotel
Poseidon Undersea Resorts LLC, President Bruce Jones
www.poseidonresorts.com

Prekestolhytta
Architect Arkitektfirma Helen & Hard
www.hha.no
Project Team Siv Stangeland, Reinhard Kropf, Dag Strass
Client Stavanger Turistforening (Stavanger Tourist Association)
Main Contractor Massive Timber Supplier
Static Engineers Wörle Sparowitz Ingenieure
Static Engineer/Wood Wörle Sparowitz Ingenieure,
Concrete, Fire, Acoustics COWI
Ventilation, Piping Modalsli Prosjektering
Electrical Engineer Ekrheim Elektro
Site Work Sivilingeniør S. K. Langeland AS
Consultants Jarle Aarstad, Treteknisk Institutt (timber work); Tor Helge Dokka, SINTEF (energy); Katharina Bramslev, Hambra (environmentally friendly materials); Tone Rønnevig, BE (universal access)

Remota Hotel
Architect Germán del Sol
www.germandelsol.cl
Project Team José Luis Ibañez, Francisca Schuler, Carlos Venegas
Client Immobiliaria Mares del Sur Ltda, Daniel Gonzalez Correa, Juan Pablo Gonzalez Correa
Building Contractor Salfa Corp.
Project Management Egar Monsalve
Structural Engineer Pedro Bartolomé

Sacred Sands Strawbale B&B
Architect Janet Armstrong Johnston
www.strongarmconstruction.com
Clients Scott Cutler and Steve Pratt
Contractor John Till Construction
Structural Engineer Pinyon Engineering of Bishop, California

SeaOrbiter
Architect Jacques Rougerie Architecte
www.rougerie.com
Project Team Michel Thodoroff (General Manager), Jean-Yves Delaune (Strategic Manager), Ariel Fuchs (Science and Media Manager).
Backers Maritime Clusterm Ifremer Oceanographic Institution, French Institute of the Sea, French Navy, Ministry of the Sea
Contractor French Navy Builders DCNS

School (high), Dano
Architect Diébédo Francis Kéré
www.fuergando.de
Client Dreyer Stiftung
Site Coordination Schulbausteine für Gando e.V.
Main Contractor EGC (Entreprise Générale de Construction), Ouagadougou
Craftsmen Binjamain Kaboré, Sanfo Saidou (master masons), Amédé Kéré, Justin Tarnagda (welders)

School (primary), Gando
Architect Diébédo Francis Kéré
www.fuergando.de
Client Schulbausteine für Gando e.V.; Village Community of Gando
Site Coordination Wénéyida Kéré
Consultant Issa Moné, LOCOMAT (training in brick production)
Craftsmen Sanfo Saidou (master mason), Minoungou Saidou (welder)

SkiBox Portillo
Architect dRN Arquitetos
www.drn.cl
Project Team Nicolás del Río, Max Núñez
Client Ski Portillo
Collaborators Cristobal Tirado
Main Contractor Ski Portillo
Structural Engineer Enzo Valladares

Chalet C7
Collaborators Heloise Galling

Ski Jump and Judges' Tower
Architect m2r architecture
www.m2rarchitecture.com
Client Landratsamt Vogtlandkreis
Main Contractor Stahlbau Schädlich
Façade Contractor Dachbau Stassfurt
Structural Engineer Arup Germany

SnowCrystals
Architect Architecture and Vision
www.architectureandvision.com
Project Team Andreas Vogler, Arturo Vittori with Altus Architects (David Nixon, Partner)
Client Palisades Glacier Mountain Hut Competition
Renderings Jean-François Jacq

Snow Show
Curator Lance Fung
www.thesnowshow.com
Fung Collaboratives Layman Lee (Assistant to Curator), Jeffrey Debany (Project Manager), Noemie Lafaurie (Project Manager), Gianni Talamini (Chief Builder), Thomas Watkiss (Press Coordinator)

Spaceport America
Architectural Lead Design Foster + Partners
www.fosterandpartners.com
Project Team Norman Foster, Grant Brooker, Antoinette Nassopoulos, Joon Paik, Ricardo Ostos, Hiroyuki Sube, See Teck Yeo
Architecture SMPC Architects
Client New Mexico Spaceport Authority (NMSA)
Tenant Virgin Galactic
Architecture and Engineering Project Manager URS Corporation
Structural and MEP Engineer URS Corporation
Environmental Design/LEED PHA Consult
Cost Estimating Balis and Company
Program Analysis Exploration-Synthesis Partner

Svalbard Global Seed Vault
Architect Peter W. Sødermann, Barlindhaug Consult AS
www.barlindhaug.no
Client The Royal Norwegian Ministry of Agriculture and Food (LMDP, The Royal Norwegian Ministry of Foreign Affairs (UD), the Royal Norwegian Ministry of the Environment (MD)
Building Commissioner Statsbygg
Property Manager Statsbygg Nord
Overall Planning Barlindhaug Consult AS
Consultant Geotechnical Engineer Sverre Barlindhaug; Multiconsult AS
Contractors Leonhard Nilsen og Sønner AS (building and technical – tunnelling, roads and open areas)
Sub-contractors Jensen Elektriske (electrical), ORAS (ventilation), Spitsbergen VVS (refrigeration)
The Art Project Public Art Norway (KORO)
Artwork ('perpetual repercussion') Dyveke Sanne

Svalbard Science Centre
Architect Jarmund/Vigsnaes AS Architects MNAL
www.jva.no
Project Team Einar Jarmund, Hakon Vigsnaes, Alessandra Kosberg, Anders Granli, Nevzat Vize, Sissil Morseth Gromholt, Thor Christian Pethon, Halina Noach, Harald Lode, Stian Schjelderup
Client Statsbygg/Norwegian Directorate of Public Construction and Property
Consultants AS Frederiksen (structural), Monstad AS (electrical), Erichsen & Horgen AS (mechanical), Grindaker AS (landscape architect), Byggforsk v/Thomas Thiis (climatic)

Tschuggen Bergoase Spa
Architect Mario Botta Architetto
www.botta.ch
Project Team Marco Strozzi, Davide Macullo, Nicola Salvadé, Carlo Falconi, Eleonora Castagnetta
Client Tschuggen Grand Hotel
Partner Architect/Project Management Fanzun AG
Civil Engineering Fanzun AG
Excavation Security Engineer Ribi & Mazzetta AG
Electrical Engineering Bühler + Scherler AG
Light Planning Engineer Büro f. innovative Lichtplanung, Jürgen Hacker
Swimming Pool Engineer Schneider Aquatec
Heating and Ventilation Engineer Hans Hermann
Acoustics IFEC Consulenze SA
Façade Engineer REBA Fassadentechnik AG
Sauna Engineer Klafs
Sanitary Fittings Engineer Felix Marco
Geometer Beck Lorenz

Walmajarri Community Centre
Architect iredale pedersen hook architects
www.iredalepedersenhook.com
Project Team Finn Pedersen, Adrian Iredale, Martyn Hook, Caroline di Costa, Johnny Belviso
Client Walmajarri Inc.
Builder Barry Baxer, Urban Building Company
Structural Engineer Bill Butler Engineering

Yacumama Lodge
Architect Travis Price
www.travispricearchitectss.com
Project Team Spirit of Place/Spirit of Design Expeditions with The Catholic University of America
Client Yacumama Lodge
Collaborators Yawari Indians, Bart Lewis
Main Contractors Students in collaboration with Travis Price employees

INDEX

Page numbers in italics refer to picture captions

Abisko Ark Hotel, Sweden 58
Absolut IceBar, Mayfair, London, UK 88
Abu Dhabi, UAE: Masdar project 11
Aga Khan Award for Architecture 9, 45, 55
air conditioning 9, 33, 41
airships 107, 152–3
Alps 91, 105–7
Altus Architects 121
Amundsen-Scott South Pole Station, South Pole, Antarctic 100–3
Andrade Morettin Arquitetos 16–21
Ant Farm 179
Antarctic 7, 57, 97
  Amundsen-Scott South Pole Station, South Pole 100–3
  Concordia Station 98, 183, 184–5
  Halley VI Antarctic Research Station 57, 96–9
  Scott's hut 57
Aquarius underwater laboratory, Florida, USA 157
Architecture and Vision 120–1, 194–5, 198–9
Arkitektfirma Helen & Hard 112–15
Artengo Menis Pastrana 24–7
artificial islands 156, 157
Atkins 11
Aurland Lookout, Sogn og Fjordane, Norway 107, 108–11
Australia
  Cape Schanck House, Victoria 12–15
  Dolphin Embassy project 179
  Field House, Perth 42
  Mardu Country housing, East Pilbara 42
  Tjunjuntjara Community Housing, Great Victoria Desert 41
  Walmajarri Community Centre, Djugerari 40–5
Austria
  Bergisel Ski Jump, Innsbruck 106, 107, 124
  Galzigbahn, St Anton am Arlberg 107, 132–5
  Nordpark Cable Railway, Innsbruck 107, 122–5

Baca 155
Bahrain, UAE
  Anwaj Islands projects 157
  World Trade Centre 11
Bannova, Olga 183

Barlindhaug Consult AS 80–3
Bearth & Deplazes Architekten 126–31
Bergisel Ski Jump, Innsbruck, Austria 106, 107, 124
Big 157
Biosphere 2, Oracle, Arizona, USA 183
Bouchain, Patrick 92, 93
Bouroullec, Ronan & Erwan 158–61
Branson, Richard 187
Brazil: House RR, Itamambuca, São Paulo, 11, 16–21
Bridging the Rift learning centre, Israel-Jordan border 11
British Antarctic Survey (BAS) 97
Broughton, Hugh 57, 97, 98
Buren, Daniel 92, 93
Burkina Faso 9, 45
  Central Market, Koudougou 9, 52–5
  school buildings, Dano and Gando 44–51

Canada 57–8
  Hôtel de Glace, Sainte-Catherine-de-la-Jacques-Cartier, Québec 86, 87
  Nk'Mip Desert Cultural Centre, Osoyoos, British Columbia 28–31
Cape Schanck House, Victoria, Australia 12–15
carlorattiassociati 172–5
Carmenna Chairlift Stations, Arosa, Switzerland 107, 126–31
Casa Segura, Sonoran Desert, Arizona, USA 22–3
Central Market, Koudougou, Burkina Faso 9, 52–5
Chalet C7, Portillo, Chile 141, 142–3
Chile
  Chalet C7, Portillo 141, 142–3
  Remota Hotel, Puerto Natales, Patagonia 70–5
  SkiBox, Portillo 140–2
Choi, Ferraro 101
Claramunt, Xavier 191, 192
Cliostraat 92
cold environments 7, 57–8, 77, 81, 91, 97, 98, 183, 185
Collins, Patrick 181
community centres 40–5
Concordia Station, Antarctic 98, 183, 184–5
Conzett, Jurg 107
cooling systems 11, 14, 39, 42, 67 see also air conditioning
Coutts, Richard (Baca) 155
cruise terminal, Dubai, UAE 155, 170–1

cultural centres 24–7, 28–31

Daversin, Denis 159
Del Sol, Germán 70–5
Delta Shelter, Mazama, Washington, USA 60–3
Denmark: superharbour project, Fehmem Belt Bridge 157
deserts 11, 23, 29, 33, 37, 41, 183, 188
digital water pavilion, Zaragoza, Spain 172–5
div.A arkitekter AS 116–19
Dolder Grand Hotel, Zurich, Switzerland 105, 106
Dolphin Embassy project, Australia 179
Dordrecht housing project, The Netherlands 155
Drid, Jannot 85
driendl*architects 132–5
dRN Arquitetos 140–3
Dubai, UAE
  floating cruise terminal 155, 170–1
  Hydropolis underwater hotel project 157, 177
  land reclamation projects 155, 157
  Palm Jumeirah development 156, 157

Echigo-Matsunoyama Museum of Natural Science, Niigata, Japan 58, 64–9
Ecole Polytechnique Fédérale de Lausanne (EPFL), Switzerland 183
energy consumption 7, 11, 23, 58
Engbarth Residence, Scottsdale, Arizona, USA 32–5
environmental issues 7, 9, 11, 30, 34, 37, 188 see also global warming
Equip.Xavier Claramunt 181, 190–3
European Space Agency (ESA) 179, 181, 185, 199
Expo 2008 173

Faber Maunsell 97
Factor Architecten BV 166–9
Federation Island, Sochi, Russia 157
Ferraro Choi and Associates 100–3
Field House, Perth, Australia 42
Fiji: Poseidon Underwater Hotel 157, 176–7
Finland: snow hotel 86
Finot, Jean-Marie 159
floating architecture 155, 158–61, 162–3, 164–5, 166–9, 170–1

flooding and floodplains 155, 167, 168
Foster, Norman 7, 92, 95, 187
Foster + Partners 7, 11, 105, 106, 181, 186–9
France
  Concordia Station, Antarctic 98, 184–5
  La Maison Flottante, Paris 158–61
Fung, Lance 90–5

Galactic Suite, Caribbean/Space 181, 190–3
Galzigbahn, St Anton am Arlberg, Austria 107, 132–5
Genberg, Mikael 157
Germany
  Olympic ski jump, Garmisch-Partenkirchen 148–51
  ski jump and judges' tower, Vogtland Arena, Klingenthal 107, 136–9
glazing 61, 65, 73, 115
global warming 13, 91, 107, 155, 197
Gormley, Anthony 42
Grand Canyon Skywalk, Arizona, USA 106, 107
Greenland 183

Hadid, Zaha 107, 124
Halley VI Antarctic Research Station, Antarctic 57, 96–9
Hertzberger, Herman 155
Herzog & de Meuron 107
Höller, Carsten 92, 93
Hong Kong 155
Horden, Richard 121
hot environments 7, 9, 11, 18 see also deserts
Hôtel de Glace, Sainte-Catherine-de-la-Jacques-Cartier, Québec, Canada 86, 87
hotels
  cold environments 58, 70–5, 84–6
  in the mountains 105, 106, 107, 140–3, 144–7 see also mountain lodges
  in space 181, 183, 191–3, 196–7
  underwater 155, 157, 176–7
Hotson Bakker Boniface Haden Architects + Urbanistes 28–31
House RR, Itamambuca, São Paulo, Brazil 11, 16–21
Hugh Broughton Architects 7, 57, 96–9
Hydropolis underwater hotel project, Dubai, UAE 157, 177

ice hotels and bars 58, 84–9
IceBar, Nordic Sea Hotel, Stockholm, Sweden 88
igloos 57, 58, 85, 194–5
India 183
Institut Polaire Français – Paul Emile Victor (IPEV) 185
insulation 37, 58, 67, 73, 98, 102
International Space Station 181, 183
iredale pedersen hook 40–5
Isozaki, Arata 91, 92
Israel: Bridging the Rift learning centre 11
Italy
 Concordia Station, Antarctic 184–5
 Snow Show, Sestriere 90–5

Japan
 Echigo-Matsunoyama Museum of Natural Science, Niigata 58, 64–9
 Kansai Airport, Osaka 155
Jarmund/Vignæs AS Architects MNAL 76–9
Jéquier, Pierre 52–5
Johnston, Janet Armstrong 36–9
Jordan: Bridging the Rift learning centre 11
Jukkasjärvi Ice Hotel, Kiruna, Sweden 84, 85
Julen, Heinz 105, 107
Jules' Undersea Lodge, Florida, USA 157

Kansai Airport, Osaka, Japan 155
Kéré, Diébédo Francis 44–51
Klein Matterhorn projects, Switzerland 105, 107

La Maison Flottante, Paris, France 158–61
land reclamation 155, 157
Lehmann, Üeli 105, 107
Leinonen, Ari 162–3
Looking Glass, Snow Show, Sestriere, Italy 95
Lunar Hotel concept 181, 196–7

Maasbommel housing project, The Netherlands 155, 166–9
Magma Arts and Congress Centre, Costa Adeje, Tenerife, Canary Islands, Spain 24–7
Maillart, Robert 106, 107
Manned Cloud project 107, 152–3
Mardu Country housing, East Pilbara, Australia 42

Mario Botta Architetto 106, 127, 144–7
Mars 181, 183, 199
MarsCruiserOne 198–9
Masdar project, Abu Dhabi, UAE 11
Massaud, Jean-Marie 152–3
modular construction 97–8, 102, 120–1, 176–7, 191–2
Monaco 157
the moon 181, 195
MoonBaseTwo 194–5
Moulmein Rise Residential Tower, Singapore 9
Mountain Lodge, Hemsedal, Norway 116–19
mountain lodges 112–15, 116–19
mountains 61, 65, 91, 105–7
m2r-architecture 107, 136–9

NASA 179, 181, 183, 199
The Netherlands
 Dordrecht housing project 155
 floating houses, Maasbommel 155, 166–9
 flooding issues 155, 167, 168
 Xtracold, Amsterdam 88
Nixon, David 121, 181
Nk'Mip Desert Cultural Centre, Osoyoos, British Columbia, Canada 28–31
Nordpark Cable Railway, Innsbruck, Austria 107, 122–5
Norway
 Aurland Lookout, Sogn og Fjordane 107, 108–11
 Mountain Lodge, Hemsedal 116–19
 Prekestolhytta, Stavanger 112–15
 Svalbard Global Seed Vault, Spitsbergen 80–3
 Svalbard Science Centre, Longyearbyen 76–9
nuclear power station, Severodinsk, Russia 155

Olson Sundberg Kundig Allen Architects 60–3
Olympic ski jump, Garmisch-Partenkirchen, Germany 148–51
Oman: Sultan Qaboos University 9
Ono, Yoko 91, 92

Page, Jeffrey H. 32–5
Palm Jumeirah development, Dubai, UAE 156, 157
Patagonia, Chile 70–5
Paul Morgan Architects 12–15

The Pearl project, Qatar, UAE 157
Pearlmutter, David 11
Penal Colony, Snow Show, Sestriere, Italy 91, 92
Perriand, Charlotte 121
Peru: Yacumama Lodge, Yarapa River 164–5
Phoenix lander, Mars 181
piloti see stilts
Pivi, Paola 92
Plensa, Jaume 92, 95
Poseidon Underwater Hotel, Fiji 157, 176–7
prefabrication 17, 97, 98, 137, 139, 177
Prekestolhytta, Stavanger, Norway 112–15
Price, Travis 164–5
Programma Nazionale de Ricerche in Antartide (PNRA) 185

Qatar, UAE: The Pearl project 157

railways 107, 122–5
Ransick, Robert 22–3
Ratti, Carlo 173
Remota Hotel, Puerto Natales, Patagonia, Chile 70–5
research stations 57, 76–9, 96–9, 100–3, 178–9, 183
Rombaut, Hans-Jurgen 181, 196–7
Rostock, Axel and Jörg (m2r-architecture) 137
Rougerie, Jacques 178–9
Russia
 Federation Island, Sochi 157
 floating nuclear power station, Severodinsk 155
 space programmes 183

Sacred Sands Strawbale B&B, Joshua Tree, California, USA 36–9
Salginatobel Bridge, Schiers, Switzerland 106, 107
Sasakawa International Center for Space Architecture (SICSA) 183
sauna, Stockholm, Sweden 162–3
Saunders, Todd 108–11
Scheiwiller Svensson Arkitektkontor 162–3
Schlaich Bergermann 11
school buildings, Dano and Gando, Burkina Faso 44–51
Scott, Robert Falcon 57
SeaOrbiter project 178–9
Séchaud, Laurent 52–5

SERVEX 184–5
shade 9, 11, 13, 41, 45, 47, 48, 55
shelters 11, 17, 22–3, 42, 57–8, 60–3
Singapore: Moulmein Rise Residential Tower 9
ski Jump and judges' tower, Vogtland Arena, Klingenthal, Germany 107, 136–9
SkiBox, Portillo, Chile 140–2
SkiHaus 121
skiing architecture 106, 107, 124, 126–31, 132–5, 136–9, 148–51
Slide Meeting, Snow Show, Sestriere, Italy 92, 93
Smith, Ian 183
Smith, Kiki 95
snow 58, 65, 78, 91–2, 97, 101, 117
Snow Show, Sestriere, Italy 90–5
Snowbeams, Snow Show, Sestriere, Italy 92, 93
SnowCrystals, California, USA 120–1
Sødermann, Peter W. 80–3
solar power 11, 23, 121, 195
SOM 11
space architecture 7, 181, 183, 191–3, 194–5, 196–7, 198–9
Space Biosphere Ventures 183
space tourism 181, 186–9, 190–3, 196–7
space training programmes 7, 157, 179, 183, 184–5
Spaceport America, Upham, New Mexico, USA 7, 181, 186–9
Spain
 digital water pavilion, Zaragoza 172–5
 Magma Arts and Congress Centre, Costa Adeje, Tenerife, Canary Islands 24–7
Spirit of Place/Spirit of Design programme 165
stilts 58, 60–3, 76–9, 97, 98, 101, 155, 157
straw bale construction 36–9, 42
Sultan Qaboos University, Oman 9
superharbour project, Fehmem Belt Bridge, Denmark 157
Svalbard Global Seed Vault, Spitsbergen, Norway 80–3
Svalbard Science Centre, Longyearbyen, Norway 76–9
Sweden
 Abisko Ark Hotel 58
 floating sauna, Stockholm 162–3
 IceBar, Nordic Sea Hotel, Stockholm 88

Index 205

Jukkasjärvi Ice Hotel, Kiruna 84, 85
Utter Hotel, Lake Mälaren 155, 157
Switzerland 105
　Carmenna Chairlift Stations, Arosa 107, 126–31
　Dolder Grand Hotel, Zurich 105, 106
　Klein Matterhorn projects 105, 107
　Salginatobel Bridge 106, 107
　space training programmes 183
　Thermal Baths, Vals 106
　Traversina Footbridge 107
　Tschuggen Bergoase Spa, Arosa 106, 127, 144–7

terrain: loenhart&mayr BDA 148–51
Tezuka, Takaharu + Yui 64–9
Thailand: Zoran Island, Phuket 157
Thermal Baths, Vals, Switzerland 106
Tjunjuntjara Community Housing, Great Victoria Desert, Australia 41
tourism 7, 105, 107, 113, 133, 171
　see also space tourism
tower block, Khanty-Mansiysk, Siberia 7
Traversina Footbridge, Viamala, Switzerland 107
tropical environments 11, 17, 18, 53, 165
Tschuggen Bergoase Spa, Arosa, Switzerland 106, 127, 144–7
Tsien, Billie 92, 93

UK
　Absolut IceBar, Mayfair, London 88
　floodplain housing projects 155
underwater architecture 155, 156, 157, 176–7
United Arab Emirates (UAE) 11, 155, 157 see also Dubai
USA
　Aquarius underwater laboratory, Florida 157
　Biosphere 2, Oracle, Arizona 183
　Casa Segura, Sonoran Desert, Arizona 22–3
　Delta Shelter, Mazama, Washington 60–3
　Engbarth Residence, Scottsdale, Arizona 32–5
　flooding issues 155
　Grand Canyon Skywalk, Arizona 106, 107
　Jules' Undersea Lodge, Florida 157
　Sacred Sands Strawbale B&B, Joshua Tree, California 36–9
　SnowCrystals, California 120–1

space programmes 157, 179, 181, 183
　Spaceport America, Upham, New Mexico 7, 181, 186–9
Utter Hotel, Lake Mälaren, Sweden 155, 157

van Egeraat, Erick 157
ventilation 9, 11, 17, 45, 46, 55, 113, 165
Virgin Galactic 7, 181, 186–9

Walmajarri Community Centre, Djugerari, Australia 40–5
water environments 155, 157, 173
　see also underwater architecture
Waterstudio.NL 155, 170–1
WATG 181, 183
Where Are You?, Snow Show, Sestriere, Italy 92, 95
Wilhelmsen, Tommie 108–11
Williams, Tod 92, 93
wind 11, 13, 58, 98, 101, 113
WOHA Architects 9
Woods, Lebbeus 95
World Trade Centre, Bahrain, UAE 11

Xtracold, Amsterdam, Netherlands 86

Yacumama Lodge, Yarapa River, Peru 164–5

Zaha Hadid Architects 106, 107, 122–5
Zoran Island, Phuket, Thailand 157
Zumthor, Peter 106

PICTURE CREDITS

7 Courtesy Foster + Partners
9 top Tim Griffith
9 bottom Albert Lim
10 Courtesy Foster + Partners
11 left Morley von Sternberg
11 right Courtesy SOM
12–15 Peter Bennetts
16–21 Nelson Kon
22–23 Courtesy Robert Ransick
24 Roland Halbe Fotografie
26–27 Hisao Suzuki
28–31 Nic Lehoux
32, 34 right Courtesy Baxter Imaging LLC
34 left Courtesy Jeffrey H. Page
35 Courtesy Baxter Imaging LLC
36–38 Greg Epperson
40–45 Shannon McGrath
46–47 Courtesy Aga Khan Award for Architecture
48, 50–51 Courtesy Diébédo Francis Kéré
52–55 Courtesy Laurent Séchaud
57 top Arcmedia Ltd
57 left Getty Images Incorporated/ Time Life Pictures/Stringer
58, 59 top Arcticphoto/Bryan & Cherry Alexander Photography
58–59 bottom Peter Rosén
60, 62 top Tim Bies
63 Benjamin Benschneider
64–66, 68–69 Katsuhisa Kida
70–71, 73, 74–75 Guy Wenborne
76–79 Nils Petter Dale
80–81, 83 Jaro Hollan
84–85 Ben Nilssen. Ben Productions © Ice Hotel
86 top Xavier Dachez
86 bottom–87 Serge Péloquin
88 left Courtesy Absolut IceBar London
88–89 Courtesy Absolut IceBar Stockholm
90–95 Jeffrey Debany
96–97, 99 bottom 7-t
99 top Andy Cheadle
100 Ferraro Choi and Associates
101, 103 bottom Courtesy National Science Foundation NSF
105 top Nigel Young/Foster + Partners
105 bottom Courtesy Vernissage-Zermatt
106 Hélène Binet
107 left Artifice, Inc/Artifice Images

107 right Getty Images Incorporated/AFP Collection/ Robyn Beck
108 Nils Vik
109–111 Courtesy Todd Saunders
112 Emile Ashley
113 Kjell Helle Olsen
114–115 Emile Ashley
116–117 Michael Perlmutter and div.A arkitekter AS
118–119 Michael Perlmutter
120 Jean-François Jacq
122–125 Hélène Binet
126–131 Ralph Feiner
132 Milli Kaufmann
133–135 Bruno Klomfar
136–138 Prof. Joachim Rostock
140–143 Max Núñez
144, 147 Enrico Cano
148–149, 151 archive_terrain.de
152–153 Courtesy Studio Massaud
155 Håkan Dahlström
156 top Stephen Frink
156 bottom Courtesy Nakheel Media Centre
157 Courtesy Crescent-Hydropolis
158–159 top Paul Tahon and R & E Bouroullec
159 centre Courtesy Studio Bouroullec
160–161 Paul Tahon and R & E Bouroullec
162–163 Cia Stiernstedt/ Scheiwiller Svensson Akitektkontor
164–165 Travis L. Price III
166–167, 169 Courtesy Factor Architecten bv
170–171 Courtesy Waterstudio.NL
172–173 Max Tomasinelli
174–175 Walter Nicolino
176–177 Courtesy Poseidon Undersea Resorts LLC
178 Courtesy Jacques Rougerie Architecte
181 left Courtesy NASA
181 right Getty Images Incorporated/AFP Collection/NASA
182 Courtesy destination design firm WATG – Wimberly Allison Tong & Goo
183 left Courtesy NASA
183 right Gill C. Kenny, Courtesy Ecotechnics Corporation

184–185 A. Manouvrier/IPEV
186–189 Courtesy Foster + Partners
190–193 Courtesy Galactic Suite
194 Courtesy Architecture and Vision/background image NASA
196–197 H-J Rombaut 2001 LUNAR ARCHITECTURE
198 Courtesy Architecture and Vision/background images NASA/ JPL-Caltech/Cornell
199 Nic Shaeffler

Author's acknowledgements

The inspiration for this book came from a long conversation with Hugh Broughton about his work on the new Halley Research Station in Antarctica. His excitement and enthusiasm were infectious, and he also put me in touch with David Nixon, who was of immense help in thinking about space architecture.

Thanks to my agent Shelley Power, to Liz Faber and Jennifer Hudson at Laurence King, who made everything much less painful than it could have been, and to the designer, Lisa Sjukur.

Finally, as always, thanks to Barry Evans for unending support and for putting up with so much, including me spelling his name wrongly on the acknowledgments of my last book.